Incentives, Cooperation, and Risk Sharing

Incentives, Cooperation, and Risk Sharing

*Economic and Psychological Perspectives
on Employment Contracts*

EDITED WITH AN INTRODUCTORY ESSAY BY

Haig R. Nalbantian

*C. V. Starr Center for Applied Economics
New York University*

Rowman & Littlefield

PUBLISHERS

ROWMAN & LITTLEFIELD

Published in the United States of America in 1987
by Rowman & Littlefield, Publishers
(a division of Littlefield, Adams & Company)
81 Adams Drive, Totowa, New Jersey 07512

Library of Congress Cataloging-in-Publication Data

Incentives, cooperation, and risk sharing.

Distillation of the proceedings of a conference held at New York University, March 1984,
and sponsored by the C. V. Starr Center for
Applied Economics.
Includes index.
1. Compensation management—Congresses.
2. Wage payment systems—Congresses.
I. Nalbantian, Haig R.   II. C. V. Starr Center
for Applied Economics (New York University).
HF5549.5.C67I56   1987   658.3'22   87-4558
ISBN 0-8476-7464-9

90   89   88   87
6   5   4   3   2   1

Printed in the United States of America

To the memory of my beloved father
Stepan Nalbantian

Contents

Part IV.   Macroeconomic Implications

Tables and Figures

Preface

In March of 1984, the C.V. Starr Center for Applied Economics at New York University sponsored a two-day conference on the Economics of Incentive, Cooperation, and Risk Sharing. This conference brought together a distinguished group of economists, industrial psychologists, and compensation/human resources specialists from industry to examine the relative merits of alternative forms of remuneration. The conference discussion touched on both individual and group incentive systems affecting all types and levels of employees. The central aim was to bring research results face to face with the burgeoning experience of American business with innovative compensation schemes.

This volume represents a distillation of the conference proceedings. It consists of a selection of papers commissioned by the Center for the conference as well as several newly commissioned ones. Together the papers offer an interdisciplinary perspective on the problems and challenges of efficient employment contract design and on some business and public policy issues arising from the growing use of performance-contingent remuneration in American industries. They provide, moreover, valuable insight concerning the pertinence of economic models of employment contracts to the design of real world compensation packages.

The volume is divided into four parts. The first deals with the central conceptual issues in incentives and risk sharing; the second with empirical evidence on the performance of various individual and group incentive plans; the third with practical issues in the design and administration of incentive schemes; and the fourth, with important policy issues, with special emphasis on the implications of flexible remuneration for macroeconomic performance and the efficacy of using tax incentives for profit sharing and employee stock ownership.

The papers in Part I review fundamental concepts and outline current theoretical approaches to the study of incentives and firm organization in the authors' respective disciplines. The papers succeed, I believe, in establishing the conceptual framework for analyzing the efficiency properties of alternative forms of remuneration. This section brings into focus some key distinctions in the perspectives of economists and industrial psychologists and underscores significant differences in the methodologies and behavioral assumptions employed. An introductory essay by the editor provides a critical analysis of the standard economic models of labor contracting in the light of some central findings of industrial psychology and the available empirical evidence.

Collectively, the papers on empirical evidence cover a wide range of incentive schemes, from individual piece rates to group productivity sharing plans. They are concerned primarily with the relationship between financial rewards and certain performance indicators. Those indicators most frequently cited are worker output, worker withdrawal (as in absenteeism and quits), and firm financial performance. The more subtle issues of economic welfare relating to the risk sharing/insurance aspects of employment contracts are not directly addressed. It is especially difficult to design empirical studies to estimate the possible losses resulting from inefficient risk allocation; the notable paucity of evidence in this domain is therefore not surprising. It is noteworthy that the body of evidence presented in this section strongly suggests that the use of financial incentives, whether of the individual or group variety, has distinctly positive effects of productivity and firm performance.

The section on practical design issues (Part II) provides for the analysis of real world experience against the backdrop of the academic research cited; it is concerned with institutional and behavioral constraints that impinge upon the compensation and employment policies of firms. Some key questions that are addressed relate to the development of adequate performance measures and the adaptation of specific kinds of incentive plans to the environmental characteristics (i.e. organizational structure, organizational culture and technological capacity) of the firm. One paper deals with the actual experience of a large international conglomerate in adapting its incentive structure to a changing economic environment. The focus is on the effective management of incentive structures in large multi-divisional organizations in which productive units operate in numerous and varied markets and where the goal of internal consistency of rewards may conflict with the imperative of offering "competitive" compensation packages. Somewhat in counterpoint, the other paper in this section presents a more academic perspective on the formation of design criteria for incentive compensation. The analysis is applied to the case of executive compensation.

Finally, the section on public policy issues (Part IV) explores the relationship between the structure of private employment agreements and macroeconomic performance. The papers are concerned with the impact of wage and employment determination in firms on macroeconomic performance, with special attention given to the effects of decentralized and staggered contract negotiations. The real focus of this section, however, is on the macroeconomic properties of alternative compensation systems, a budding area of economic research. Alternative views of the consequences of flexible remuneration are represented among the contributors to this section and the rationale for the standard fixed wage contract is discussed. The lines of debate are clearly drawn.

This volume is truly comprehensive in scope and provides a balanced overview of the central theoretical and empirical issues that arise in the study of alternative incentive systems. The approach is interdisciplinary and some highly technical material has been translated in terms accessible to intelligent nonspecialists. The volume therefore should function both as a basic introduction to the field and as a practical source book for those interested in the theory and practice of compensation design.

Acknowledgments

A number of people contributed to the realization of this volume and the conference on which it is based. I am most indebted to Dr. R. Robert Russell, former Director of the C.V. Starr Center and currently Professor of Economics at the University of California, Riverside, for his unreserved support for the idea of holding an interdisciplinary conference of this nature. Dr. Russell was receptive to the idea from its inception and put the resources of the Center behind it. He was extraordinarily magnanimous and self-effacing in allowing me to pursue this project despite the clear perils of such an interdisciplinary endeavor and in giving a young colleague the opportunity to run with an idea. I am sincerely grateful for all that he did to make this project viable.

I am grateful to Dr. Bruno Stein, Professor of Economics and Director of the Institute of Labor Relations at New York University, for his advice and encouragement in the planning of the conference program and his participation as a session moderator.

In organizing the conference I relied on the expert, practical advice of Robert Korchak, Budget Director of the Faculty of Arts and Sciences at New York University, Eliana Covacich, then administrator of the Department of Economics, and Michael Dobie of the C.V. Starr Center. Their contributions to budgetary and logistical planning were indispensible; moreover, when family illness interrupted my work and threatened the final preparations for the conference, they came to the rescue insuring that nothing essential fell through the cracks so that the conference could proceed on schedule. I will never forget the extreme kindness and support of *all* the Center staff during this particularly trying period of my life.

The preparation of this volume has been greatly facilitated by the administrative support accorded me by the C.V. Starr Center. I am grateful to Professors William J. Baumol and Andrew Schotter, co-directors of the Center, for authorizing continuation of this support even though my current affiliation with the Center is on an adjunct basis. They have been gracious and generous in allowing me to see this project through to completion.

Finally, I wish to express my sincere appreciation to all the contributors to this volume and to the other conference participants from industry and organized labor. This project would never have gotten off the ground had it not been for the receptivity of the scholars and practitioners whom we approached as potential participants and their willingness to prepare papers addressing the specific issues that we requested. They recognized the potential fruitfulness of sharing their knowledge and expertise with colleagues from other disciplines and of engaging in a collaborative exploration of the dilemmas of employment contract design.

It is my profound hope that this volume will serve as an impetus to further interdisciplinary exchange and research on this important subject.

H. R. N.

INTRODUCTION

1

Incentive Compensation in Perspective

Haig R. Nalbantian

I.

Introduction

Incentive compensation of one form or another has become a common feature of employment contracts in the United States.[1] Profit sharing, productivity gain sharing, bonus systems and employee stock ownership plans (ESOPs) have gained a strong foothold in the American economy and their incidence has grown dramatically in recent years.[2] American firms are increasingly turning to incentive programs as a possible remedy for the declining productivity growth rates of their work forces and as a means of introducing greater cost flexibility to their operations. As in Japan, West Germany, and other West European countries, the standard fixed wage system is gradually giving way to a more diversified system of remuneration, one in which a significant portion of employee income is contingent upon some measure of firm or group performance (usually pretax profits).[3]

The resort to incentives, particularly of the group variety, has been highlighted in some of the more prominent and highly publicized contract settlements of the early eighties. In steel, autos, airlines, communications, construction, rubber, and a number of other industries, recent collective bargaining agreements have featured the introduction or expansion of profit sharing and other participatory measures, often in exchange for wage and work practice concessions (see Mitchell 1982; Flanagan 1984). In most instances, such "concession bargaining" has been a reflection of acute economic distress in the affected industry. Growing international competition and the continued trend toward domestic deregulation of industries has created an extremely competitive economic environment which in some sectors is forcing a fundamental readjustment in the terms of employment. The readjustment frequently demands changes in both the level and structure of corporate costs, of which the wage bill is almost always the most significant component. The indexing of individual compensation to measures of firm performance is emerging as a key mechanism facilitating the adaptation of internal labor market conditions to new economic realities.

While the plight of distressed industries has certainly contributed to the expansion of group incentives, it would be a mistake to interpret this development as simply a temporary accommodation to transitory economic forces. The growing use of incentive systems is not simply the consequence of defensive maneuvers on the part of beleaguered or failing firms. Most often, the institution of incentive pay systems is a positive action taken by firms in recognition of the strategic role of compensation in furthering corporate goals. In an ever changing economic environment, driven by rapid technological innovation, frequent external shocks and intense competition, expeditious adaptation to new contingencies is essential to corporate profitability. Compensation systems that provide more direct and immediate linkage between labor costs and actual business conditions increase the flexibility of firms in responding to changes and meeting competitive pressures. Compensation systems that succeed in promoting the perception of a harmony of interest between employer and employee foster improvements in labor-management relations that are useful in inducing cooperative efforts to attain corporate objectives. The recognition of these potential benefits has spurred firms to adopt a more sophisticated approach to compensation. American firms are devoting substantial resources to designing and implementing incentive programs tailored to their specific needs and characteristics. Compensation policy is thus pursued as an instrument of human resource management which seeks as its principal aim to establish congruence between the attitudes, abilities and behaviors of employees and the firm's objectives.[4]

The growth in incentive compensation is also a reflection of long-term changes in the nature of work and in the composition and attitudes of the work force (see Lawler, this volume). In the emerging knowledge/information-based economy, the expanding sectors are precisely those in which variations in employee motivation and initiative have greatest significance for firm performance. Providing incentives for skill acquisition and development, information sharing and cooperative behavior becomes equally important to the motivation of individual effort or "hard work." These are areas that are most amenable to the application of incentivized reward systems and where group measures of performance are more easily tracked than are individual contributions. In short, the modern economy is expanding those sectors that have traditionally used various elements of performance-contingent pay and where group incentives are most viable.

The recent surge in group incentive systems is in fact an acceleration of a long-term trend that has marked the entire post-war period, especially in the case of profit sharing. The growth of profit sharing took its initial impetus from a report issued in 1939 by the Vandenberg-Herring Subcommittee on Finance that heralded profit sharing as a vital and workable concept that had already proven effective in improving labor-management relations and increasing industrial efficiency. Indeed the report went so far as to declare profit sharing as "essential to the ultimate maintenance of the capitalist system."[5] In the wake of these findings, legislation was passed that accorded special tax treatment to qualifying profit sharing plans.[6] The federal government created compelling incentives for employees and their employers to come to terms regarding profit sharing.

The records of the treasury department indicate that there were 2,113 qualified deferred and combination-cash plans operating in the United States in 1945. By 1974 that figure had risen to 186,499; ten years later the number stood at 374,557. Except for a brief period of decline in the mid-seventies and more recently in 1984–85, the pace of growth evidenced in the intervening period has been steadily increasing.[7] It is estimated that of the more than 450,000 profit-sharing firms in the U.S. a little over one quarter maintain immediate cash plans.[8] While larger firms predominate among the profit sharers (indeed many of this countries largest firms are conspicuous among the profit sharers), an increasing number of small and medium sized firms have adopted profit-sharing programs, a fact reflected in the persistent decline, throughout the sixties and seventies, in the average number of employees covered by each plan. The distribution of these plans is broad, ranging across the entire spectrum of American industry. In the banking industry, retail trades, department stores, petroleum, publishing and printing, textiles and apparel, and other industries, profit sharing is extremely widespread and its incidence in manufacturing now exceeds one quarter of all firms.[9] If public utilities and hospitals where profit sharing appears most infrequently are excluded, it is estimated that 25 percent of firms have some form of profit sharing in operation.

All in all, the evidence clearly indicates that incentive compensation is already well established in some of the most important sectors of American industry. In these sectors, the prevailing system of incentive and reward, the mechanism by which risk is allocated among employers and employees is slowly but unmistakeably being transformed, in ways that could vitally affect the performance of the American economy.

While the increasing use of incentive compensation may well be apparent, it remains to assess what impact this development is having on company performance and on general economic welfare. On an empirical level, there is already a considerable body of evidence concerning the relationships between financial incentives, employee productivity and firm performance. The evidence has been garnered from case studies of specific incentive programs, frequently relying on subjective evaluations by program organizers and management personnel, and from more sophisticated, controlled studies of the effects of various incentive programs. Some of this evidence is summarized and evaluated in Part II of this volume. Generally speaking, it reveals that financial incentives, both individual and group, are effective as motivators of performance and will *on average* result in improvements in the performance indicator they are designed to affect. However the results also indicate substantial variance in the effectiveness of specific types of incentive plans, suggesting that a number of environmental and human factors operate to influence the motivating powers of contingent pay systems.

Despite the plethora of empirical studies concerning productivity performance, there is still little evidence with which to evaluate the significance of incentive systems for the broader questions of economic welfare.[10] There is a host of issues that must be addressed before we can even presume to make judgments about the general economic consequences of particular contractual regimes. The complexity of the issue arises from the complexity of function of employment contracts themselves.

Employment contracts, whether explicit of implicit, are economic instruments that serve a wide variety of functions. Far more is involved than the mere pricing of labor inputs, the provision of work incentives or the specification of job descriptions. Employment contracts serve also as the primary vehicle for the allocation of employment-related risks. They are an important means of allocating a heterogeneous labor force across firms and projects, and a determinant of the degree of labor mobility within the economy. They serve as a device for signaling information regarding privately observed contingencies that are pertinent to production choices and for delivering incentives for information generation and distribution among economic agents along with the requisite level and quality of decision making. The list could go further, but the point should be clear. In determining the structure of compensation and the terms of employment contracts, the parties to the bargain are in fact making complex choices that have welfare consequences beyond the parties themselves for society at large. A comprehensive evaluation of the merits of alternative reward systems must consider their effects in at least some of the most important of these areas before any basic judgments are reached.

On the theoretical level, understanding of the nature of labor contracting has grown considerably during the past decade or more due to the extensive research in this area by economists, industrial psychologists, and compensation/human resources specialists in industry and academe. Within the economics discipline, there has emerged over this period an extensive literature on the theory of contracts that together with studies in labor management, property rights, organization theory and principal-agent relationships significantly expands our understanding of the economic properties of various contractual forms and of the conditions under which share arrangements, in particular, emerge. Much of this work has sought to characterize the "optimal contract" under alternative assumptions concerning the level and distribution of information and the attitudes of the contracting parties towards risk. (See for instance Arrow 1970; Stiglitz 1974). The literature has probed the relation between the efficient allocation of risk and the appropriate provision of incentives and has identified the circumstances in which the two are in apparent contradiction.[11] Indeed, the implications of adverse incentives or what is termed "moral hazard"[12] for the efficiency of alternative types of contracts have been closely examined and conditions for attenuated or "second best" solutions advanced[13] (Harris and Raviv 1978; Holmstrom 1979 and 1982; Shavell 1979). The analysis of these issues together with a consideration of the role of differential costs of negotiating and implementing the various contractual forms has helped explain the existence of hierarchies within organizations (Cheung 1969; Calvo and Wellisz 1978).

Within this framework, the literature has focused on four factors judged to be important in determining the structure of employment contracts: the existence of imperfect and asymmetric information among economic agents (employers and employees), differences in the motivation of agents and in their respective attitudes towards risk, and differences in the transactions costs associated with alternative contractual arrangements. The models formulated have generally dealt with the interplay of two or more of these factors and their implications for optimal sharing rules. They have resulted in a series of propositions that go a long way in explaining observed patterns of economic organization and are useful in evaluating their consequences for economic efficiency.

Psychological research relating to incentive systems has pursued a different though closely related track. Typically, industrial psychologists have been concerned with the nature of motivation, its sources and consequences for employee behavior (Whyte 1955; Vroom 1964; Lawler 1971; Locke et al. 1980). They have focused on the interaction between the stimulus of external rewards and the internal, cognitive evaluations that spur productive activity. A distinction has been drawn between intrinsic and extrinsic motivation, the central concern being the impact that one has upon the other (See for example, Deci 1971, 1975; Scott 1975; Pritchard et al. 1977). Industrial psychologists have spent considerable effort delineating the types of rewards that are potentially motivating and identifying the various contextual factors that render them most potent in eliciting productive behavior (Guzzo and Katzell, this volume). In this connection the analysis has probed the dynamics of group behavior; the emphasis has been on the role of interagent transfers and externalities in determining the effectiveness of programs based on financial incentives.

Thus, there is a wide body of knowledge concerning employment contracts. The research cited in these two disciplines has proceeded independently; for the most part, there has been little cross referencing involved and few attempts to provide a synthesis of the research findings.[14] This is especially curious given the apparent divergence in some of the central research conclusions that can be gleaned from these disciplines, particularly regarding assessments of the benefits of performance-contingent pay generally and the relative effectiveness of individual versus group incentive programs. The divergence reflects not so much inconsistency in the findings, but differences in the breadth of analysis and in interpretation. There is much to be gained from a synthesis of research findings and it is to this purpose that this volume and, to a more modest degree, this essay are devoted. In identifying some of the sources of the perceived disparities, we can point the way to prospective alterations of the assumptions of formal analysis and of the standard approaches to the modelling of labor contracting, such that research results can provide more reliable guidelines to practitioners for the design and implementation of compensation packages.

II.

The Basic Economics of Labor Contracting

The diversity of employment contracts has long been of interest to economists, but until rather recently many of the important features of these arrangements have been essentially camouflaged behind the central proposition that, in a competitive labor market, "hired" employees would be paid the value of their marginal products.[15] It was the emergence of that branch of inquiry called the Economics of Information that propelled the economics discipline into a more rigorous analysis of specific features of employment contracts as they relate to the provision of incentives and the allocation of the risks associated with productive activity.

The origin of incentive problems or moral hazard lies in imperfections and asymmetries of information confronting the contracting parties under condition of employee risk aversion.[16] In a world of perfect information the criteria for the efficient allocation of resources might well be fulfilled by any contractual regime. No incentive problems would arise. All productive inputs would be paid the value of their marginal products and the particular contractual regime adopted (whether it be a fixed wage, rental, or some hybrid mixture of fixed and share components) would be inconsequential to the satisfaction of efficiency criteria. Once uncertainty in the relation between actions and their consequences is introduced, the allocation of risk becomes a central function of the market mechanism and information itself becomes a coveted commodity. Not all contracts will be equivalent in terms of the economic welfare they generate. The specific contract adopted will reflect the special adaptation of the contracting parties to the data pertinent to their choices and the particular "state of knowledge" with which they are individually endowed. In a competitive market, the employment contract will be designed to best utilize all information that is available to the contracting parties and that is relevant to sorting the various parties' specific contributions to the outcome of the productive activity.

Much of the theory of employment contracts has been developed through the use of the principal-agent paradigm.[17] In the standard bargaining situation represented in the principal-agent model, the employee (the agent) supplies labor inputs to the employer (the principal) in exchange for income and other nonpecuniary rewards. These inputs combine with other factor inputs to produce output(s) of economic value. Under conditions of uncertainty, the input(s)-output(s) relation is not uniquely identified. There are sources of variability in output or its value that are not directly tied to variations in the inputs provided by employees or, to be more precise, that are not reflective of specific choices that employees have made.[18] Thus, a given level of labor input can correspond to different levels of output, depending upon the particular contingency that is realized. The actual realization of such external or "exogenous" contingencies is characterized by economists as the "state of the world." This analytic construct subsumes all factors affecting output that are beyond the direct control of individual employees. It is the device by which "exogenous" or "environmental" risk is introduced into the analysis of contracting, so as to capture the stochastic nature of productive activity in the real world. Adverse weather conditions, materials supply disruptions, product demand and price fluctuations are examples of the kind of external contingencies that affect production or, more generally, performance levels in actual business operations.

In a competitive labor market, the central problems of contract selection are to generate and then apportion a stochastic outcome among the contracting parties in a manner that maximizes their welfare. The efficiency of any particular reward system is determined largely by its ability to track or meter individual employee contributions and to distinguish them from the influences of exogenous factors. The risks associated with stochastic disturbances to output (or value of output) are themselves commodities to be allocated among employer and employee according to principles of efficient risk management. The latter requires that those most willing and able to bear risk assume the risk burden by taking on the role of insurer, usually charging a fee (premium) for the insurance services they provide.

Typically, the firm is cast in the role of insurer of employment-related risks. This is consistent with the observations that firms generally enjoy a comparative advantage in risk bearing and are thus able to assume the burden of risk at less cost, in welfare terms, than are those they employ. For one thing, shareholders are usually wealthier individuals than are employees; if risk tolerance increases with the level of wealth, then it is fair to assume that employers are likely to be less averse to risk than are employees. Even more importantly, the capital market facilitates the diversification of wealth among a wide variety of real and financial assets. Shareholders can lower the overall burden of risk they face through diversification of their wealth among alternative projects. It is far more difficult and costly to diversify the investment of one's portfolio of human capital; employees can hardly spread their services across a variety of projects in a manner than efficiently reduces their risk exposure. Thus, it is not surprising that we most often see owners of capital assuming the major burden of income uncertainty rather than the suppliers of labor services. The provision of complete or partial insurance against the effects of exogenous contingencies becomes a central function of the employment contract.

The basic information asymmetry that gives rise to moral hazard is the inability of employers to monitor directly the level or quality of labor inputs supplied by employees. The labor inputs that actually contribute to productive output are difficult if not impossible to observe directly, and assessments of their quality are even more problematic. The employer is usually forced to rely on proxies or estimators of the actual labor inputs of concern.

When individual inputs are directly observable, the problem of adverse incentives can be avoided through the use of a so-called "forcing contract." Such a contract simply specifies that the agreed-upon reward will be paid, if and only if the requisite input levels are observed to be forthcoming. Otherwise the employee will be penalized. Given the appropriate penalty, this reward system ensures that employees have the proper incentives to provide the input levels that equate the marginal costs of their input expenditure (the marginal disutility from supplying inputs) with the expected marginal benefits derived from this exchange, namely, the expected marginal utility of income.[19] Obviously, if we abide the common assumption that supplying inputs like effort generates disutility to the agent, then for any given level of reward, there is always an incentive to withdraw inputs and thereby increase one's net return. If such withdrawal can go unnoticed, that is, if no responsibility can be attached to the diminished product levels it creates, then shirking is the predicted response.

The natural correction to shirking, in this context, is to ensure that the agent pays some penalty for this activity, one that is commensurate with the employees evaluation of the subjective gains from shirking. A forcing contract does this through direct monitoring of input levels and the imposition of penalties for any perceived shortfall. Individual output-based reward systems, such as piece rates, accomplish the same thing by linking the reward directly to performance, such that, *ceteris paribus,* withdrawal of inputs is automatically reflected in a proportional reduction in reward. But whereas the forcing contract can accomplish the provision of incentives without imposing on employees the risk associated with fluctuations in factors exogenous to employees, the output-based systems inevitably subject them to some of the risk burden.

Whenever there is imperfect observation of the level (and quality) of inputs supplied by employees and, as a consequence, rewards must be based on some proxy or estimator of their inputs, the uncertainty associated with the values of these estimators will impact upon employees. The employee's income is thereby affected by factors unrelated to the input choices he has made and assumes stochastic properties. To a greater or lesser extent, the employee is forced to assume an excess risk burden. Assuming that employees are risk averse, or at least, more risk averse than the firm, the resulting contract cannot be (Pareto) efficient. Incentives can only be provided at the cost of inefficient risk bearing. Those who have a comparative advantage in bearing risk cannot absorb that risk to the extent that is socially optimal. Both parties could be made better off if the risk burden could be transferred to the least risk-averse party. The employee would willingly pay a premium to unload this risk, perhaps in the form of a lower guaranteed compensation level. The employer would willingly assume this risk burden because in so doing compensation would be paid in a form that is less costly to him (in fact, zero cost if the employer is risk neutral). But such a transfer of risk is not feasible in this instance because the employee simply cannot make a credible promise to supply the requisite level of productive inputs, even though, *ex ante,* it is in his interest. Without the ability to directly observe input levels, the employer cannot be sure that in taking on the function of insurer against exogenous risk, he is not thereby stimulating a withdrawal of the very inputs for which he has contracted. Whatever benefits the employee would reap from unloading this risk, there remains upon contracting an incentive to shirk. As such, no self-enforcing agreement to engage in such exchange is feasible. Without direct observations on input levels, remedies relying on policing or external enforcement are insufficient to insure that the employment contract is efficient. Hence, the outcome of this bargaining situation (or contract) is what economists call "second best." The deviation from a first-best solution (optimum) and the resulting misallocation of risk is the true cost of the information imperfections that characterize the typical employment situation.

In the face of moral hazard, as just described, the challenge of designing an efficient employment contract becomes one of finding the appropriate reward formula that generates incentives for the supply of the desired inputs at the least cost in terms of inefficient risk sharing. The object of the employer is to encourage self-selection of requisite input levels without exposing the employee to appreciable risk emanating from the factors beyond the employee's control. Again, it must be emphasized that it is not altruism that drives the employer's response here. If the employer enjoys a comparative advantage in risk bearing, it actually pays for him to absorb as much of the risk as is consistent with the provision of incentives. Otherwise, his overall compensation bill will be higher than it need be to retain the level and quality of labor inputs that he requires. Or, if compensation does not adjust to reflect the risk burden assumed by the employee, then it can be expected that the employee will either seek employment elsewhere under terms preferable to him or engage, if possible, in activities that minimize the risk to which he is exposed. This situation is especially pertinent to executive compensation. If managers are overly exposed to risk in their capacity as agents for shareholders, they are likely to have their decisions influenced by their own dislike of risk and thereby undertake projects that reduce their own risk exposure even at the cost of reducing shareholders prospective returns. Such behavior can delay or forestall productive activities that would be economically beneficial to the parties themselves and for society at large. Clearly there is a substantial social cost involved in such decisions.

Of course, if employees are not, in fact, averse to risk, say, they are risk neutral, designing an efficient contract becomes trivial. In this case, a fully performance-contingent reward system under which the principal is paid a fixed fee will be optimal. Under the performance-contingent regime, the incentive problem is completely internalized. Since the agent bears the full cost of his actions, and his actions affect the probability distribution of the (stochastic) outcome, he is driven, thereby, to select that level of activity that equates the marginal costs of supplying the labor inputs with the expected marginal return. A risk-neutral individual is indifferent to fluctuations in income so long as expected income remains unaffected. Thus, exposure to exogenous risk under the performance-contingent regime will not result in a welfare loss to the risk neutral agent if it does not affect the expected returns that govern his choice both of the activity engaged in and the level of activity undertaken.

We see then the central role of information constraints in shaping contract choices. When firms cannot directly observe the level and quality of labor inputs and those supplying them are risk averse, the condition of moral hazard will be present and a first best optimum will not be obtainable. The extent of the welfare loss this imposes is determined both by the degree of sensitivity of the supply labor inputs to expected return and by the quality of estimators used to track the actual supply of employees' inputs forthcoming to the firm. The elasticity of supply of labor inputs is in large measure a function of subjective evaluations by individual employees of the value of the particular kinds of rewards deriving from their activities within the firm and of the true costs to them of supplying the particular labor inputs for which the job calls. Psychological research on motivation sheds much light on the process by which such calculations are actually made. More will be said on this matter at a later point in this essay.

The quality of estimators of labor inputs is assessed in terms of their ability to convey accurate information about the underlying variable of interest, namely the supply of labor inputs. The estimator is useful as a basis of the reward to the extent that it allows the firm to draw inferences concerning the actual level of inputs supplied. In selecting an estimator on whose value outputs will be contingent, the parties to the contract should seek a statistic that gleans from all the available information that which is strictly pertinent to assessing the employee's contribution.[20] If the statistic used embodies information that is irrelevant to discerning the employee's contribution, the resulting reward will assimilate the randomness associated with the statistic itself and additional income uncertainty will be generated. This is not in the interest of either party to the bargain. Ultimately, the search for the optimal reward formula can be interpreted as, in part, a search for a "sufficient statistic" for the prevailing exogenous contingencies ("state") with respect to employee inputs.[21]

The quality of estimators can of course be influenced by the level of direct monitoring of employee activity used by the firm. Monitoring can be conceived as both a substitute and complement to incentives within organizations (see Stiglitz 1975). The aim of an incentive system is to induce employees to self-select the requisite levels of inputs for which the firm has contracted. Monitoring, on the other hand, is an activity designed to increase the level of information concerning employee inputs. With monitoring, employers seek to overcome or ameliorate the information gaps that give rise to moral hazard in the first place. If, for instance, monitoring succeeds in raising the probability of detection of shirking behavior, it lowers the employee's expected gains from shirking and thereby alters the calculus of benefit and cost that governs the employees selection of input levels. Moreover, to the extent that it provides information on the ability of employees (or the quality of inputs, generally), monitoring reduces the need to rely on compensation systems as the mechanism for sorting employees from the labor pool according to ability.[22]

Nonetheless we have noted that the effectiveness of incentive systems depends on the quality of the estimators on which they base rewards; in this sense they inevitably rely on monitoring to make them functional. Monitoring activity by managers, on-line supervisors, time-study experts, and industrial engineers, etc., is the primary source of the information used to develop estimators on which rewards are necessarily based. When monitoring is flawed or incomplete when it itself is affected appreciably by stochastic disturbances, then the estimators of employee contributions that it produces may well serve to demotivate employees and generate inefficient risk sharing.

Furthermore, in the context of multiple employees and team production, monitoring can be the central instrument for ensuring the coordination of individual activities by fostering employee confidence that the behaviors of co-workers will be complementary to the individual employee's actions. It has been suggested that the very structure of modern organizations is an adaptation to the inability of purely market transactions to credibly meter and distribute the payouts from team production (Alchian and Demsetz 1972). By this interpretation, economic agents actually seek the intermediation of an external party, the employer, to monitor the activities of all parties to production so as to ensure that they engage in the appropriate behaviors to maximize joint product.

Incentive problems and the dual nature of monitoring also have implications for the structure of authority and control within organizations. Proponents of the "efficiency wage hypothesis" explain organizational hierarchies and the attendant pay differences across layers of the organization as an adaptation to an incentive structure that relies primarily on differences between returns to working within a firm and those anticipated as a consequence of separation from the firm. According to the efficiency wage scenario, firms offer employees a premium over general market wages in an effort to provide incentives for the appropriate supply of labor inputs. If all firms simultaneously pursue such an incentive policy, the market wage will rise, creating in its wake, a higher rate of unemployment. The existence of unemployment serves to raise the penalty for those caught shirking and thereby diminishes the incentive for employed workers to shirk. Unemployment appears as a "discipline device" (Shapiro and Stiglitz 1984).

In this theory, monitoring is a central element of the incentive structure. On the one hand, monitoring is the instrument that enforces incentives through its impact on the probability that shirkers will be detected. At the same time monitoring and supervision also act as substitutes for pay incentives. If the probability of detecting shirkers falls with firm size, incentive problems are aggravated and constraints on firm size may ensue. Further wage premia may be required to overcome adverse incentives. Alternatively, the prospect of escalating wages may justify, on a cost basis, the introduction of layers of supervisors within the organization and hence the creation of hierarchies. The higher pay that supervisors typically receive will simply reflect the greater damages that would result from the shirking of the supervision function (Calvo, this volume). In sum, monitoring and financial incentives interact to produce the optimal incentive package.

The essential outlines of contract theory have now been drawn. Some important issues relating to the sorting of labor inputs by quality, the impact of turnover costs, and the distortions of input supply decisions due to signaling imperatives have been neglected in order to highlight what is perceived to be the central dilemma of labor contract design: the trade-off between the provision of incentives and the efficient allocation of risk. We are now in a position to characterize some generic forms of compensation systems in terms of the criteria presented. Our focus is principally on the properties of the estimators employed in these systems and their ability to mediate the inherent tension between incentives and risk-sharing considerations.

III.

Incentive Systems in Practice

Several categories of estimators can be discerned in the actual compensation practices of firms. Input-based estimators use surrogate inputs as measures of the underlying inputs of concern. Time spent on the job, observations on physical exertion, and the level of complementary inputs expended (i.e. logged mileage for sales personnel) are examples of such estimators that are commonly used by firms as the basis of payments to employees. The standard hourly wage is the still the characteristic form of remuneration in industry. Payments are geared to hours worked, usually subject to certain minimum performance standards. Under this system, performance contingency operates strongly at the lower bounds of employee effort but beyond the penalty threshold (the minimum performance standard below which the penalty comes into play), there is little incentive for marginal effort on the part of employees. There is no mechanism under the time standard for increased effort or other labor input levels to translate into increased pay. On the other hand, the time rate effectively immunizes tenured employees from the effects of exogenous risk and is less susceptible to measurement errors than are other input estimators. Measurement error is an additional source of uncertainty and is, in fact, a major avenue through which income uncertainty is introduced in real-world situations. The simplicity of measurement under the time standard is one of its most compelling assets as a compensation system.

Output-based estimators utilize individual or group performance indicators as surrogate measures of labor inputs. There are a variety of such estimators used by firms for compensation purposes. The piece rate is the oldest and most common form of individual incentive system. Rewards are contingent on the number of units of output produced, subject usually to a minimum quality standard. In practice, the piece rate often comes into play only after an established output quota is achieved. The piece rate is almost universally recognized as a strong motivator of individual performance because it tracks variations in individual effort fairly well. But even in this domain its capacities are not unqualified. Changes in job difficulty brought on by new technologies or production methods can be obscured by employee behaviors; hence, it is often the case that the firm cannot properly attribute the performance improvement to its proper source. The idiosyncratic risks specific to individual employees (illness, sudden inspiration, failure of an individual employee's equipment) will affect employee performance and will thus be reflected in their rewards. Thus, there is the potential of inefficient risk sharing under the piece rate system. Finally, in a multiple agent setting, the piece rate tends to generate strategic behavior on the part of employees seeking to affect rate determination by modifying both their own behavior and that of their peers. The upshot is that piece rates introduced into a group setting very often lose the characteristics of individualistic reward systems.

An important class of compensation systems that is not individualistic is the competitive compensation scheme based on relative performance evaluation.[23] These can be either of the individual or group variety. Competitive compensation systems base pay on the ordinal rank of the employee or employee group, rather than on actual performance levels measured cardinally. The classic example is the so-called rank order tournament in which payoffs are based on the employee's rank alone, and where the margin of differential performance is completely immaterial to the rewards earned. Such a system renders employee income a two-part structure, with a safe income component reflecting the actual value of the employee's productivity and a lottery income reflecting the potential prize to the employees participating in the contest. The expected earnings of the employee are determined by the probability of winning, which, in turn, is affected by a number of factors including the employee's own effort (inputs), his competitor's effort, and the realization of idiosyncratic contingencies, i.e. stochastic disturbances pertaining uniquely to individual employees. Competition within firms for a limited number of executive positions with the attendant financial rewards is perhaps the most pervasive manifestation of competitive compensation systems in U.S. industry.

In many instances competitive compensation schemes provide strong incentives for effort and high performance. The deviation of reward from marginal product is the central motivating factor in these schemes.[24] Where employee's outputs are not independent, that is, where they are affected by common uncertainties, the employee's rank order has valuable properties as an estimator of employee contributions to output. Rank order is a powerful statistic for filtering out the effects of common environmental risks. In addition, it is generally true that ordinal measures require less information than do cardinal measures of performance and, thus, are less costly to the firm to acquire. It is often easy to determine that one employee performs better than another, though one might be hard pressed to state *how much* better. On the other hand, in practice ordinal measures are frequently dependent on subjective evaluations and this can serve to introduce new sources of uncertainty and thereby diminish employee's welfare. Finally, as noted, employees' income is affected by idiosyncratic risk so that individual contestants will still have their income affected by factors unrelated to their input choices. However, a major asset of the programs is that they force automatic adjustments to changing contingencies, which is surely welfare enhancing. The structure of rewards ensures that changes in job difficulty will induce the requisite changes in the level of labor inputs supplied.

Profit sharing and productivity gain sharing are examples of reward systems based on group performance indicators. These two types of programs are distinguished primarily by the scope of the estimators of labor inputs that they utilize to determine bonus payments to employees. Profit is, of course, the broadest of the performance indicators commonly used for compensation purposes. As a statistic on output, it meters changes in *all* factors affecting the supply and demand side of company operations. It incorporates a whole body of information that is, practically speaking, irrelevant to assessments of the employee's actual contributions to the firm's production. Accordingly, it is a seriously flawed estimator of labor inputs to production.

In addition, in many instances information on profit levels is not equally available to all parties to the contract. Employers are usually in a better position to accurately assess firm profitability. If profit serves as the basis of reward, the employer will have incentives to behave opportunistically in reporting profit levels to employees (see Stiglitz, Bull, Taylor, this volume). Hence, another source of income uncertainty is introduced. The prospective costs of risk misallocation under profit sharing may be quite substantial. These must be weighed against the various benefits that profit sharing can confer in the form of incentives for cooperation and information sharing, and flexibility of adaptation to new contingencies.

The various gain-sharing programs base bonus payments on changes in economic or physical labor productivity measures with respect to an agreed-upon base period. These productivity measures are more narrowly defined than profit. They are devised essentially to estimate the labor content of output and are calculated in terms of some surrogate measure of the labor inputs of the group, i.e. total payroll cost, total hours worked. In each case improvements in productivity measures are distributed between employer and employee according to a pre-specified share formula.

There are three major gain-sharing plans now in use in the United States. The Scanlon plan bases bonus payments on changes in the ratio of total payroll costs to the sales value of production. The Rucker plan, a variant of Scanlon, also uses total payroll in its rewards formula, but valued added in production is adopted in place of sales value in an effort to discount the effects of changes in materials cost and bought-in services and/or the ratios of materials employed in production. Improshare, the most recent of the gain-sharing plans, dispenses entirely with economic productivity ratios; instead it bases rewards on changes in the ratio of actual labor hours expended per unit of production to "standard hours," where the latter reflects the labor hour content of a unit of output in the base period.[25]

An evaluation of the quality of the estimators used in these group incentive plans must address two principal issues. First, how well do the various productivity formulae track the actual labor inputs of the *team*? That is, to what extent do they filter out those factors that are exogenous to the actions of team members? Second, how well can a group statistic function as an estimator of the labor inputs of individual employees under team production? To what extent can firms use aggregate output, or its value, to draw inferences about individual contributions?

The productivity formulae adopted in these gain-sharing plans function as estimators of actual labor inputs to production. Since the formulae involve intertemporal comparisons of productivity, they are not analagous to competitive compensation schemes in their handling of exogenous uncertainties. Random disturbances to labor productivity in either the current or base period will affect the level of bonus payments distributed to employees. Of the three plans mentioned, Improshare is the most refined in terms of the quality of the estimator of labor inputs that it employs. Because economic valuations of inputs and outputs are excluded entirely, bonus payments to employees are unaffected by changes in the relative prices of inputs and of outputs. Thus, some factors external to the input choices of employees, which do nonetheless affect bonus payments under profit-sharing and the other gain-sharing plans, are discounted from employee rewards under Improshare. On the other hand, the omission of dollar values obstructs or delays the transmission of product market signals concerning the valuation of labor inputs, signals that play an important role in facilitating the efficient allocation of labor across firms and projects.

Most gain-sharing plans contain mechanisms to differentiate between productivity improvements induced by changes in capital investment and those that follow from changes in the level or use of labor inputs. Some also contain "buy-back" provisions that essentially, permit productivity improvements beyond a certain ceiling level to be, in part, capitalized. Incentives for productivity improvement beyond the ceiling level can thus be sustained over time. This provision also allows for productivity gains attributable to employer decisions and other employer inputs to be properly discounted from employee rewards. Finally, since the productivity formulae are calculated with respect to "acceptable product" ready for shipment, they provide some mechanism for changes in the quality of labor inputs to be detected as well (Fein 1977, p. 43).

However, no matter how refined the estimators used in these gain-sharing plans, the firm must still confront the most compelling practical problem of group incentives generally, namely, their tendency to stimulate "free-rider" behaviors. The free-rider syndrome is a form of moral hazard that can arise under team production even when there is no uncertainty in aggregate output. It is the consequence of the inadequacy of aggregate output, under team production as an estimator of individual employee's labor inputs. When the level of individual inputs cannot be directly observed and aggregate output alone is used as a signal for these input levels, incentives are generated for individuals to reduce their supply below the levels required for economic efficiency. These incentives are present because in the costs of incremental changes in input levels are fully borne by the individual supplying them, while the consequences for output are diluted among the entire membership. Changes in the individual's rewards are not proportional to changes in the levels of labor inputs he supplies. In effect, the employee is taxed on any marginal contribution to product that he makes. The resulting deviation of marginal private benefit from marginal social benefit will bolster the employee's incentive to economize on the inputs he supplies to the firm. This incentive is manifested in shirking, an activity that will likely persist so long as the shirker cannot be identified.

The separation of ownership from labor combined with the application of group penalties or bonuses that, respectively, waste or exceed team output has been presented as a viable solution to the free-rider problem (Holmstrom 1982). In fact, the joint stock company or capitalistic firm, which is the characteristic form of business organization in the industrial economies, is explained in part as an adaptation to this free-rider phenomenon. Of course, another way to counteract these behaviors is to institute incentive systems that effectively transform the process of team production into a cooperative game.[26] Group incentives could succeed in overcoming the free-rider problem either by stimulating monitoring activity among employees themselves such that shirkers are detected, or by creating a social environment that confers social sanctions and benefits in support of cooperative behavior. These possibilities will be addressed at greater length in part IV of this essay.

The preceding discussion was not meant to offer a comprehensive analysis of the overall merits of the various types of compensation systems identified. We sought instead to place these systems in the context of contract theory and to characterize the properties of the estimators that they employ. A more meaningful assessment of these systems requires consideration of their impact on employee motivation and of some practical constraints that pertain to the design and administration of these systems in real-world situations.

IV.

Critique

In the preceding section, we set forth a general framework for analyzing the problems of incentives and risk sharing as they relate to the efficiency of alternative systems of employment and compensation. An understanding of the nature of the trade-offs involved in providing incentives under conditions of imperfect and asymmetric information has contributed to the widespread skepticism among economists about the utility of *explicit* incentive systems *per se* and of the wisdom of various tax and other public policy measures designed to promote the expansion of incentive compensation in American industry. Generally speaking, there is indeed a bias among mainstream economists in favor of the fixed wage-cum-supervision system. That the fixed wage remains the predominant form of compensation in the private sector is taken as *prima facia* evidence of its inherent merits relative to alternative share arrangements. The limited use of partnerships as a form of business organization is also cited as evidence of inherent inefficiencies of employee share ownership and the intractability of moral hazard problems within closed organizations (Holstrom, this volume). As we have seen, economic models of labor contracting place great emphasis on the insurance properties of employment contracts. In this respect, what most commends the fixed wage system is that it permits the transfer of risk from the labor to the capital market where it can be more efficiently dealt with.

Moreover, economists take exception to the notion that incentives need be explicit in order to have productivity consequences. Implicit incentives are present in most if not all employment relationships; they are manifested primarily in the adjustment (under competitive conditions) of wages to productivity changes, in opportunities for promotion within firms, and for lateral movements across firms. It has also been suggested that in many industries, especially those which are heavily unionized, certain forms of implicit profit sharing are in effect whereby workers share in the economic rents earned by the firm (Bull, this volume).

Where economists do recognize the necessity for explicit incentives, they tend to favor individual over group incentive systems. This position reflects an assessment of the prevalence and strength of the free-rider problem under group incentives; it is also based on the judgment that group performance indicators do tend to shift excessive risk to employees and that the social costs of this inefficiency are quite substantial.

Finally, there has been growing recognition among economists of the efficiency properties of competitive compensation schemes; recent research results on tournaments have led to rather sanguine views of their effectiveness in spurring productive performance among employees with little attendant losses in terms of inefficient risk sharing. Moreover, the properties of these systems in promoting quick adaptations to changing technology and other factors that affect job difficulty lend added weight to assessments of their value within institutions. Furthermore, it is noted that tournaments are in fact widely used in industry, particularly among sales staffs and management personnel.

It is interesting that these conclusions are in basic contradiction to developments in the American economy and to the prevailing views of psychologists and practitioners most directly involved in the design and administration of compensation systems. We have already noted the evidence on the performance of individual and group incentive systems in American industry. There appears to be a growing consensus among industrial psychologists and compensation specialists that explicit incentive devices are effective in motivating employees to improvements in productivity performance, and that they are valuable in creating an organizational climate conducive to high performance and the attainment of corporate goals. Among these observers, one also finds a much more favorable view of group incentives than what prevails among economists. There is greater emphasis on the negative externalities involved in individual piece rates and an affirmation of the powers of group incentives, properly formulated, to encourage worker involvement and interest in the firm's operations and to stimulate cooperative behavior among employees and between employees and management. These are seen as crucial elements in the effort to improve productivity performance.

Industrial psychologists and practitioners also tend to stress the value of participative or consultative management that aims to tap the information resources of employees and to involve them more directly in decision-making processes with respect to production decisions, work organization, and the design and implementation of reward systems. The argument for these arrangements is that they increase the supply of valuable information to the firm and improve communication on performance issues. It is also claimed that they give employees a greater sense of responsibility and autonomy in the fulfillment of their work, thereby increasing job satisfaction.

In the same vein, we are also seeing greater efforts in the field to promote flatter, less hierarchical organizations with compensation systems that relate pay to skills rather than to relative positions within the corporate hierarchy. The view is that payment according to knowledge and skill provides stronger incentives to the work force at large to acquire and develop skills that are requisite to the firm's success in a rapidly changing economic environment. Skill-based pay, it is thought, better tracks the employee's true contributions to the firm's productive potential and establishes more credible linkages between pay and employee performance. It also encourages decision making on the basis of expertise rather than in consideration of an employee's position in the hierarchy.

To this writer, the discrepancies between the conclusions just outlined are indeed significant and raise important questions about the practical relevance of economic models of labor contracting, in particular, the principal-agent paradigm. How do we account for these discrepancies? What are their sources? And, to what extent does the emphasis on risk sharing considerations and free-rider tendencies accurately convey the true posture of employees vis à vis the problems of work and reward? It is to these questions that we now turn.

A critical analysis of the view of labor contracting presented in Section II of this essay must deal with three areas of concern: the characterization of labor inputs, the conception of rewards, and the specification of individual preferences, particularly with regard to employee attitudes towards risk and the supply of labor inputs. In each of these areas there are considerations that render the formulations of principal-agent models overly simplistic and perhaps misleading in the conclusions to which they give rise. These areas are linked since the activities of economic agents within organizations are closely interrelated. Both on the input and reward side, there are inter-agent transactions that transform the basic decisions that economic agents are required to make and that interpose a complex of constraints and opportunities that ultimately determine the level of labor inputs supplied and the structure of employment contracts adopted. We examine each of these areas in turn.

Vector-Valued Inputs

It is common to hear human resources and compensation practitioners assert that their central task is to make workers "work smarter, not harder." The basic insight underlying this comment is that individual employees are typically the source of multiple inputs to the firm, inputs that are diverse in nature and that cannot be characterized as a single function or activity as is customary in the standard specifications of principal-agent models. Changes in an employee's productive contribution to the firm are accomplished not only through changes in the level of a particular input, such as effort, but in the composition of the bundle of inputs that the employee supplies.

A fundamental dilemma of contract design, largely overlooked in the economic analysis of employment contracts, is that the greater the precision of estimators used in tracking the levels of any specific input supplied by an employee, the more demanding are the requirements on the firm to identify precisely those inputs for which it is actually contracting. In practice, it is extremely difficult to pre-specify all the inputs that make up a given job. To a greater or lesser degree, most jobs entail elements of information generation and processing, decision making and capital maintenance. The optimal supply of such inputs depends, from the vantage point of the firm, on the particular contingency that obtains.

Theoretically, an efficient contract would pre-specify each and every activity required in response to all anticipated contingencies. In practice, however, the complexity of such a contract would impose enormous administrative costs upon the firm and most likely blur the employee's perception of the relationship between pay and performance. But complexity aside, information constraints on the contracting parties impose serious limitations on the kind and extent of contingency clauses that can be incorporated in any employment contract. For the institution of contingency clauses requires that the relevant contingencies be observable to both parties; otherwise there exist strong incentives for the privileged party to represent the actual contingency in a manner more favorable to his own interests. Without further contractual stipulations to ensure truth-telling, the differential information among the parties would render the contingency clauses incompatible with the provision of appropriate incentives for the supply of productive inputs (see Stiglitz, this volume).

It is for this reason that we generally see considerable latitude in the job descriptions of employees (particularly in the growing service and information sectors of the economy). Broader, more general job descriptions allow employer and employee greater flexibility in their responses to specific contingencies as they arise; in effect, they allow the employer to determine the specific set of inputs that is required in a given condition or circumstance. Whether such adjustments do actually occur depends largely on the kind of incentives that are in place. In this respect, there are clear advantages, therefore, in having a compensation system that induces automatic and timely adjustment of both input levels and input selection to changes in the economic environment of the firm. A rewards system that is too finely honed to certain inputs, specified at the time of contracting, may fail entirely to track and then "incent" employees to supply other inputs that are called for in the actual situation. A piece rate system may adequately assess and motivate the pace of production, but fail to encourage the level of care and work precision that ensure high levels of quality, especially when material defects or operations failures suddenly present themselves. In contrast, a compensation system that bases rewards on broader, more general, performance indicators, such as profit or group productivity, will provide at least some mechanism for the provision of such inputs (optimal though not specifically contracted for) to influence his rewards. This is a very real benefit that must be weighed against the costs of potential risk misallocation that the broader performance measures impose.

From what I have gleaned from the testimony of practitioners, the major sources of efficiency earnings potentially available to the firm are in changes in the organization of work, in cooperative efforts to uncover and eliminate organizational impediments to productivity, and in facilitating the introduction of new processes and techniques that permit more efficient use of labor and capital resources. Ultimately, these efficiency earnings are attributable to specific behaviors of employees and can thus be conceived as inputs to production. The inputs associated with information sharing, innovation, monitoring activity, coordination, and decision making will tend to have more impact on group performance indicators than on individual ones: when provided unilaterally, they do not materially affect the performance measures of the individual supplying them. In other words, these inputs have productivity effects external to the individual employee and, as such, individual performance indicators may fail to detect changes in their supply to the firm.

Employees will only have incentives to provide such inputs if their rewards are linked in some fashion to the group performance indicators that are affected by these inputs. Moreover, the incentives will be stronger if employees are convinced that the "best responses" of their co-workers will be complementary to their own actions and thereby allow the full economies to be realized at the plant or firm level. Where the reward system is strictly individualistic, or where it contains a competitive component, as in rank order tournaments, the appropriate incentives will not be generated. This is especially true when the activity involves direct costs or risks to the employee who undertakes it.

Consider, for instance, the piece rate system. The output of an individual under a piece rate system serves not only as a signal for the employee's input levels but of his ability and of the difficulty of the task being performed. In this latter respect, an employee's performance has ramifications beyond his own welfare. Where the productivity of high effort or most able employees is considered in the determination of the rates applied to the entire work group, a significant and potentially demotivating externality is created. The prospective income of the least able or low effort employees is affected by the superior performance of their co-workers. Thus, there are incentives for those so affected to take actions to reduce the performance of their more productive peers. Usually, this is accomplished through the administration of various penalties in the form of peer pressure, negative feedback, or social ostracization. Sometimes, however, employees resort to direct action to impede the productive performance of the so-called "rate busters." These actions can involve the withdrawal of cooperation and, sometimes, downright sabotage. They can be viewed as negative inputs to production. The potential divisiveness of piece rates, well documented in numerous case studies, is one of the major deterrents to their institution in firms, even though their inherent motivating powers are recognized.

Similar behaviors can be discerned in the case of competitive compensation schemes. While the deviation of income from marginal product may well produce strong incentives for employees to supply appropriate levels of their own inputs to the firm, the competitive structure of the game generates incentives for employees to seek to undermine the productive performance of their adversaries. In a contest, the behavior of each party affects not only his own expected income, but that of the other contestants as well. An employee's activity simultaneously affects his own and his competitor's probability of winning the contest. Again, negative externalities such as these can create incentives for nonproductive behaviors. Apart from direct sabotage, the negative responses can show up as a refusal to cooperate or the hoarding of private information; these are common methods by which employees act to shape the outcome of the contest. Since these activities do represent inputs to production, the competitive compensation scheme can, in some circumstances, actually generate incentives for the withdrawal of certain inputs, which, if supplied, would contribute positively to the overall productivity of the firm.

The ability of group incentives to enhance organizational performance is perhaps clearest in the areas of information sharing and monitoring activity. Employees engaged in the routine day-to-day fulfillment of a task are usually in a position to detect inefficiencies in operations that diminish productivity. They are also likely to acquire important information concerning the actual productive contributions of their co-workers. In essence, information processing and monitoring activity are joint products of the employee's productive activity in the firm, products that are usually produced at insubstantial cost to the employee himself. The information derived from such activity is potentially very valuable to the firm as an input to production. Yet such information transfers will not be induced under an individual performance-based rewards system since it does not directly affect his own performance measures. The apparent lack of incentives is compounded by the fact that under individual incentives, the activity may in fact be detrimental to the interests of co-workers and adversely affect their net income. But under the group system, the appropriate incentives are much more likely to be present. The performance indicators most affected by these information flows are the very ones used to calculate the individual employee's rewards. If there are indeed positive externalities associated with these information inputs and all the relevant group members are subject to the same incentives, then there is reason for the employee to identify his own interests with those of the firm and to furnish the inputs requisite to the firm's success.

With respect to monitoring activity, a group incentive system will succeed in promoting productivity improvement if it facilitates the transfer of monitoring activity from the firm to the employees themselves; that is, if it generates adequate self-monitoring by employees and at less cost than that required for direct monitoring by supervisors. Furthermore, it cannot be overlooked that the firm's managers and supervisors are themselves in an agency relationship with the firm's shareholders. Under some conditions they too are are in a position to shirk or have incentives to make decisions at odds with the interests of the firm's shareholders. The costs of managerial shirking can at times be even more substantial to the firm than employee shirking. A group incentive plan, properly designed, can be a useful instrument for encouraging employees, or their representatives to monitor the performance of their supervisors and managers and thereby provide valuable information to the firm's shareholders.

It is clear then that while profit sharing and other group incentives may be deficient as a motivator of individual effort or some other prespecified labor inputs, it may at the same time succeed dramatically in fostering behaviors that have a substantial impact on the overall productivity of the team. The group plan may deliver financial rewards for labor inputs that are completely neglected under the standard piece rate or hourly wage system. In sum, when we consider the multidimensional character of the labor input, it is not at all surprising that the system that delivers rewards may need to be multifaceted as well.

Vector-Valued Rewards

Just as labor inputs are vector-valued, so too are the rewards generated by productive activity. In their studies of work motivation, industrial psychologists have identified a variety of outcomes associated with work—outcomes that are quite diverse in nature. Clearly individuals engage in work for a variety of reasons. Financial gain is certainly a highly important motivator of work effort, but it is by no means the only one. Others prominently featured in the psychological literature are: security, prestige, friendships and social milieu, feelings of accomplishment and appreciation. It is misleading to make judgments of the relative merits of alternative compensation schemes without explicitly considering their effectiveness in delivering some of these other rewards that the affected employees value.

In their synthesis of the findings of over two hundred productivity improvement "intervention programs," Guzzo and Katzell (this volume) find that financial incentives, in fact, are not on average the most successful motivator of individual productivity improvement. Several of the programs, including goal setting and training, rank appreciably higher in their impact on targeted productivity measures. Especially striking in their findings was the high variability in the impact of financial incentives in the numerous cases surveyed. In fact, the variation was so high as to render the strong average productivity effect detected for financial incentives statistically insignificant.

This is not to suggest that financial incentives do not substantially affect productivity performance. Rather it indicates that certain contextual factors are of great consequence to the impact of financial incentives. The effectiveness of financial incentives varies with the type and level of employees within organizations, as well as by the type of organization in which they are introduced. The organizational environment and the particular experience of the employees covered will have bearing on the ability of financial incentives to spur productivity improvement.

Most importantly, the ability of financial incentives to motivate increased productivity depends on the existence of other rewards deriving from individual work effort. Some rewards bear a complementary relationship to financial incentives; others appear to operate as substitutes. The entire array of rewards available in a given work situation will determine the effectiveness of planned changes in any one component.

Industrial psychologists are generally concerned with analyzing the nature of employee motivation and in understanding the relationship between reward structures in the broadest sense of the term and individual behavior. Psychologists tend to distinguish between extrinsic and intrinsic motivation. The former are those generated from sources outside the individual, as with financial compensation. The latter arise from internal self-evaluations that are made by individuals, involving feelings of self-worth, competence, and self-determination. An important debate within the psychological profession concerns the interrelationship between these two broad classes of motivation. Some evidence has been produced that shows that extrinsic rewards can, in certain circumstances, undermine the individual's intrinsic motivation to fulfill a task (De Charms 1968; Deci 1971, 1972; Pritchard et. al. 1977). This does not mean that there is an inverse relation between the level of external rewards and the level of activity; only that extrinsic rewards can supplant, to some degree, the intrinsic motivation to work and hence will have less impact on performance than might otherwise be conjectured. These effects will be even more pronounced if the reward system is accompanied by other organizational structures or bureaucratic processes that directly undermine the individual employee's sense of autonomy and responsibility in the performance of his work.

The importance of preserving and indeed augmenting the employees intrinsic motivation to accomplish a task has not been lost on compensation administrators. A number of different programs have been developed that are geared primarily to affecting the intrinsic motivation of employees in the work place. Goal setting, feedback and appraisal, and job enrichment are three such programs that have been notably successful in improving productivity performance (Guzzo et. al. 1985).

A most interesting example of the pertinence of intrinsic motivation to employee behaviors might be drawn from some recent experimental studies of competitive compensation systems. (Bull et. al. 1985). These studies were designed to test some basic postulates of the theory of tournaments through experiments using paired competitors operating under circumstances simulating actual tournament conditions. One intriguing finding was that in uneven tournaments, the level of activity ("effort") undertaken by disadvantaged ("high cost") competitors was greater than that predicted by theory. That is, disadvantaged competitors, knowing their state, neither withdrew from the contest nor provided levels of activity that were consistent with optimal behavior given their constraints.

The implication of this result is that some other factor beyond expected monetary return was at work motivating behavior in this contest. The authors ruled out the hypothesis that the satisfaction derived from "winning," as opposed to expected return, was the factor governing the contestants' responses: the activity levels of the advantaged contestants did not bear out this speculation.

A more likely explanation, as I see it, is that the uneven tournament as designed by the experimenters stimulated in the disadvantaged contestants a high level of intrinsic motivation: the desire to overcome the odds and meet the challenge of their designation as high-cost contestants. The advantaged contestants, on the other hand, were probably demotivated by the knowledge that they were endowed with such an advantage and hence had less incentive to augment their expenditure of effort in the game. This seems a tenable explanation for the asymmetrical responses on the part of the high- and low-cost contestants. While both might derive satisfaction from winning, in one instance the satisfaction is particularly great because winning is an unexpected accomplishment and represents the conquest of a challenge; in the other, winning generates little if any satisfaction beyond that associated with the expected monetary return, since the challenge is minimal, the outcome entirely expected.

Evaluations of these results based purely on economic theories of employment contracts that neglect or obfuscate such factors as intrinsic motivation will find the observed behaviors in the uneven tournament to represent quite an anomaly. Explicit consideration of intrinsic rewards proves essential to an understanding of many of the behaviors routinely observed in employment situations.

The social environment of work is without question a major determinant of the effectiveness of pay as a motivator of work effort. In a group context, it is not only the employer who is in a position to assess and administer rewards and penalties but employees as well. The activities of peers and co-workers comprise an important part of the reward structure that confronts an individual employee in any organization. This is most clearly evident in cases where the activites of employees are interrelated, where the performance of one employee affects the performance of another, and where the rewards obtained by one employee have bearing, immediate or eventual, on the rewards obtained by others. Such situations given rise to interagent transactions that can fundamentally alter the operation of the incentive system in use. We noted earlier the kind of negative externalities associated with piece-rate systems. More generally, the emergence of protective social norms of production is a common by-product of individual incentive systems in many organizations. These norms effectively define the limits of individual performance; violators are subject to a variety of social sanctions or penalties designed to curb their productivity.

Similarly, social sanctions can work to spur individual employees to higher productivity performance, and to counter the tendency of employees to engage in free-rider behaviors under a group incentive system. Indeed, group incentives seem to work best when applied to smaller, cohesive groups of employees within which social sanctions and social benefits are more readily conveyed, and with greater clout with individual employees. Yet, remarkably, many of the largest Japanese trading companies seem to have succeeded in establishing a collective ethos of high productivity, backed up by what appears to be a powerful system of social sanctions and rewards that works to enforce an implicit contract among employees to desist from shirking behaviors.

The contingency between pay and performance and the perception of pay equity are crucial factors cited by industrial psychologists as complementary to financial reward in its effect on productivity. In truth, the perception of a pay-performance link is more important as a motivator of work effort than is actual, *ex post* linkage. Performance measures that accurately sort individual contributions from exogenous influences on productivity can actually have negative consequences for overall productivity if their use results in reward allocations that run counter to the assessments of the affected employees. Thus, we should take note of the substantial risks inherent in complicated reward formulas. If too many contingencies are covered, confusion and misunderstanding can be generated, and the system may convey to employees the misimpression that noncontrollable factors are determining the levels of rewards obtained. Incorporating various indices of environmental factors in an effort to filter out external influences on productivity may be valid in the sense of sufficient statistics, but if, in the process, employee perceptions of controllability over their rewards is lost or distorted, the use of such indices will be counterproductive in terms of motivational impact.

It is no wonder, then, that compensation practitioners stress so forcefully the role of communication or "process" mechanisms in the success or failure of any compensation scheme. The more complicated the pay plan formula, the greater the necessity of devoting resources to ensuring the employees' understanding of the system. Education and communication activities are themselves costly to the firm. These additional costs must, of course, be weighed against the benefits of basing rewards on more accurate assessments of the factors influencing productive performance. If refining the estimators of individual input contributions increases the complexity of the firm's compensation system, the informational value of the estimators may, in fact, be offset by a loss of motivation due to employee misunderstandings of the pay-performance link.

Even piece-rate systems can generate losses of this kind. The process of rate setting and rate adjustments in face of technological change invariably involves subjective judgments on the part of program administrators and managers. If the adaptation of rates to exogenous changes undermines the credibility of rates in the eyes of employees, the perception of linkage between pay and performance may be damaged and thus the motivational value of the system diminished.

The same kind of distortions can occur under competitive compensation schemes. Where the ordinal rankings of employees rely primarily on subjective evaluations by supervisors, the prospect of judgment errors arises. This can lead to the perception that factors beyond job performance most influence the outcomes of the contest. Should this perception indeed take hold, employee motivation can radically deteriorate. Moreover, since idiosyncratic risks connected with individual work effort play an important role in determining the outcome of competitive compensation schemes, the impression of randomness in employee income may be what is primarily conveyed. With the labor input-reward link thus impaired, the motivational value of the competitive compensation scheme can well be lost.

Employee perceptions are also at issue in evaluating the relationship between pay equity and employee motivation. Some psychological studies have shown that the degree of equity in the distribution of rewards has a notable effect on the motivational impact of financial incentives. Equity signifies a perception on the part of employees of a balance between the inputs they deliver to firms and the rewards obtained in exchange where the balance is assessed both relative to peers within the organization, or similarly endowed individuals in other organizations. An interesting finding in the empirical literature concerns the responses of employees to situations where there is a perception of inequitable payment. Specifically, some studies purport to show that employees who are overpaid will increase work effort under such circumstances, as if to rectify the perceived imbalance between inputs and rewards.[27] The observed behavior is then interpreted as an indication that employees act to remove inequity, even when the inequity is in their favor.

Another interpretation of these results is more consistent with the findings of economic theory. It is most likely that individuals who feel overpaid undertake protective action to insure that they remain in their more advantaged position. If the situation of overpayment represents, for instance, access to above-market wages, the fear of losing this privileged position would generate incentives for efforts to improve productivity performance both in qualitative and quantitative terms. Thus, the findings appear as a confirmation of the incentive properties of the "efficiency wage."

In this connection, there is also evidence in the literature that the actual level of wages is not an important determinant of performance, that contingency between pay and performance is the central mechanism by which financial incentive stimulates performance. This suggests that the tactic of paying higher than market wages will have little impact on employee work effort unless it is combined with very real and viable threats of job loss for those found to be shirking. This result calls into question the notion that the efficiency wage is somehow a substitute for monitoring. The augmentation of the wage must be accompanied by an appreciable increase in the level of unemployment for there to be meaningful incentive effects on employees.

As noted earlier, incentive problems and the resort to efficiency wages have been used to explain the emergence of hierarchies in business organizations. The hierarchical form of organization, with pay contingent on the employee's level in the hierarchy rather than on actual marginal products, is viewed as an efficient adaptation to incentive problems that otherwise would produce rapidly escalating wages or severely limit firm size.

It is curious however, that the recent trend in modern organizations is away from hierarchical organizational structures; we find instead new organizational forms emphasizing participative or consultative management, less hierarchy and skill-based rewards. These are regarded by many compensation specialists to be more compatible with high productivity states than the more traditional structures associated with hierarchies. Psychological research lends credence to the view that, in some circumstances, hierarchical structures can have strong demotivating consequences for employees; rather than being a mechanism for the application of work incentives, they introduce incentive problems of their own. Hierarchical structures are likely to undermine the perception of pay-performance linkages and magnify the employee's sense of pay inequity. They are also likely to weaken the intrinsic motivation of employees to accomplish their work. The presumed benefits derived from supervision-cum-threats of termination may well be offset by diminished individual incentives for work effort and high performance.

Observers like Lawler (this volume) emphasize that changes in the nature of work and in the values and expectations of the work force are highly significant with respect to the evolving trends in compensation practices and organizational forms. As previously argued, the kind of jobs available in the expanding information economy are typically less conducive to performance measurement on an individual basis, especially in the sense of cardinal measurement. These jobs require greater reliance on ordinal measures of performance that tend to introduce new risks in the form of measurement and judgment error. We know the kind of welfare losses that can result from excess risk burdens on employees. But it should also be noted that risks of this kind can interact with employee motivation to disort incentives for work effort. Specifically, if measurement error or failed judgment affect employee perception of the pay-performance link, or if they undercut the employee's sense of equity concerning the allocation of rewards, then it is very possible that diminished incentives will result from these reward structures in addition to the introduction of new risks. Whether, in fact, the perceptions are valid is of little relevance to these concerns, since perception, as we have noted, is the central force behind employee behaviors.

The difficulty of devising sound, accurate measures of employee input contributions based on individual output suggests that the resort to group incentives is a prudent response to incentive problems in the kind of work that is predominant in the modern economy. Perhaps parodoxically, group measures are likely to result in less damage to the employee's perceptions of a pay-performance link and of equity in the distribution of rewards.

Feedback Mechanisms

Another major issue that differentiates the approaches of economists and psychologists to the study of incentive systems relates to the treatment of employee preferences with respect to income, input expenditure, and risk. Whereas economic models of contracting characteristically proceed from *a priori* specifications of employee preferences and analyze their consequences for the structure and content of employment contracts, psychologists emphasize the feedback mechanisms through which the prevailing reward system impacts employee preferences themselves and, as such, determine the ultimate shape of the employment contracts utlized by the parties.

Thus it is important, for instance, to consider how a particular contractual arrangement may affect the propensity of employees to bear risk and engage in risk-taking ventures within the firm. A contract that emphasizes entrepreneurial activity on the part of all or some employees and rewards these activities as well can prove both an effecitve device for sorting employees according to risk preferences and as an instrument for promoting more positive attitudes toward risk. Such entrepreneurial contracts, aimed at creating a climate conducive to "intrapreneurship," are most prevalent in the high-tech, electronics, and consumer goods industries where intense international competition and rapid technological change mean that strong explicit incentives for creative activity are required if firms are to keep pace with their competitors.

The aim of such contracts is usually two-fold: to retain high-ability employees by thwarting lateral moves to other firms or to start-up companies; and to encourage skill development and human captial investments, largely firm-specific, that invariably entail a degree of risk taking on the part of employees. In offering such possibilities to employees, the firms affect the environment or culture of the organization and help create collective values that support and actually stimulate the kind of individual activities that they seek to encourage.

An overreliance on the static assumptions of economic models of contracting can lead to a misplaced emphasis on the costs of risk misallocation, neglecting in the process the essential fact that the disutility associated with risk is not absolute. It varies not only with income, but with the specific environment in which the individual operates. It is based on the extent of employee knowledge and understanding of the nature of the risks that they confront. And, as with any unknown contingency, acceptance of risk requires exposure to risk and an understanding, on the part of those concerned, of the relationship between risk and return.

In sum, the preference function of an individual is not part of the data of the economic system, but a fluid and evolving network of relationships whose parameters are constantly modified by the prevailing reward structure and the environment in which the individual operates. Compensation and human resource practitioners in modern industry can ill afford to operate under the blanket assumption that the provision of income insurance is the central aim of employment contracts, especially if they are operating in industries where rapid technological change is the rule and quick adaptation to environmental changes requires the willingness of employees to expose themselves personally to risks that only they can assume.

V.

Conclusion

In this essay, a wide array of compensation systems has been surveyed. The methodologies and findings of two disciplines have been tapped in an effort to illuminate the central problems and challenges of employment contract design.

Unquestionably, the models of labor contracting are extremely powerful devices for analyzing compensation systems. They yield valuable insights into the properties of alternative compensation systems. They clarify the kind of trade-offs involved in addressing the incentive problems that arise in face of the information constraints that commonly exist within organizations. Moreover, these models have also improved our understanding of the role of employment contracts, generally, in determining resource allocation in the economy at large.

Yet, the analysis presented points out the inherent dangers in simply extrapolating from these models in evaluating real-world compensation systems. The problems posed by the need for incentives in modern organizations are complex and idiosyncratic. Providing incentives usually calls for the application of custom-made incentive plans tailored to the specific circumstances, environment, and objectives of the individual firm. These plans must take into consideration the attributes of employees and employer, the complexity of job function, its vulnerability to external shocks, and the kind of employee behaviors that are most significant for company performance.

To this writer, the models of labor contracting give rise to an excessive preoccupation among economists with free-rider tendencies and the potential for risk misallocation. It is true that the existence of moral hazard in the form of free-rider behaviors is a major impediment to the successful implementation of group incentives. Within the limited scope of principal-agent models, individual incentives are indeed more likely to stimulate optimal input levels than are group incentives. However, seldom are such limited conditions present in business organizations. Where labor inputs and rewards are both vector-valued, it is not at all clear that the free-rider problem will manifest itself as the overriding issue for incentive schemes to address. There is abundant evidence to suggest that group plans are effective in motivating productivity improvement. It is quite conceivable that group incentives are more successful than individual incentives in furnishing some of the various rewards deriving from work that employees value. In any event, the evolution of job descriptions and the make-up of the work force indicate that the world is becoming less not more amenable to individual incentives, both because cardinal measurement of individual performance is becoming increasingly problematic and because service sector jobs involve a good deal more information processing and decision making than do the standard manufacturing jobs. In such a climate, it is hard to see how explicit individual incentives can dominate.

On the matter of risk sharing, the principal-agent models of labor contracting assess the efficiency of risk allocation from a distinctly microeconomic perspective. It is clear that the structure of employment contracts adopted by firms has profound consequences for the overall performance of the labor market in adapting to external shocks and cyclical fluctuations in various economic aggregates. There are externalities involved in contract selection that impact the general state of the labor market. It has been suggested by Weitzman (1983, 1984, this volume) that the widespread adoption of share arrangements in the form of profit or revenue sharing would create a "tight" labor market characterized by permanent excess demand for labor. This condition would counteract the tendency for employment variations across the business cycle and would, in the view of Weitzman, reduce the aggregate uncertainty relating to labor income.

There is no room here to join the debate concerning the effect of wage flexibility on macroeconomic performance. (See Part IV of this volume.) The issues are considerable and at this point further empirical investigation is required to meaningfully evaluate the contesting theoretical positions. What is clear, however, is that assessments of the efficiency of risk sharing among employer and employees can not be made strictly in terms of the welfare of the contracting parties themselves, but must take into account external effects on labor income as a whole. If, by smoothing out fluctuations in the income of individual tenured workers, fixed-wage contracts create conditions that increase the variability of national income, then the efficiency of risk sharing at the macroeconomic level will be cast in doubt. There exists a potential conflict between micro and macro efficiency. A deeper understanding of the nature of this conflict is essential before any firm determinations of the risk-sharing properties of group incentives can be made.

Notes

1. In this essay, the term "employment contract" denotes both explicit contractual agreements such as those negotiated under collective bargaining, and other "implicit contracts," those informal agreements between employer and employee that stipulate the terms of employment and the means by which they can be altered.

2. The data on profit sharing and other group incentives on which I have based my judgments concerning its prevalence and scope are drawn from a variety of sources, Among those consulted are: Bureau of Labor Statistics, 1984; Hewitt Associates, 1984; Kendrick, this volume; Latta, 1979; Metzger, 1975; New York Stock Exchange, 1982; Profit Sharing Research Foundation, 1985 and U.S. Chamber of Commerce, 1984.

3. As a percentage ot *total* payroll, profit-sharing payments have actually remained remarkably constant over the past three decades, around 1% according to the U.S. Chamber of Commerce Survey (1984). This low figure does not, in my judgment, accurately convey the true extent of performance-contingent pay in the U.S. nor the relative importance of profit sharing *per se* in the process of wage determination. Profit sharing and other human resource programs are not uniformly distributed across the economy. They are far more prevalent in some industries than in others and tend to be associated with larger firms. In smaller firms where less structured implicit contracts dominate, employee income will tend to be more responsive to industry conditions. Moreover, it is estimated that for employees who are covered by profit-sharing plans, the payments constitute 9–10% of total payroll.

4. For a more extensive discussion of the strategic use of compensation, see the papers of Lawler, Larson and Rich, and Armstrong in this volume.

5. U.S. Congress, Senate Subcommittee of the Committee on Finance, Survey of Experiemces in Profit Sharing and Possibilities of Incentive Taxation (Washington, D.C.: U.S. Government Printing Office, 1939) p. 5.

6. Under the Internal Revenue Code, deferred payments to employees (upon retirement or full vesting) were not taxable until the time of distribution; lump-sum payments distributed to employees at retirement were treated as long-term capital gains and were thus subject, generally, to a lower rate of tax. The employer's contribution under a qualifying plan could be deducted as a business expense so long as it did not exceed 15% of the total compensation.

7. Profit Sharing Research Foundation, 1985 and supplement to report, 1986.

8. Estimates are based on Hewitt Associates, 1984; Latta, 1979.

9. In each of these industries the percentage of companies paying profit-sharing bonus exceeds 35%. For instance, among Department stores the percentage is 43%; in banking it is 39%. For estimated percentages in other industries, see U.S. Chamber of Commerce, 1984.

10. It is especially difficult to design empirical studies to estimate the possible losses

resulting from inefficient risk allocation. The notable paucity of evidence in this domain is therefore not surprising.

11. Economists use the word "efficient" to denote something very specific. An outcome is efficient or "Pareto optimal" if there exists no action that can improve the welfare of one party (or parties) without damaging, simultaneouly, the welfare of at least one other party. In the context of labor contracting, a contract is efficient if it is impossible to improve the well-being of employees without reducing profits.

12. Moral hazard is a term adopted from the insurance literature. It denotes that condition where the provision of insurance against some contingency (event) actually increases the probability that the insured-against contingency will occur. As applied to contracting, it serves to characterize the adverse incentives that can arise when income guarantees (insurance) are offered to employees. Providing employees insurance against income variation can stimulate behaviors on the part of employees that actually increase the overall variability of the firm's income.

13. Second best solutions pertain to situations where information constraints on the behavior of employees or other market imperfections preclude the simultaneous satisfaction of *all* the conditions for efficient resource allocation. They are the best outcomes that can be realized in the remaining markets when one or more markets contain imperfections that are irremediable.

14. A major exception to this generalization is the important work of Leibenstein, 1976. His analysis represents an integration of modern psychological concepts and microeconomic theory.

15. The marginal product of labor is defined as the change in output attributable to a unit change in labor input, all other inputs held constant. Marginal product thus assesses the productivity of labor at current (given) input proportions.

16. An individual is classified as risk averse if he is unwilling to play a game (enter a lottery) that is actuarially fair, that is, the cost of which is precisely its expected value. Thus, a risk-averse employee is one who is *not* indifferent between receiving a guaranteed income of Y^* or participating in a lottery which generates an expected income of Y^*. (Note: expected income is simply the income the employee will earn *on average* under the lottery.) Indeed the risk-averse employee will willingly take a deduction from his wage to avoid the income variability associated with the lottery.

17. A classic exposition of the principal-agent paradigm is found in Ross, 1973. See also Grossman and Hart, 1983.

18. It is important to note that the channel of influence of exogenous factors on output often is through *unplanned* changes in labor inputs. For instance, an interruption in materials supplies or machinery breakdowns generally result in changes in the actual level of labor inputs supplied to the firm, *ex post*. Here the *ex ante* (planned)–*ex post* (realized) distinction becomes crucial. Exogenous factors can influence output by creating a divergence between the planned labor input levels and realized input levels. In other words, the choices of employees are not fulfilled due to factors beyond their control. Thus the distinction between exogenous and endogenous for our purposes really revolves around the issue of employee choices.

19. In models of labor contracting, the preference system of an individual is represented by the "utility function." This function is an analytic device designed to represent the level of satisfaction derived by the individual from the consumption of commodities. It generates rankings of alternative market baskets of goods and services that the individual consumes. In the principal-agent paradigm, the utility function consists of two arguments: income and effort (or labor inputs). Income is a source of utility; effort generates disutility. Effort is usually treated as an expenditure on the part of the employee that has a monetary equivalent. Individual's make this expenditure in order to obtain net income. The assumption of effort disutility is a fundamental element in the analysis of labor contracting.

20. This does not mean that every variable incorporated in the compensation function need be one that is controllable by the employee. Holmstrom, in his contribution to this volume, points out that under certain circumstances, variables completely external to employees should be considered in the allocation of rewards to the extent that they allow the employer to draw more accurate inferences about employee behaviors. For instance,

data on general economic conditions, (GNP or price level statistics, industry profit levels) can convey extremely useful information regarding the prevailing exogenous "state," which can help assess actual employee contributions.

21. For interesting discussions of the concept of "sufficient statistics," see Holmstrom, 1982 and Nalebuff and Stiglitz, 1983.

22. For an understanding of the sorting properties of piece-rate systems, see Stiglitz, 1975 and Weiss, this volume.

23. Among the seminal contributions to the theory of competitive compensation schemes are: Lazear and Rosen, 1981; Green and Stokey, 1983; Nalebuff and Stiglitz, 1983; O'Keefe et. al, 1984.

24. There are some circumstances under which the structure of the contest will actually stimulate shirking behavior. When the random component of individual performance is very small, the equilibrium solution to the contest can involve arbitrarily small prizes (and hence losses). Since supplying inputs will at most result in only a small gain over what is earned in losing the contest, there is an incentive for contestants to shirk and save thereby on the costs, in terms of utility, of supplying inputs. See Nalebuff and Stiglitz, 1983 for a more thorough analysis of this "non-convexity problem."

25. More detailed discussions of the various gain-sharing plans can be found in the following: Fein, 1977; White, 1979; Ringham, 1984; and Kendrick, this volume.

26. The analysis of the free rider problem presupposes that team production is best modelled as a non-cooperative game where the reaction functions (or best responses) of individual players are constructed on the assumption that the input levels of other players remain unchanged in response to any individual change in inputs.

27. A full review and evaluation of the evidence on employee responses to inequitable pay can be found in Lawler, 1971, chapter 8.

References and Selected Bibliography

I. Economics

Akerlof, G. 1970. "The Market for Lemons: Qualitative Uncertainty and the Market Mechanism." *Quarterly Journal of Economics* 84 (August): 488–500.

——. 1976. "The Economics of Caste and of the Rate Race and Other Woeful Tales." *Quarterly Journal of Economics* 90 (November): 599–617.

Akerlof, G. and J. Miyazaki. 1980. "The Implicit Contract Theory of Unemployment Meets the Wage Bill Argument." *Review of Economic Studies* 47 (January): 321–38.

Alchian, A.A. and H. Demsetz. 1972. "Production, Information Costs and Economic Organization." *American Economic Review* 62 (December): 777–95.

Arrow, K.J. 1970. *Essays in the Theory of Risk Bearing.* Chicago: Markham.

——. 1985. "Informational Structure of the Firm." *American Economic Review* 75 (May): 303–7.

Azariadis, C. 1975. "Implicit Contracts and Underemployment Equilibria." *Journal of Political Economy* 83 (December): 1183–1202.

Baily, M.N. 1974. "Wages and Unemployment Under Uncertain Demand." *Review of Economic Studies* 41 (January): 37–50.

——. 1977. "On the Theory of Layoffs and Unemployment." *Econometrica* 45 (July): 1043–64.

Becker, G.S. and G. Stigler. 1974. "Law Enforcement, Malfeasance and Compensation of Enforcers." *Journal of Legal Studies* 3 (January): 1–18.

Bell, L.A. and R.A. Freeman. 1985. "Does a Flexible Industry Wage Structure Increase Employment?: The U.S. Experience." National Bureau of Economic Research Working Paper No. 1604, April.

Borch, K. 1962. "Equilibrium in a Reinsurance Market." *Econometrica* 30 (July): 424–444.

Bull, C., A. Schotter, and K. Weigelt. 1985. "Tournaments and Piece Rates: An Experimental Study." C.V. Starr Center for Applied Economics, Economic Research Report #85–21, June.

Bureau of Labor Statistics. 1984. *Employee Benefits in Medium and Large Firms, 1983* (Bulletin 2213). Washington, D.C.: U.S. Government Printing Office.

Calvo, G.A. 1979. "Quasi-Walrasian Theories of Unemployment." *American Economic Review* 69 (May): 102–7.

———. 1985. "The Inefficiency of Umemployment." *Quarterly Journal of Economics* 100 (May): 373–87.

Calvo, G.A. and S. Wellisz. 1978. "Supervision, Loss of Control and the Optimum Size of the Firm." *Journal of Political Economy* 86 (August): 943–52.

———. 1979. "Hierarchy, Ability and Income Distribution." *Journal of Political Economy* 87 (August): 991–1010.

Cheung, S.N.S. 1969. *The Theory of Share Tenancy*. Chicago: University of Chicago Press.

———. 1969. "Transactions Costs, Risk Aversion and the Choice of Contractual Agreements." *Journal of Law and Economics* 19.

Demski, J.S. and D.S. Sappington. 1984. "Optimal Incentive Contracts with Multiple Agents." *Journal of Economic Theory* 33: 152–71.

Domar, E.D. 1966. "The Soviet Collective Farm as a Producer Cooperative." *American Economic Review* 56 (March): 734–57.

Drèze, J. 1976. "Some Theory of Labor Management and Participation." *Econometrica* 44 (November): 112–39.

Flanagan, R.J. 1984. "Wage Concessions and Long-term Union Wage Flexibility." *Brookings Papers on Economic Activity I:* 183–216.

Furubotn, F.G. and S. Pejovich. 1972. "Property Rights and Economic Theory." *Journal of Economic Literature* 10 (December): 1137–57.

Green, J.R. and N.L. Stokey. 1983. "A Comparison of Tournaments and Contracts." *Journal of Political Economy* 91 (June): 349–65.

Greenwald, B.C. and J.E. Stiglitz. 1986. "Externalities in Economies With Imperfect Information and Incomplete Markets." *Quarterly Journal of Economics* 101 (May): 229–64.

Grossman, S. and O. Hart. 1983. "An Analysis of the Principal-Agent Problem." *Econometrica* 51: 7–46.

Hall, R.E. and D.M. Lilien. 1979. "Efficient Wage Bargains Under Uncertain Supply and Demand." *American Economic Review* 69 (December): 868–79.

Harris, M. and A. Raviv. 1978. "Some Results on Incentive Contracts With Applications to Education and Employment, Health Insurance and Law Enforcement." *American Economic Review* 68 (March): 20–30.

———. 1979. "Optimal Incentive Contracts With Imperfect Information." *Journal of Economic Theory* 20 (April): 231–59.

Hewitt Associates, in cooperation with the Profit Sharing Council of America. *1984 Profit Sharing Survey (1983 Experience)*, Lincolnshire, Ill.: Hewitt Associates, 1984.

Holmstrom, B. 1979. "Moral Hazard and Observability." *The Bell Journal of Economics.* 10 (Spring): 74–91.

———. 1982. "Moral Hazard in Teams." *The Bell Journal of Economics* 13 (Autumn): 324–41.

Internal Revenue Service, Department of the Treasury. News Release (IR–86–113): Determination Statistics For Various Employee Benefit Plans, 1985 and January through June, 1986. August 21, 1986.

Jensen, C.M. and W.H. Meckling. 1976. "Theory of the Firm: Managerial Behavior, Agency Costs and Ownership Structure." *Journal of Financial Economics* 3 (October): 305–60.

Kihlstrom, R.F. and J.J. Laffont. 1979. "A General Equilibrium Entrepreneurial Theory of Firm Formation Based on Risk Aversion." *Journal of Political Economy* 87 (August): 719-48.

Kihlstrom, R. and M. Pauly. 1971. "The Role of Insurance in the Allocation of Risk." *American Economic Review* 61 (May): 371–79.

Klein, B, 1984. "Contract Costs and Administered Prices: An Economic Theory of Rigid Wages." *American Economic Review* 74 (May): 332–38.

Knight, F.H. 1921. *Risk, Uncertainty and Profit.* Boston: Houghton Mifflin.

Latta, G.W. 1979. *Profit Sharing, Employee Stock Ownership, Savings and Asset Formation Plans in the Western World.* Philadelphia, Pa.: Industrial Research Unit, The Wharton School.

Lazear, E.P. and S. Rosen. 1981. "Rank Order Tournaments as Optimum Labor Contracts." *Journal of Political Economy* 89 (October): 841–64.

Leibenstein, H. 1966. "Allocative Efficiency vs. X-Efficiency." *American Economic Review* 56 (June): 392–415.

———. 1975. "Aspects of the X-Efficiency Theory of the Firm." *The Bell Journal of Economics* 6 (Autumn): 580–606.

———. 1976. *Beyond Economic Man.* Cambridge, Mass.: Harvard University Press.

Leonard, H.B. and R.J. Zechauser. 1985. "Financial Risk and the Burdens of Contracts." *American Economic Review* 75 (May): 375–80.

Leontief, W. 1946. "The Pure Theory of the Guaranteed Annual Wage Contract." *Journal of Political Economy* 56 (February): 76–79.

Marcus, A.J. 1982. "Risk Sharing and the Theory of the Firm." *The Bell Journal of Economics* 13 (Autumn): 369–78.

Marschak, J. and R. Radner. 1972. *The Economic Theory of Teams.* New Haven: Yale University Press.

Meade. J.E. 1972. "The Theory of Labour-Managed Firms and of Profit Sharing." *Economic Journal* 82 (March Supplement): 402–28.

———. 1974. "Labour-Managed Firms in Conditions of Imperfect Competition." *Economic Journal* 84 (December): 817–24.

Mirrlees, J.A. 1976. "The Optimal Structure of Incentives and Authority Within an Organization." *The Bell Journal of Economics* 7 (Spring): 105–31.

Mitchell, D.J.B. 1982. "Gain-Sharing: An Anti-Inflation Reform." *Challenge* 25 (July/August): 18–25.

———. 1982. "Recent Union Contract Concessions." *Brookings Papers on Economic Acitivty* I: 165–204.

———. 1985. "Wage Flexibility in the United States: Lessons From the Past." *American Economic Review* 75 (May): 36–40.

Miyazaki, H. and H.M. Neary. 1983. "The Illyrian Firm Revisited." *The Bell Journal of Economics* 14 (Spring): 259–70.

Nalebuff, B.J. and J.E. Stiglitz. 1983. "Prizes and Incentives: Towards a General Theory of Compensation and Competition." *The Bell Journal of Economics* 14 (Spring): 21–43.

New York Stock Exchange Office of Economic Research. 1982. *People and Productivity: A Challenge to Corporate America.* New York: New York Stock Exchange.

O'Keefe, M., W.K. Viscusi, and R. Zeckhauser. 1984. "Economic Contests: Comparative Reward Schemes." *Journal of Labor Economics* 2 (January): 27–56.

Pauly, M.V. 1968. "The Economics of Moral Hazard." *American Economic Review* 58 (June): 531–37.

Radner, R. 1968. "Competitive Equilibrium Under Uncertainty." *Econometrica* 36 (January): 31–58.

———. 1981. "Monitoring Cooperative Agreements in a Repeated Principal-Agent Relationship." *Econometrica* 49 (September): 1127–48.

Riley, J.G. 1975. "Competitive Signalling." *Journal of Economic Theory.* 10 (April): 174–86.

Ross, S.A. 1973. "The Economic Theory of Agency: The Principal's Problem." *American Economic Review* 63 (May): 134–39.

Rothschild, M. and J.E. Stiglitz. 1970. "Increasing Risk. I: A Definition." *Journal of Economic Theory* 2: 225–43.

———. 1976. "Equilibrium in Competitive Insurance Markets: An Essay on the Economics of Imperfect Information." *Quarterly Journal of Economics* 90 (November): 630–49.

Salop, S.C. 1979. "A Model of the Natural Rate of Unemployment." *American Economic Review* 69 (March): 117–25.

Schotta, C. 1963. "The Distribution of Profit Sharing Plans: An Analysis." *Southern Economic Journal* 30 (July): 59.

Schultze, C.L. 1985. "Microeconomic Efficiency and Nominal Wage Stickiness." *American Economic Review* 75 (March): 1–15.

Shapiro, C. and J.E. Stiglitz, 1984. "Equilibrium Unemployment as a Worker Discipline Device." *American Economic Review* 74 (June): 433–44.

Shavell, S. 1979. "Risk Sharing and Incentives in the Principal and Agent Relationship." *The Bell Journal of Economics* 10 (Spring): 55–73.

Spence, A.M. 1973. "Job Market Signaling." *Quarterly Journal of Economics* 87 (August): 355–74.

———. 1973. *Market Signaling: Information Transfer in Hiring and Related Processes.* Cambridge, Mass: Harvard University Press.

———. 1974. "Competitive and Optimal Responses to Signals: An Analysis of Efficiency and Distribution." *Journal of Economic Theory* 7 (March): 296–332.

Spence, A.M. and R. Zeckhauser. 1971. "Insurance, Information and Individual Action." *American Economic Review* 61 (May): 380–87.

Steinherr, A. 1977. "On the Efficiency of Profit Sharing and Labour Participation in Management." *The Bell Journal of Economics* 8: 545–55.

Stigler, G.J. 1976. "The Xistence of X-Efficiency." *American Economic Review* 66 (March): 213–16.

Stiglitz, J.E. 1974. "Incentives and Risk Sharing in Sharecropping." *Review of Economic Studies* 41 (April): 219–56.

———. 1975. "Incentives, Risk and Information: Notes Towards a Theory of Hierarchy." *The Bell Journal of Economics* 6 (Autumn): 552–79.

———. 1983. "Risk, Incentives and Insurance: The Pure Theory of Moral Hazard." *The Geneval Papers on Risk and Insurance* 8 (January): 4–33.

Stiglitz, J.E. and A. Weiss. 1981. "Credit Rationing in Markets With Imperfect Information, Part I." *American Economic Review* 71 (June): 393–410.

———. 1983. "Incentive Effects of Terminations: Applications to the Credit and Labor Markets." *American Economic Review* 73 (December): 912–27.

U.S. Chamber of Commerce. 1984. *Employee Benefits: 1983* Annual Report. Washington, D.C.

Vanek, J. 1970. *The General Theory of Labor-Managed Market Economies.* Ithaca: Cornell University Press.

Ward, B. 1958. "The Firm in Illyria: Market Syndicalism." *American Economic Review* 48 (September): 566–89.

Weiss, A. 1980. "Job Queues and Layoffs in Labor Markets With Flexible Wages." *Journal of Political Economy* 88 (June): 526–38.

Weitzman, M.L. 1974. "Prices vs. Quantities." *Review of Economic Studies* 41 (October): 477–92.

———. 1980. "The 'Ratchet Principle and Performance Incentives." *The Bell Journal of Economics* 11 (Spring): 302–8.

———. 1983. "Some Macroeconomic Implications of Alternative Compensation Systems." *Economic Journal* 93 (December): 763–83.

———. 1984. *The Share Economy.* Cambridge, Mass.: Harvard University Press.

———. 1985. "The Simple Macroeconomics of Profit Sharing." *American Economic Review* 75 (December): 937–53.

White House Conference on Productivity. 1984. *Productivity Growth: A Better Life for America.* Springfield, Va.: GPO.

Wiliamson, O.E. 1975. *Markets and Hierarchies: Analysis and Antitrust Implications.* New York: The Free Press.

Wilson, C. 1977. "A Model of Insurance Markets with Incomplete Information." *Journal of Economic Theory* 16 (December): 167–207.

Wilson, R. 1968. "The Theory of Syndicates." *Econometrica* 36 (January): 119–32.

Yellen, J. 1984. "Efficiency Wage Models of Unemployment." *American Economic Review* 74 (May): 200–205.

Zeckhauser, R. 1970. "Medical Insurance: A Case Study of the Trade-Off Between Risk Spreading and Appropriate Incentives." *Journal of Economic Theory* 2 (March): 10–26.

II. Industrial Psychology and Compensation Practice

Bourdon, R.D. 1980. "A Basic Model For Employee Participation." *Training and Development Journal* 34 (April): 24–29.

Deci, E.L. 1971. "Effects of Externally Mediated Rewards on Intrinsic Motivation." *Journal of Personality and Social Psychology* 18: 105–15.

———. 1972. "The Effects of Contingent and Noncontingent Rewards and Controls on Intrinsic Motivation." *Organization Behavior and Human Performance* 8: 217–29.

———. 1975. "Notes on the Theory and Metatheory of Intrinsic Motivation." *Organizational Theory and Human Performance* 15: 130–45.

DeCharms, R. 1968. *Personal Causation: The Internal Affective Determinants of Behavior.* New York: Academic Press.

Fein, M. 1977. *Improshare: An Alternative To Traditional Managing.* Norcross, Ga.: Institute of Industrial Engineers.

———. 1982. "Improved Productivity Through Worker Involvement." Hillsdale, N.J.: Mitchell Fein Inc., mimeo.

———. 1983. "Managing Philosophy Affects Productivity Improvement," Hillsdale, NJ: Mitchell Fein Inc., mimeo (August).

Frost, C.F., J.H. Wakely, and R.A. Ruh. 1974. *The Scanlon Plan for Organization Development: Identity, Participation and Equity.* East Lansing: Michigan State University Press.

Guzzo, R.A. 1984. "Programs for Productivity and Quality of Work Life." Mimeo.

Guzzo, R.A. and J.S. Bondy. 1983. *A Guide to Worker Productivity Experiments in the United States: 1976–81.* New York: Pergamon.

Guzzo, R.A., R.D. Jette, and R.A. Katzell. 1985. "The Effects of Psychologically-Based Intervention Programs on Worker Productivity: A Meta Analysis." *Personnel Psychology* 38 (Summer): 275–91.

Howard, B. and P.O. Dietz. 1969. *A Study of the Financial Significance of Profit Sharing.* Chicago, Ill.: Council of Profit Sharing Industries.

Jenkins, G.D. and E.E. Lawler. 1981. "Impact of Employee Participation in Development of a Pay Plan." *Organizational Behavior and Human Performance* 28 (August): 111–28.

Katzell, R.A., P. Bienstock, and P.H. Faerstein. 1977. *A Guide to Worker Productivity Experiments in the United States 1971–75.* New York: New York University Press.

Katzell, R.A. and R.A. Guzzo. 1983. "Psychological Approaches to Productivity Improvement." *American Psychologist* 38: 468–72.

Latham, G.P. and D.L. Dossett. 1978. "Designing Incentive Plans For Unionized Employees: A Comparison of Continuous and Variable Reinforcement Schedules." *Personnel Psychology* 38 (Spring): 47–61.

Latham, G.P., T.R. Mitchell, and D.L. Dossett. 1978. "Importance of Participative Goal Setting And Anticipating Rewards on Goal Difficulty and Performance." *Journal of Applied Psychology* 63 (April): 163–71.

Lawler, E.E. 1971. *Pay and Organizational Performance: A Psychological View.* New York: McGraw Hill.

———. 1981. "Merit Pay: An Obsolete Policy?" Graduate School of Business, University of Southern California. Working Paper G80–1.

———. 1981. *Pay and Organizational Development.* Reading, Mass.: Addison-Wesley.

———. 1984. "The Strategic Design of Reward Systems," in *Leaders and Managers,* edited by C. Fombrun, N. Tichy, and M. Devanna, 127–47. New York: Wiley & Sons.

———. 1984. "Whatever Happened to Incentive Pay?" *New Management* 1: 37–41.

Ledford, G. E. and E. E. Lawler. 1985. "Skill-Based Pay." *Personnel* 62: 30–37.

Lesieur, F., ed. 1958. *The Scanlon Plan: A Frontier in Labor Management Cooperation.* Cambridge: M.I.T. Press.

Locke, E.A., D.B. Feran, V.N. McCaleb, K.N. Shaw, and A.T. Denny. 1980. "The Relative Effectiveness of Four Methods of Motivating Employee Performance," in *Changes in Working Life,* edited by K.D. Duncan, M.M. Gruneberg, and D. Wallis, 363–88. New York: Wiley.

Metzger, B.L. 1966. *Profit Sharing in Perspective,* second edition. Evanston, Ill.: Profit Sharing Research Foundation.

———. 1975. *Profit Sharing in 38 Large Companies, I and II.* Evanston, Ill.: Profit Sharing Research Foundation.

Metzger, B.L. and J.A. Colletti. 1971. *Does Profit Sharing Pay?* Evanston, Ill.: Profit Sharing Research Foundation.

Mirvis, P.H. and E.E. Lawler. 1977. "Measuring the Financial Impact of Employee Attitudes." *Journal of Applied Psychology* 62 (February): 1–8.

Neider, L.L. 1980. "An Experimental Field Investigation Utilizing an Expectancy Theory

View of Participation." *Organizational Behavior and Human Performance* 26 (December): 425–42.

Poole, M. 1975. *Workers' Participation in Industry.* London: Routledge & Kegan Paul.

Preiwisch, C.F. 1981. "GAO Study on Productivity-Sharing Programs," in *Productivity Improvement,* edited by V.M. Buehler and Y.K. Shetty. New York: AMACOM. 177–200.

Pritchard, R.D., K.M. Campbell, and D.J. Campbell. 1977. "Effects of Extrinsic Financial Rewards on Intrinsic Motivation." *Journal of Applied Psychology* 62: 9–15.

Pritchard, R.D., P.J. Deleo, and C.W. Von Bergen. 1976. "A Field Experimental Test of Expectancy-Valence Incentive Motivation Techniques." *Organizational Behavior and Human Performance* 15. (April): 355–406.

Profit Sharing Research Foundation. 1985. "Cumulative Growth in Number of Qualified Deferred Profit Sharing Plans and Pensions in the United States, 1939 through 1984. Mimeo.

Ringham, A.J. 1984. "Designing a Gainsharing Program to Fit a Company's Operations. *National Productivity Review.* (Spring).

Rosenberg, R.D. and E. Rosenstein. 1980. "Participation and Productivity: An Empirical Study." *Industrial and Labor Relations Review* 30 (April): 355–67.

Scott Jr., W.E. 1975. "The Effects of Extrinsic Rewards on Intrinsic Motivation: A Critique." *Organizational Behavior and Human Performance* 15: 117–29.

Sibson & Company, Inc., 1985. *Executive Compensation: Facts and Issues, 1985* An Annual Report.

Smart, T. 1985 "The Take at the Top." *Inc.* (September).

U.S. Department of Labor, Bureau of Labor Statistics. 1984. *Employee Benefits in Medium and Large Firms, 1983* (Bulletin 2213). Washington, D.C.: Government Printing Office.

Vroom, V.H. 1964. *Work and Motivation.* New York: Wiley.

White, J.K. 1979. "The Scanlon Plan: Causes and Correlates of Success." *Academy of Management Journal* 22: 292–312.

White, W.L. 1984. "Creative Solutions to the Pay-for-Performance Dilemma." The Hay Group, Hay Management Consultants. Mimeo, May 14.

Whyte, W.F. 1955. *Money and Motivation: An Analysis of Incentives in Industry.* New York: Harper & Row.

Part I

CONCEPTUAL ISSUES

2

The Design of Labor Contracts: The Economics of Incentives and Risk Sharing

Joseph E. Stiglitz

During the past two decades, economists have spent a considerable amount of effort analyzing the nature of the employment relationship. They have been concerned with all the facets of this relationship, including the structure of compensation, delegation of authority, and lay-off policies. They have been concerned not only with explicit contracts, which may be enforceable under law, but also with what they call implicit contracts—"understandings" between management and workers, which when violated may result in reduced worker effort or quitting, with the result that firms may have greater difficulty hiring workers in the future. Economists have been particularly concerned with characterizing *efficient* contracts (where we use the term "contracts" loosely, to include both explicit and implicit contracts), contracts that stipulate that workers cannot be made economically better off without lowering profits.

Economists believe that, in general, the employment relationship is *not* a zero sum game, that by structuring the employment relationship appropriately, both workers and the firm can benefit. When no further improvements to the employer-employee relationship can be found, we say that the employment relationship is efficient. In this chapter, I propose to review "some of the basic findings concerning the structure of efficient contracts. Some of these findings seem at variance with the kinds of employment relationships (e.g. compensation plans) commonly found. This presents a puzzle, a puzzle upon which perhaps the discussions in this volume may throw some light: have we, as economists, omitted something important from our analysis,[1] or have firms not been

Financial support from the National Science Foundation and the Hoover Institution is gratefully acknowledged.

sufficiently thoughtful about the design of the employment relationship?

The Premises Underlying the Analysis

Our analysis of the nature of efficient employment relationships is based on several premises. It may be well to spell out these premises as clearly as possible in the beginning. Not all of the results cited herein depend on the validity of all of these premises. I shall attempt, in presenting each of the results, to try to make clear precisely what is assumed in each case.

1. *Risk-averse workers.* The first assumption is that workers do not like risk, they do not like variability in their incomes. Income variability imposes a heavy cost on workers. While they may be able to make small adjustments relatively easily, their assumption of large fixed commitments (like mortgages) make large variations in income (such as those that result from unemployment) particularly hard to deal with.

2. *Limitations on insurance provided by the market.* Normally, when individuals face large risks, they attempt to divest themselves of at least part of this risk through the purchase of insurance. They purchase medical insurance to insure themselves against high medical bills and automobile insurance to insure themselves against losses arising from automobile accidents. The risks associated with being unemployed are at least as significant as these risks, and one might have thought that this would give rise to a demand for "employment insurance." Yet, the private market does not provide such insurance.[2] If the individual is to obtain insurance for employment-related risks, he must do so through his employer.[3]

3. *Risk-neutral firms.* The earlier literature on employment contracts (Bailey 1964, Azariadis 1965) assumed that firms were risk-neutral: they only cared about average profits, not their variability.[4] The owners of the firm were sufficiently well diversified that the variability in profits had a relatively small effect on them. (What was critical for most of the results was not the assumption of risk neutrality but that firms were less risk-averse than workers.) This view has been criticized on two grounds. First, most individuals do not have a widely diversified portfolio and hence are not indifferent to the variability in profits of the firms in which they hold shares; and secondly, most of the decisions of the firm are made by its managers, and managers are, in fact, significantly affected by what happens to the firm; they are not risk-neutral.[5] (In some more recent theories, the opposite assumption, that firms are risk averse, has played a critical role, as we shall see.)

4. *Imperfect information and information asymmetry.* The information available to employers and employees is imperfect and different. This is important because it limits the scope of possible contracts. Because of

imperfect information at the time a contract is signed, there is very imperfect knowledge concerning possible future conditions. Hence, it is often desirable to write contracts with contingency clauses that specify what should be done when various possible future events occur. But the things upon which the contract can be made contingent depend on what is easily observable. When only one of the two parties can observe whether a particular event has occurred, there can obviously be difficulties in contract design: that party may have an incentive to misrepresent whether the event has occurred. The contract must be designed with that possibility in mind in such a way as to ensure that the party with the access to the information does not have an incentive to misrepresent existing conditions.[6]

Here is an example. One can imagine writing a contract that specifies that if the fortunes of the company turn adversely, the workers will share in the risk by lowering their wages. But managers are more likely to be better informed than workers concerning the true health of the firm. They may have an incentive to misrepresent the state of the firm, claiming that it is in difficulty simply to get the workers to accept a lower wage. (There may be ways of designing a contract so that the managers only say that the firm is in a bad shape when it is in fact the case. We shall provide examples of this later.)

This is not the only information problem. Managers cannot observe the actions of their workers perfectly; they cannot monitor them costlessly. Similarly, owners of firms cannot fully observe the actions of their "employees"—the managers—and even when owners can observe their managers' actions, they seldom have all the requisite information to judge whether the action was the appropriate one to take in a particular circumstance.[7]

5. *Conflict of interest between managers and workers.* We noted that the employment relationship is not a zero sum game: there are ways of designing the relationship so that both workers and firms gain. At the same time, it is important to realize that the interests of management and workers do not coincide, that they are often in conflict. Workers may wish to shirk, to enjoy more leisure at the workplace, managers wish the worker to work harder. Workers may wish to have a steady income, but this may conflict with the firm's profit-maximizing strategy, which may entail layoffs. However, the extent of the conflict should not be overstated. There is a general principle that if firms offer contracts that workers find more attractive, then the firm will be able to hire workers for lower wages than it otherwise could.[8] Thus, it is in the interests of employers to construct employment relationships that are attractive to workers. In competitive markets, firms will be "forced" to provide such efficient contracts. It is this observation that provides the link between normative contract theory and the positive theory: while the normative

theory seeks to characterize what efficient contracts look like, the positive theory asserts that in competitive markets, these are the kinds of contracts we should expect to find. When we don't find these contracts, we have a puzzle, and these puzzles are a central part of the topic I wish to address.

There is a similar conflict of interest between owners and managers. Owners may be concerned with the long-term market value of the firm; managers may be more concerned with the short-term market value if their compensation is tied to the performance of the firm at present and in the immediate future.[9]

Efficient Contracts

There are three critical aspects of efficient contracts:

1. *Risk-sharing.* Efficient contracts should provide for *risk-sharing.* Risks should be borne by those most able to bear them; and the burden of any risk can be significantly reduced by sharing that risk among a large number of individuals. *If* firms are risk-neutral, and individuals are risk-averse, then it would seem that firms are in a better position to bear the risks associated with cyclical fluctuations than the workers. Firms should thus be able to provide income insurance to workers. Similarly, the firm is in a much better position to bear the risks associated with the individual's being ill-suited to the job (either in tastes or productivity).

Recall from our earlier discussion that there are market incentives for firms to provide what we have called efficient contracts: they can obtain and retain workers of a given quality at a lower wage, or they can obtain higher quality workers at the same wage. (Effectively, firms can obtain a return from providing insurance, a return to absorbing risk, just as insurance firms do.) This gives rise to some clear predictions: the employment contract should provide for guaranteed incomes,[10] and to the extent that there are income fluctuations, they should be shared among the workers. Training and moving costs should be borne by the firm.[11] All contracts should be fully indexed, so that the firm, not the individual, bears the risks associated with inflation. None of these predictions conform to what is actually observed. Few firms have offered guaranteed incomes; in the United States, the prevalent way of responding to a decrease in the demand for labor is by lay-offs, not by work-sharing (which is much more common in Europe). A significant fraction of the specific training and moving costs are often borne by the individual (so that it turns out that he is ill-suited to the firm, and quits or is fired, his lifetime income may be significantly reduced); and few contracts have full indexation.

The marked contrast between efficient risk-sharing contracts and what is observed obviously calls for explanation. Part of this explanation lies in a second aspect of efficient contract design.

2. *Incentives.* Efficient contracts must provide appropriate incentives. If individuals' incomes are guaranteed, workers will obviously have only a limited incentive for putting out greater effort for the firm. There is thus a fundamental trade-off between the provision of insurance (risk-sharing) and the provision of incentives.[12] The contract design must represent a compromise between these two objectives. The more the individual's pay depends on measured output, the greater the risk faced by the individual, but also the greater his incentives. If incentive problems are not very significant—the worker can easily be monitored, so that shirking can be avoided—then the risk sharing considerations predominate.

Incentives can be provided to workers in a number of different forms, and the efficient employment relationship requires the appropriate mix of incentive devices. The most obvious incentive plan relates compensation to some measure of performance.[13] Some plans base pay on relative performance—the pay of the individual depends on how his performance compares with others, either in the firm or outside, performing similar tasks.[14] Promotions based on past performance provide another way of rewarding effort. Management is frequently rewarded with stock options, and since their value depends on the performance of the firm, they can be viewed as an indirect incentive. Profit-sharing programs are often described as incentives for workers (though the relationship between the individual's pay and his effort is usually so weak as to cast doubt on the efficacy of such schemes, apart from their effect on morale).

Incentives may be provided by negative means: the threat of being fired or demoted is also effective.[15]

Economists are concerned not only with work incentives, but also with mobility incentives. The economy often faces disturbances that change the relative (marginal) productivity of workers in different firms. One firm finds that the demands for its products have risen, while another firm finds that the demand for its products have fallen. Efficient labor allocation requires that workers move *from* the firm where the productivity has fallen. If individuals have perfect insurance, they will have no incentive to move.[16]

Similarly, if the firm absorbs all the firm-specific training costs, then the worker will not have the correct incentives to stay: he may move to a better firm even though the total costs of moving (including the specific training costs) exceed his slight gain.[17]

A concern for incentives explains some of the "failures" to provide complete risk-sharing contracts to workers. Because the firm is concerned with excessive turnover, it may make the worker share in some of the costs of training. Because the firm is concerned with the worker moving to other firms where he may be more productive, the firm does not provide complete income insurance. Still, firms provide less complete insurance than the theory would predict, and often in a quite different form.

Thus, there are no incentive issues associated with the firm providing insurance against the effects of inflation: all contracts should be fully indexed. And even if firms do not provide complete income insurance, there should be work-sharing, not lay-offs.

Some recent theories have attributed the failure to provide adequate insurance to the fact that firms are risk-averse. If firms are risk-averse, then they will not provide insurance against cyclical fluctuations, against temporary decreases in the demand for their commodity. They will want the worker to share this risk with them. (In contrast, large firms can easily absorb the risks associated with specific individuals, e.g. risks associated with whether the individual is well suited to the firm.) But while a firm's risk-aversion can provide an explanation for imperfect income insurance, it cannot explain lay-offs. Efficient contracts should still entail full employment. (Workers would be laid off only if their productivity is less than their reservation wage [the minimum wage at which the worker is willing to supply the specified quantity of labor services.])

To explain lay-offs, some economists have combined the hypothesis of firm risk-aversion with that of informational asymmetry.[18] Workers do not know the health of the firm, i.e., whether the firm is in a good or bad condition. The efficient contract requires that if the firm is in poor condition, the wage is low, that is, the risk is shared between the worker and the firm; but the contract has to be designed so that the firm only announces that it is a bad state when in fact it *is* in a bad state. To ensure that the firm tells the truth, an appropriate incentive scheme must be devised. By insisting that whenever the firm announces that it is in a bad state it must take certain other actions (actions that are costly if it is, in fact, in a good state), the firm can be induced not to misrepresent itself. Thus, a restriction that the firm must cut back on its employment if it says it is in a bad state does induce truth telling.

This theory, at least as it stands, is an unpersuasive explanation of unemployment. Typically, unions do bargain wage cuts against cutbacks in employment. If asymmetric information considerations were paramount, they would not be doing this.[19] Furthermore, there are variables that are observable by both managers and workers, which are correlated with the unobservable variables of interest; such variables ought to be included within the contract. Finally, information asymmetries do not explain a number of the central aspects of risk-sharing in labor contracts, such as the use of lay-offs rather than work-sharing. The theory, moreover, is incomplete: it does not explain why unemployment is concentrated within particular groups in the labor force. It explains unemployment only by assuming that layed-off workers are not hired in the spot market, and it does not explain the absence of substantial lay-off pay. It predicts, counterfactually, that with optimal lay-off pay, workers prefer to be layed off.

To explain lay-offs, one evidently needs a more complicated theory. Two explanations have been put forward. One of these is based on the *efficiency wage hypothesis.* This states that the productivity of the labor force increases with the wage (or more generally, with the attractiveness of the employment relationship). There are several reasons for this relationship. One is the incentive effect discussed earlier: by paying workers "above the market," the worker is induced to work harder; he knows that if he looses his job, he will be worse off. The other reason is that, at higher wages, the firm attracts more productive workers (or a larger pool of applicants from among which it can choose more suitable workers).[20] There are still other reasons for the relationship between the productivity of the labor force and the wages they receive. Labor turnover is likely to be lower at higher wages, and so long as the firm bears some of these turnover costs, the net profit of the firm will thereby be increased. (Stiglitz 1972) Akerlof has presented several sociological explanations of the wage-productivity nexus. (Akerlof 1984) For a survey of alternative theories, see Stiglitz (1986), and Yellen (1984).

If this effect is important, firms—even risk-averse firms—may not lower wages much in response to a decline in the demand for their products; they will pay a high wage to the workers they retain, but they may reduce the number of workers they employ. The result of this is that even if firms are better able to bear risks than workers, the workers actually bear the risks.

Another explanation of lay-offs has to do with the nature of search costs. It may be more "efficient" to induce a few workers to search for alternative employment intensively, than to have a large number of workers search half-heartedly. Lowering the wage—work-sharing—thus may not induce as efficient a search as do lay offs.[21]

3. *Contract flexibility.* An efficient contract needs to be able to respond to changing circumstances. What are appropriate incentives in one circumstance may not be appropriate incentives in another. What may be an appropriate risk-sharing arrangement in one circumstance may not be an appropriate risk-sharing arrangement in another. It is difficult to anticipate all possibilities; but the contract needs to concern itself with at least a few of the more important possibilities. Clearly, these include the risks associated with unemployment and inflation.

Piece-rates have often been criticized for a lack of flexibility. As technology changes, the appropriate piece-rate changes; but the process of adjusting piece-rates (and determining what the appropriate piece-rate is) is often difficult and the subject of contention.[22]

One of the virtues of relative performance schemes is that, under certain circumstances, they provide automatic adjustments of pay to the difficulty of the task being undertaken. This is the reason that teachers usually grade on the curve (which is like a relative performance compensation plan). The advantages in the case of firms are even greater. When the task is easier, not only is pay per unit of output reduced, but the incentives for exerting effort are also automatically adjusted. Because of the greater ease of the task, each competitor may work a little harder, as he should. At the same time, his pay does not vary with the difficulty of the task. Relative performance plans introduce another source of uncertainty: that relating to relative abilities of different individuals. And there are some circumstances in which these schemes do not work well. (Nalebuff and Stiglitz 1983b.)[23]

Profit-sharing plans and end-of-the-year bonus schemes similarly have marked advantages in flexibility, particularly when the firm is risk-averse. The wages of the worker are automatically adjusted to the circumstances the firm finds itself in. If the firm finds that the demand for its products has decreased, its wage bill adjusts automatically. Though such plans are good on grounds of flexibility, they do make the worker bear a larger proportion of the income risks (at least this is true for the workers who are retained). Depending on the rules by which profits are shared, these profit-sharing plans work much like work-sharing schemes.

The Puzzles of Current Employment Relations

In the previous section, we discussed three central aspects of an efficient contract design: incentives, risk-sharing, and flexibility. Limitations on information imply that no contract can simultaneously provide for perfect risk-sharing, perfect incentives, or even a suitable balance for each set of circumstances. Still, it seems to me that there is great room for improvement: we can design contracts that provide better incentives and more risk-sharing. (The mere fact that periodically, large fractions of our work force are unable to find gainful employment—a massive waste of resources—suggests that something is wrong, that something can be done better.)

In this section, I want to discuss some of the provisions of contracts that the theory of efficient contracts says we should find, but seem rarely found in practice. As I noted in the beginning, I am somewhat puzzled by this: have we left out something important from our analysis? Of course, it may be that both labor and management have not been inventive enough, have not fully considered all of the consequences of current employment practices, and that by thinking these through, they will come to the realization that there are better ways of designing employment relations. With that in mind, in the final section, I shall present several possible suggestions for more efficient contracts.

There are four identifiable kinds of risks: (1) risks peculiar to the individual and the extent to which he is well matched with the firm; (2) risks specific to the firm (these include risks associated with the demand for the firm's products, or particular managerial problems among others; (3) risks that affect all firms within an industry simultaneously (including risks associated with the demand for the products of the industry, risks associated with the supply of products by foreign competitors, risks associated with taxes and other government policies that affect the industry); and (4) macro-economic risks that affect the economy as a whole (recessions, inflation, tax policies). It is my contention that employment contracts should be able to do better (than they are doing at present) on all but the second category of risks.

The first puzzle to which I have alluded on several occasions is the failure of the market to deal adequately with macro-economic risks: on the one hand, the failure of employment contracts to provide income insurance, and, on the other, the wage rigidities that seem, in many instances, to lead to unemployment (and to exacerbate income fluctuations).

Prior to the government's provision of income insurance during the Great Depression, few firms provided it. Even today, with unemployment insurance covering only a fraction of the loss in income, relatively few firms provide much in the way of supplemental unemployment benefits. Indeed, it was not until 1955 that the first important Supplemental Unemployment Benefit plan was negotiated (between Ford and the United Auto Workers). Interestingly enough, coverage by these plans has actually declined during the past decade, from 67% of workers in manufacturing in 1970, to 51% in 1980 (from 48% of agreements, to 25% of agreements). In nonmanufacturing, these supplemental benefits remain insignificant: only 4.4% of all workers are covered.[24]

Similarly, the magnitude of the employment fluctuations is hard to understand. Surely, it does not represent an efficient utilization of our human resources to allow 10% or more of those able and willing to work to go unemployed. Yet this is what happened in the United States in the early 80s (and the situation in Britain is even worse).

There is a tendency to blame the government, but the root of the problem lies in the employment relationship, which is the subject of this volume. The employment contract, as presently designed, induces firms to lay off workers. The lack of wage flexibility means that when the demand for the firm's products decreases, the firm is better off laying off some of its workers. If wages fell—at least if they fell enough—some firms would be able to keep their labor force employed, or at least not to reduce it by as much. The firm could lower its prices, leading to an increase in the demand for its products. It could accumulate an inventory of goods, ready for sale when demand picks up again. Workers have, perhaps, been concerned that they would get a relatively small increase in employment for a large decrease in wages, and thus have resisted the introduction of more flexibility.[25] I suspect that the extent to which this concern is valid depends both on the nature of the industry and the manner in which flexibility is introduced. When the economy goes into a recession, it is not only the level of wages that are of concern to the firm, but also the uncertainty about the price at which it will be able to sell its output. A profit-sharing plan, by allowing some of the risk to be transferred from the firm to workers, may thus induce a greater increase in employment (avert a greater decrease in employment) than a wage reduction with the same expected value.[26]

In our previous discussions, we have noted several reasons why firms may not provide complete income insurance and why employment contracts are characterized by such high variability in employment.

(a) *Risk-averse firms.* In well functioning capital markets, firms should not be very risk-averse; certainly they should be better able to absorb income variations than workers. An important exception arises from the fact that when firms are in particularly severe straits, they may be unable to borrow, and so may face severe liquidity constraints. In that case, when a firm's survival may be at stake, it is not surprising that it may act in a very risk-averse manner. This suggests that we can identify two different situations: for small fluctuations in demand, when the survival of the firm is not threatened, the firm should be able to provide fairly complete income insurance; in situations where the survival of the firm is threatened, there should be risk-sharing between firms and their workers. To some extent, firms do behave as this theory suggests they should: firms frequently do not lay off workers in response to small fluctuations in their demand. Still, there are many fluctuations of intermediate size, still too small to represent any significant threat to the firm's survival, in which workers are asked to share significantly in the risk.

In formulating appropriate risk-sharing policies, the problem arises in distinguishing between those situations where the firm is in a better position to bear risks than the worker (where its survival is not threatened) and where there should be risk-sharing. This is the problem of asymmetric information to which I referred earlier. The firm may have an incentive not to disclose its true financial state. Accounting records may not provide a completely accurate depiction of the true state of the firm. Limitations on information imply that the distinction will not be made with perfect accuracy; yet it seems to me that the distinction can be made with sufficient accuracy to provide a basis for more efficient risk-sharing contractual arrangements than are, at present, commonly provided. In cases where the relevant risks are industry-wide disturbances, and the industry is reasonably competitive, then data on industry profits (or other similar indices) provide a basis for employee income adjustment. (In these circumstances, no single firm has an incentive to distort his accounting information in order to induce his employees to accept a lower income.) In other cases, providing a basis for income adjustment may be more difficult. Still, I suspect that even in these circumstances more can be done to stabilize income than is done at present.[27]

(b) *Risk-averse managers.* Part of this puzzle may be explained by the risk-aversion of managers. We noted earlier than the interests of shareholders and of managers need not coincide. Managers are frequently paid on the basis of compensation plans that place a heavy emphasis on the short-run performance of the firm. Thus, if the firm faces a fluctuation of intermediate size, the managers may attempt to cut short-run costs, to raise current profits by laying off workers, even though doing so may in some sense lead to an increase in long run costs (because the firm is less attractive, it may have to pay higher wages to attract the same quality of labor force as it previously did).[28] There are two ways of remedying this problem: change the incentive structure of managers to ensure that they are more concerned with the long-run interests of the firm, or change the employment contract to ensure that when managers face a situation of the kind just described, it is not in their short-run interest to reduce the income of workers.

(c) *Efficiency wage considerations.* We have already noted that wage cuts may have a deleterious effect on the productivity of the labor force (both because it affects the effort provided by workers and because it affects the quality mix of workers that remain with the firm). Laying off workers also may seriously affect the productivity of remaining workers, particularly if they feel that they are likely to be let go in the near future. That is why firms often employ clear rules for who gets laid off: *most* workers with significant seniority know that they will not be laid off; for them, the firm has provided income insurance.

Though I believe that efficiency wage considerations go a long way in explaining the rigidity of market wages (and the corresponding fluctuations in employment), it does not really explain the market's failure to provide income insurance. Indeed, the failure of the firm to provide adequate income insurance for new employees may increase its (expected present discounted value of) total labor costs—making it necessary to pay higher current wages than it otherwise would to elicit effort (since what workers are concerned about is not just their current wage, but the expected present discounted value of their future wages, and this is reduced if there is significant probability of being laid off). Again, I suspect that the discrepancy between the short-run interests of the manager and the long-run interests of the firm provides part of the explanation for the firm's behavior.[29]

(d) *Incentives for reallocating labor.* With perfect income insurance, workers would have no incentive to reallocate themselves to where they may be more productively employed. The present system, in which a significant number of individuals are laid off, does motivate those individuals to look for alternative employment. But still, optimal risk-sharing between the employer and employee would provide severance (lay-off) pay at a far higher level than is usually provided.[30]

Though these arguments provide part of the rationale for limitations on income insurance and for wage rigidities, I remain unconvinced that they provide a full explanation. I have suggested that modifications in the contractual arrangements between manager and firms, resulting in managers more frequently taking into account the long-run interest of the firm, might result in contractual arrangements between workers and the firm with more income insurance and less employment variability.

I have discussed several proposals for risk-sharing (greater use of contingency contracts, profit sharing). If properly designed, these proposals may reduce average income fluctuations by reducing employment fluctuations (though in general, these increase the income variability of workers with seniority, those who would, in any case, have been retained). Profit-sharing plans, by reducing the risk to the firm associated with employment, encourage the employer to hire more laborers.[31]

The second puzzle is the failure of firms to provide insurance against inflation—to have appropriately indexed contracts. One would not expect full indexing on the Consumer Price Index, since that index probably does not fully reflect the risks facing most individuals. Still, it should be possible to construct (on the basis of data collected by the Bureau of Labor Statistics) a more appropriate index, and even if this isn't done, to index much more than is currently done. The explanations for incomplete indexing follow closely along the lines discussed above: firms may be risk-averse (particularly if they have contracts, such as loans or sales contracts, which are denominated in money terms) when their survival is threatened, and even when it is not, managers may act in a risk-averse manner. Again, it seems possible to distinguish among these cases: the contract can have the workers' income partially indexed on the costs of other inputs and the price of output. The contract should probably be highly nonlinear. For firms with limited debt, and with limited long-term contracts for inputs or sales denominated in money terms, there should be close to full indexing. For other firms, there should be close to full indexing, provided inflation rates are not too high. (But when inflation rates become high, it is likely that other contracts become indexed, again suggesting that the firm should provide income insurance.)[32]

The third puzzle is the form taken by adjustments to the demand for labor. We argued before that if workers are risk-averse, there should be work-sharing. Yet in the United States, layoffs are prevalent. These force a few workers to bear the brunt of the risks associated with variations in demand.

The puzzle is particularly acute given the structure of public unemployment compensation plans in the United States. Though firms are experience rated (so firms with higher lay-off rates pay more in unemployment taxes), many firms are at the maximum rate. For these firms, an increase in unemployment causes no increase in taxes. If the firm rotated its unemployed workers, having one set of workers layed off for two months, followed by another set, there would be effective work-sharing. The income fluctuations would be greatly moderated. And since no individuals would then face the cut-off of benefits after 26 weeks, the total amount that the workers (as a group) would receive from the government would be increased, at no expense to the firm.

In the case of union contracts, there is one perhaps not very attractive explanation: that unions are not pursuing the interests of the workers as a whole so much as they are pursuing the interests of the "established" workers, those with sufficient seniority to be affected only in the severest recessions. The analogy with old-style fraternity hazings may be instructive: each cohort believes, having paid a price in terms of periodic unemployment while lacking seniority, that it is only "fair" to make the next cohort face the same risks. This is the case even though a more humane (or in economists' terms, a more efficient) system would entail work-sharing among all the workers.[33] There are problems of designing appropriate compensations for the generation caught in the transition to a more efficient employment relationship. Those who have earned sufficient seniority to be relatively immune to employment fluctuations might argue that though some alternative system is more efficient, switching to a work-sharing system would make them worse off. It should be possible to provide cohort-specific compensation to these workers through the pension system.

The fourth puzzle is the limited use of explicit incentive schemes. Relatively few workers are paid on a piece-rate basis. Most workers have a high degree of job security. For many workers, their pay is not linked to performance. We argued earlier that risk-averse workers will not wish to have their pay depend completely on performance, but that there is a trade-off between "insurance" and incentives. It is my opinion (and I cannot prove this) that many contracts go too far in the direction of "insurance," that unions have been unduly concerned with job security, without realizing, at the same time, that there may be a price that has to be paid for this security. I have emphasized that the employment relationship is not a zero sum game: giving greater job security does not just represent a transfer of a certain set of prerogatives away from management. If the consequence is lower worker productivity, then the size of the pie, which is to be divided between the firm and its workers, is smaller. Fortunately, we have not gone as far in this direction as some European countries have, or as far as academics in the United States have. In both cases, the consequences for productivity have been, I suspect, very deleterious.

Profit-sharing plans are often put forth as one method of providing greater incentives to workers. The difficulty with most such plans is that the pay of the individual depends on the profits of the entire firm; there is little relationship between what a single individual does and the firm's profits. Such plans thus provide little incentive at the individual level, but they do serve one important function. They make it clear that the interests of the firm and its workers are not totally divergent.[34]

It is curious that incentive plans are more prevalent as compensation for managers than for workers. It is not apparent why. Indeed, the fact that managers are more likely to get more enjoyment from their work suggests the contrary. It may, of course, be that management simply uses "incentives" as a justification for paying themselves high salaries. Indeed, the form in which they receive much of their compensation poses another puzzle in the design of efficient compensation plans.[35] Many managers receive a significant part of their compensation in stock options. They justify this in terms of the incentive effects *and* in terms of the tax advantages: the compensation may effectively receive capital gains treatment. Both arguments are dubious. (There is no necessary link between the two; pay may be made contingent on share prices without actually taking the form of stock options.)

The question the shareholders should be concerned with, in deciding whether to give stock options, is how much do they have to give up, after tax, to give the manager a dollar of after-tax income. When the manager is paid a wage that is tax deductible, $100 of wages reduces dividends by $50 (assuming a 50% corporate tax rate); if dividends are thereby reduced by $50, and the shareholder is in the 50% tax bracket, his after-tax income is reduced by $25. The manager's income after tax (if he too is in the 50% tax bracket) is increased by $50. Thus, the shareholder, by paying wages, can give the manager $2 in after-tax income for every dollar in after-tax income that he gives up. Contrast this with stock options. Stock options are not costless. They dilute the ownership rights of the shareholders. If the company gives its managers $100 in stock, the value of the stock of other shareholders should, in a well functioning stock market, decrease by $100. Assume that the manager is in the 50% tax bracket, and the stock options receive favorable capital gains tax treatment; then his after-tax income has increased by $80. On the other hand, so long as the shareholder does not sell his shares, he does not receive any tax reduction. It is not until many years later, when he eventually sells his shares (and they are worth less than they otherwise would have been) that he gets his tax reduction. The consequence is that (in present value terms) to give the manager a dollar in after-tax income costs the shareholder more than a dollar. Stock options are clearly unfavorable. The prevalence of their use is testimony either to the attempt of managers to take advantage of unwary shareholders or the failure of managers to realize the full tax consequences of their actions. Either is a serious indictment.

Moreover, most stock option plans impose unnecessary risk while providing only limited incentives. Much of the variation in the price of shares is determined not by the actions of the firm, but by general market conditions. One would have thought that the managers pay should be made contingent on the performance of the firm relative to that of other similarly situated firms, and at the minimum, the manager should neither be rewarded nor punished for general variations in the stock market.

Some Prescriptions

I have attempted to suggest that there is considerable scope for designing better labor contracts, that there are many features of the kinds of contracts currently employed that seem inconsistent with efficient contract design. In the remaining pages, I want to put forward several proposals. Some of these may be more appropriate for some firms than for others; some may be inappropriate for any firm. The objective of these proposals is to encourage those who are involved in the practice of contract design to think imaginatively about its fundamental objectives (risk-sharing, incentives, flexibility), and how these objectives may be better served.[36]

The first set of proposals concerns the provision of greater risk-sharing; the extension of profit-sharing, inflation, indexing, and supplemental unemployment benefits can all be helpful. There are two other proposals that can make a significant contribution. The first I have already alluded to: more extensive use of indexing wages on indicators of profitability and labor scarcity, on indices such as industry profits or sales, or industry unemployment, or aggregate unemployment.[37] These could introduce greater flexibility into wage setting and provide greater sharing of risks between firms and workers in recessionary periods, and thus reduce some of the variability in employment. The second proposal is the establishment of unemployment savings and loan funds. I noted earlier that the institutionalization of savings for retirement (social security, pensions) resulted in the elimination of an important buffer upon which individuals whose income was temporarily reduced could draw. By setting up individual savings and loan accounts, a worker could contribute a percentage of his salary to the account. When he was unemployed, he could draw from the account. When the account was depleted, he could borrow using his pension benefits as security. In this way, the individual could smooth out income fluctuations.[38]

The second set of proposals is concerned with the improvement of workers' incentives. Here, I am less sanguine than many others about the role to be played by profit-sharing plans because of the greater importance that I (like most other economists) place on individual incentives. On the other hand, I think there is considerable room for devising more effective systems of worker incentives; these may entail a reduction in workers' job security. It is not in the interest of management to act in a capricious way, to fire workers who do not deserve to be fired. Firms that treat their workers well establish good reputations, and can attract better quality workers. Paying excessive attention to job security may have an undue effect on workers' productivity, more than can be compensated for by the reduced risk faced by workers. (In addition, profit-sharing plans may, by encouraging workers to recognize their mutual interests as well as those they hold with the firm, result in greater peer monitoring.)

The final set of proposals is concerned with the improvement of managerial incentives, and in particular, the incentive of managers to respond to fluctuations in the demand for their product by laying off workers. Proposals similar to those given previously (where the wage adjusts automatically to the firm's employment, so that the marginal cost of hiring an additional worker is less than its average cost), provide managers with incentives not to lay off workers; they provide an incentive for the firm to bear a larger share of the cyclical risks than they do at present.

Profit-sharing schemes, in which the total share of profits going to workers is fixed in the short run, do provide good incentives in this respect. Indeed, so long as the direct wage (base pay) component of the compensation package is sufficiently small, the short run-response (with the profit-sharing rule fixed) of the firm may entail hiring as many workers as it can get.[39]

I have touched on only a few of the important aspects of the employment relationship. I have not discussed the role of authority, worker participation in management, routinization, supervision, job rotation, and a host of other issues that affect both the quality of the life of workers, their productivity, and the profitability of the firm. The issues, primarily concerned with the design of compensation and employment policies, are central. I have suggested that there are three criteria on which such policies can be judged: their effects on risk-sharing and incentives and the extent to which they adjust to changes in circumstances, that is, their flexibility. Many commonly observed compensation and employment policies look markedly different from those that would seem to characterize efficient contractual arrangements.

Notes

1. Any analysis represents some simplifications from the complexities of the "real world." Hopefully, our analysis captures the essential features of the situation under examination. Thus, it is not a criticism of a theory that something has been omitted. It must be shown that what has been omitted would alter the basic predictions of the theory. Thus, in our analysis below, we shall argue that efficient contracts may entail lay-off policies that look markedly different from those commonly observed. It is not a criticism of our analysis to point out that we have omitted important psychological aspects of the employment relationship (which we have) unless one can show that, were these to be explicitly introduced into the analysis, the nature of the efficient lay-off policy would be quite different, and closer to what is actually observed, than to what we have characterized as efficient lay-off policies based on more narrowly defined economic considerations.

2. There are good reasons that the market fails to provide such insurance: it may, for instance, be very difficult for a third party (the insurance firm) to ascertain whether an individual is unemployed. There would be an incentive for those who expect to be unemployed to purchase the insurance, while those who do not expect to be unemployed would not. (This is known as the adverse selection problem; though it affects all insurance markets, it may be particularly significant in the case of unemployment insurance provided by the market.) Furthermore, the provision of the insurance might provide incentives for individuals to become unemployed (to quit, or to take actions that will induce the employer to fire him. This is referred to as the moral hazard problem. A moral hazard problem arises whenever the provision of insurance increases the likelihood of the insured-against event occurring. This problem, like the problem of verifying that the insured-against event has occurred, affects public as well as private insurance.) On the other hand, the private insurance market was slow to provide a number of forms of insurance for which these problems are not so severe (forms of insurance that they eventually have provided).

3. Individuals can, to some extent, self-insure by saving. As a matter of fact, many lower- and middle-income individuals (particularly younger individuals) do not have enough liquid assets to hold them over for an extended period of unemployment, without hardship. The substantial increase in pension funds and social security has exacerbated these problems: private savings for retirement can also serve as a buffer stock against short run fluctuations in income, but "savings" in pension funds and social security cannot serve these functions.

4. This is in contrast to risk-averse workers who are concerned not only by the average value of their income but also its variability. When the threat of bankruptcy is important, firm behavior is particularly likely to deviate from risk neutrality. If firms are concerned with their expected profits, which are zero if the firm goes bankrupt, and increase with the returns to investment if the firm does not go bankrupt, then firms will act like a risk lover, i.e. prefer greater variability. On the other hand—and more realistic in our view—managers are likely to act in a particularly risk-averse manner when the firm is near bankruptcy. What is critical for most of the analysis is that firms are sufficiently less risk-averse than workers (or that the risks facing the two are sufficiently different) that firms should be willing to absorb some of the employment-related risks for their workers.

5. In this view, moreover, the owners of the firm have only limited control over the actions of the manager. And the market exerts only limited discipline on firms, to ensure that they act in a way which maximizes the market value of the firm. Though this new

theory is closely related to the more traditional "managerial theory of the firm," it provides an explicit rationale for why managers' compensation should depend in a significant way on the outcome of the firm (an explanation that is part of the theory of efficient employment relations, the subject of this chapter) and for why markets provide only limited discipline on managers. Both are based on costs of information.

6. Asymmetric information creates another problem: e.g., if the workers believe that the employers have superior information concerning the likelihood that certain contingencies will occur, then they may infer that the firm is willing to provide extra income in a certain contingency only because they believe it will not occur. This problem is analogous to the standard adverse selection problem.

7. Indeed, the whole problem of delegation of authority and responsibility arises from information costs.

8. This view has been put forward, for instance, in Stiglitz 1975.

9. There are also important conflicts between the interests of bondholders and equity owners. For a more extensive discussion of all of these conflicts and their implications, see Stiglitz 1985.

10. See, for instance, Bailey 1974 and Azariadis 1975.

11. Provided that they are specific to the firm. See Becker, 1975.

12. This is the problem of moral hazard to which we referred earlier. For a discussion of the nature of these trade-offs in the context of labor contracts, see Stiglitz 1975.

13. There are a variety of ways in which this relationship can be specified. A piece-rate system has pay increase proportional to some measure of output. A bonus scheme is an example of a "non-linear" compensation scheme; a minimum output, which must be met before the individual qualifies for his base pay, is another example of a "non-linear" compensation scheme.

14. There are a variety of relative performance schemes. In some, pay is based on rank order—that is, the individual who has the highest sales gets the first prize, the individual with the second highest sales gets the second prize; the individual with the lowest sales gets fired. In others, pay may be related to the extent to which the individual's performance (his sales) exceeds the average.

For a discussion of relative performance compensation schemes, and their relative merits, (compared to individualistic performance schemes where compensation depends simply on the individual's own performance) see Nalebuff and Stiglitz 1983b., or Lazear and Rosen 1981.

15. The role of terminations as incentive devices has recently been explored by Stiglitz and Weiss 1983 and Shapiro and Stiglitz 1984. See also Calvo 1979 and Calvo and Wellisz 1979.

16. See Arnott, Hosios, and Stiglitz 1983.

17. See Arnott and Stiglitz 1985.

18. For a discussion of these theories, see Azariadis and Stiglitz 1983, Hart 1983, and Stiglitz 1986. The recent literature on this has included papers by Grossman and Hart (1981, 1983), Greene and Kahn 1983, Chari 1983, and Azariadis 1983.

19. There are a large number of other technical objections to the theory. For instance, under plausible conditions, the theory generates over-employment in good states, not under-employment in bad states. And it implies either that there is over-employment in all states of nature but one, or under-employment in all states of nature but one. Moreover, the theory is really based on a one period model of explicit contractual arrangements, rather than a long term implicit contract; but explicit contracts virtually never have the form that the theory would suggest. The theory assumes that some variables such as employment levels and capital transfers are more easily monitored than they probably are, while others (such as profits and sales) are assumed to be less easily monitored than they are. See Stiglitz 1986.

20. This assumes, as is realistically the case, that firms are imperfectly informed concerning the attributes of potential employees, and that they cannot, or do not, base pay simply on performance. The effect of the wage on the quality of the labor force through this mechanism has been recently discussed by Weiss 1980, Stiglitz 1976a, and Nalebuff and Stiglitz 1983.

21. Unless the firm can identify who are efficient searchers, lay-offs have the disadvantage of forcing a random selection of workers to search intensively. If all individuals had the same productivity, but differed only in search costs, then lowering wages would induce those who had the lowest search costs to seek out alternative employment. See Arnott, Hosios, and Stiglitz 1983.

22. This is, of course, not the only objection to piece-rates. Another important objection is the difficulty of finding adequate measures of performance; if there is some possibility of varying quality (as there frequently is), then the quality has to be monitored.

23. When pay is based on relative performance of workers within an organization, it may adversely affect cooperation.

24. From A. J. Oswald, "Unemployment Insurance and Labor Contracts under Asymmetric Information: Theory and Facts," Princeton University, Dec. 1983, mimeo.

25. In some industries, where efficiency wage considerations are important, the resistance to wage decreases and work-sharing may come from the firms, and not from the workers.

26. This is predicated on the assumption that firms act in a risk-averse manner in recessionary periods. For a more extended discussion of this, see Greenwald and Stiglitz 1986a.

27. The other explanation for limited risk-sharing on the part of the firm is that efficiency requires that workers move from jobs where they have low productivity to jobs where they have high productivity; they will only have incentive to search for such jobs if they are provided with incomplete income insurance. This argument is particularly applicable to firm- or industry-specific disturbances, not to economy-wide disturbances (in which case the productivity of individuals at all firms is altered simultaneously, and efficiency does not require labor mobility). Thus, our first puzzle is particularly concerned with the provision of income insurance against macro-economic risks. Moreover, lump sum severance pay does not have adverse incentive effects.

28. In cases where wages are not competitively set, then there may not be any long-run trade-off: there may already be an excess of applicants. The question, in these circumstances, is why unions did not bargain for a contract that was more in accord with the interests of their workers. We shall return to this question later.

29. Another part of the explanation has to do with imperfect capital markets; if firms are credit or equity rationed, and the implicit cost of capital rises in a recession, the savings in current labor costs may be more valuable than the long run increase in labor costs resulting from income fluctuations.

30. Indeed, it should equate the marginal utility of income to those retained with the (expected) marginal utility of income of those layed off; this implies that under certain circumstances, those layed off may actually be better off than those not layed off.

31. Any contract in which the wage paid the worker is reduced the greater the number of workers the firm hires results in the marginal cost of hiring workers being less than the wage, and thus encourages employment. I shall return to these alternative proposals in the final section of this chapter.

32. An argument against firms providing indexation is that, when inflation rates are small (or more accurately, when variations in the inflation rates are small), the workers should be able to absorbe the risk; the gain from transfering or sharing risks is less than the transaction costs involved in designing the appropriate contracts, while when inflation rates are large (or more accurately, when variations in the inflation rate are large), but loan and other contracts are not indexed (as they have not been in the U.S. until recently), then there should be risk-sharing between the firm and the workers.

33. There are some arguments that the younger workers are in a better position to absorb the income fluctuations, since they have fewer commitments. But they also have fewer resources (savings). Younger workers may have both a greater capacity and a greater incentive to search; our earlier analysis suggested that under certain circumstances that it would be efficient to lay off those workers who have a greater ability to search. But this argument does not have much validity for industry-wide, or economy-wide, lay-offs, where relatively few of those who are layed off obtain employment.

34. This is the context in which the economists' narrow focus on individual incentives

may be most misleading. Theories that suggest that workers' productivity is related to their sense of fair treatment imply that profit-sharing plans may still lead to an increase in productivity even when the individual's own effort has a negligible effect on profits.

35. This discussion is based on the tax law in place prior to the 1986 tax reform act. Under the new tax law, the advantages of paying executives direct cash benefits (possibly contingent upon the firm's performance) are even strengthened.

36. Economic theorists are apt to ask, at this juncture, why, if these proposals are welfare enhancing, have they not already been adopted by profit maximizing firms. The several puzzles which we described in the previous section should at least alert us to the possibility that firms are not, in fact, profit maximizing. There are several further answers to this query. First, there is, I believe, scope for social innovation, just as there is scope for technological innovation: firms (or unions) may not be fully aware of the advantages which might accrue from alternative contractual forms. Secondly, in economies with imperfect information and incomplete risk markets—that is, in all economies—market equilibrium is not (constrained) pareto efficient, and there are important externalities; the gains to society from adopting income and employment stabilizing policies may exceed those to any single firm.

37. Another proposal concerns the sharing of risks among workers: the use of work-sharing rather than lay-offs. In the absence of efficiency wage considerations, work-sharing would seem to dominate. As I argued earlier, I suspect that there is scope for more extensive use of work-sharing. Whether efficiency wage considerations, however, provide a sufficient argument against a significant increase in work-sharing remains moot.

38. The advantage that these accounts have over supplemental unemployment benefits programs is that they do not suffer from the same moral hazard problem: while the supplemental unemployment benefits (so long as the magnitude of the benefits are related to the length of time that the individual is unemployed) reduce individual's incentives to search for a better job, this is not true of the loan programs. For most individuals, the period for which they are unemployed is relatively short, and the fraction of lifetime income that is lost is relatively small. The major problem they face is a liquidity problem: the lack of funds to maintain their consumption levels (to pay the mortgage, e.g.). Unemployment Savings and Loan Funds meet this need.

39. That is, in the short run, the firm will hire workers so long as the value of the marginal product of the worker exceeds the base pay. In the extreme, if the base pay were set at zero, the firm would hire workers so long as the value of the marginal product of the worker is positive.

In the long run, of course, the terms of the contract—the fraction of profits which go to workers—will have to adjust in the same way that wages adjust in conventionally run labor markets, to reflect the demand and supply of labor.

References

Akerlof, George. 1984. "Gift Exchange and Efficiency Wage Theory: Four Views." *American Economic Review Proceedings.*

Akerlof, G. and H. Miyazaki. 1980. "The Implicit Contract Theory of Unemployment Meets the Wage Bill Argument." *Review of Economic Studies* 47: 321–38.

Arnott, R., A. Hosios, and J. Stiglitz. 1983. "Implicit Contracts, Labor Mobility and Unemployment." Mimeo. Princeton University. (revised version of a paper presented at NBER-NSF conference, Dec. 1980)

Arnott, R. and J. Stiglitz. 1985. "Labor Turnover, Wage Structures and Moral Hazard." *Journal of Labor Economics.*

Azariadis, C. 1975. "Implicit Contracts and Underemployment Equilibria. *Journal of Political Economy* 83: 1183–1202.

———. 1979. "Implicit Contracts and Related Topics: A Survey." Z. Hornstein et al., eds., *The Economics of the Labour Market.* London: HMSO.

————. 1983. "Employment with Asymmetric Information." *Quarterly Journal of Economics* 98: 157–72.

Azariadis, C., and J. E. Stiglitz. 1983. "Implicit Contracts and Fixed-Price Equilibria", *Quarterly Journal of Economics* 98: 1–22.

Baily, M. N. 1974. "Wages and Employment Under Uncertain Demand". *Review of Economic Studies* 41: 37–50.

Becker, Gary S. 1975. *Human Capital: A Theoretical and Empirical Analysis with Special Reference to Education.* New York: National Bureau of Economic Research, Columbia University Press.

Calvo, Guillermo. 1979. "Quasi-Walrasian Theories of Unemployment". *American Economic Review.* Vol. 69, No. 2: 102–107.

Calvo, Guillermo and E. S. Phelps. 1977. Appendix: employment contingent wage contracts. *Stabilization of the Domestic and International Economy* Vol. 5. Eds. Karl Brunner and Allan H. Meltzer. Carnegie-Rochester Conference Series on Public Policy. *Journal of Monetary Economics Supplement:* 160–68.

Calvo, Guillermo and Stanislaw Wellisz. 1979. "Hierarchy, Ability and Income Distribution". *Journal of Political Economy* 87: 991–1010.

Chari, V. V. 1983. "Involuntary Unemployment and Implicit Contracts." *Quarterly Journal of Economics* 98: 107–22.

Cooper, R. 1981. "Risk-Sharing and Productive Efficiency in Labor Contracts Under Bilateral Asymmetric Information." Mimeo. University of Pennsylvania.

Eaton, B. Curtis and William White. 1982. "Agent Compensation and the Limits of Bonding." *Economic Inquiry* 20: 330–43.

Gordon, D. F. 1974. "A Neoclassical Theory of Keynesian Unemployment." *Economic Inquiry* 12:431–59.

Green, J. and C. Kahn. 1983. "Wage-Employment Contracts." *Quarterly Journal of Economics* 98:173–87.

Greenwald, B. and J. E. Stiglitz. 1986a. "Information, Finance Constraints, and Business Fluctuations." Paper presented at a Conference on Monetary Economics, Taipei, January.

————. 1986b. "Externalities in Economics with Imperfect Information and Incomplete Markets." *Quarterly Journal of Economics.* 101:229–264.

Grossman, S. and O. Hart. 1981. "Implicit Contracts, Moral Hazard and Unemployment." *American Economic Review* 71:301–7.

————. 1983. "An Analysis of the Principal-Agent Problem." *Econometica* 51:7–46.

Grossman, S., O. Hart, and E. Maskin. 1983. "Unemployment With Observable Aggregate Shocks." *Journal of Political Economy* 91:907–26.

Hall, Robert. 1975. "The Rigidity of Wages and the Persistence of Unemployment." *Brookings Papers on Economic Activity* 2:301–35.

Hall, R. 1980. "Employment Fluctuations and Wage Rigidity." *Brookings Papers on Economic Activity.* pp. 91–124.

Hall, R. and E. Lazear. 1982. "The Excess Sensibility of Layoffs and Quits to Demand." *NBER Working Paper.* no. 864.

Hall, R. and D. Lilien. 1979. "Efficient Wage Bargains Under Uncertain Supply and Demand." *American Economic Review* 69:868–79.

Hart, O. 1983. "Optimal Labor Contracts Under Asymmetric Information: An Introduction." *Review of Economic Studies* 50:3–36.

Holstrom, B. 1983. "Equilibrium Long-Term Labor Contracts." *Quarterly Journal of Economics* 98:23–54.

Lazear, E. and S. Rosen. 1981. "Rank Order Tournaments as Optimum Labor Contracts." *Journal of Political Economy* 89 (October): 41–64.

Malcolmson, James. 1981. "Unemployment and the Efficiency Wage Hypothesis." *Economic Journal* 91: 848–66.

Nalebuff, B. J. and Stiglitz, J. E. 1983a. "Information, Competition and Markets." *American Economic Review* 73: 278–83.

————. 1983b. "Prizes and Incentives: Towards a General Theory of Compensation and Competiton." *Bell Journal.* 14, 21–43.

Newbery, D. and J. Stiglitz. 1982. "Wage Rigidity, Implicit Contracts and Economic Efficiency: Are Market Wages Too Flexible?" Mimeo. Princeton University.

Oswald, A. J. 1983. "Unemployment Insurance and Labour Contracts under Asymmetric Information: Theory and Facts", Mimeo. Princeton University.

Salop, Steven. 1979. "A Model of the Natural Rate of Unemployment." *American Economic Review* 69: 117–25.

Schlicht, Ekkehart. 1978. "Labour Turnover, Wage Structure and Natural Unemployment." *Zeitschrift fur die Gesamte Staatswissenschaft* 134: 337–46.

Shapiro, Carl and Joseph Stiglitz. 1984. "Equilibrium Unemployment as a Worker Discipline Device." *American Economic Review* 74 (June): 433–44.

Solow, Robert. 1979. "Another Possible Source of Wage Stickiness." *Journal of Macroeconomics* 1: 79–82.

———. 1981. "On Theories of Unemployment." *American Economic Review* 91: 848–66.

Stiglitz, J. E. 1974. "Alternative Theories of Wage Determination and Unemployment in LDC's: The Labor Turnover Model." *Quarterly Journal of Economics* 88 (May): 194–227.

———. 1975. "Incentives, Risk, and Information; Notes Towards a Theory of Heirarchy," *Bell Journal of Economics and Management Science* vol. 6 (Autumn). 552–79.

———. 1976a. "Prices and Queues as Screening Devices in Competitive Markets." IMMSS Technical Report no. 212. Stanford University.

———. 1976b. "The Efficiency Wage Hypothesis, Surplus Labor and The Distribution of Income in L.D.C.'s." *Oxford Economic Papers*. vol. 28. no. 2: 185–207.

———. 1978. "Lectures in Macro-economics". Mimeo. Oxford University.

———. 1982a. "Ownership, Control, and Efficient Markets: Some Paradoxes in the Theory of Capital Markets," in *Economic Regulation: Essays in Honor of James R. Nelson,* Kenneth D. Boyer and William G. Shepherd eds., Ann Arbor, Michigan: Michigan State University Press, pp. 311–41.

———. 1982b. "The Wage-Productivity Hypothesis: Its Economic Consequences and Policy Implications." Paper presented at the New York Meetings of the American Economic Association.

———. 1985a. "Equilibrium Wage Distributions". *Economic Journal*. 95, 595–617.

———. 1985b. "Credit Markets and the Control of Capital," *Journal of Money, Banking, and Credit* 17: 133–52.

———. 1986. "Theories of Wage Rigidity," in *Keynes Economic Legacy,* edited by James L. Butkiewicz, Kenneth J. Koford, and Jeffrey B. Miller. New York, N.Y.: Praeger.

Stiglitz, J. E. and A. Weiss. 1983. "Incentive Effects of Terminations: Applications to the Credit and Labor Markets." *American Economic Review* 73: (December) 912–27.

Stoft, Steven. 1982. "Cheat Threat Theory: An Explanation of Involuntary Unemployment." Mimeo. Boston University.

Strand, J. 1983. "The Structure of Implicit Contracts with Word of Mouth Reputational Enforcement." Mimeo. University of Oslo.

Weiss, A. 1980. "Job Queues and Layoffs in Labor Markets with Flexible Wages." *Journal of Political Economy* 88 (June): 526–38.

Yellen, J. 1984. "Efficiency Wage Models of Unemployment." *American Economic Review* 74 (May): 200–205.

3

Pay for Performance: A Motivational Analysis

Edward E. Lawler III

The idea of pay for performance is so widely accepted that almost every organization says that it has it. A recent survey of 557 large companies found that 80% of them rate pay for performance as a *very* important compensation objective (Peck 1984). Even the United States government calls its system a merit pay system and, under the Carter administration, legislation (the Civil Service Reform Act) was passed that calls for wage increases more related to merit. The major reason for the popularity of merit pay is the belief that it can motivate job performance and increase organizational effectiveness. Psychological research clearly supports this view. There has been, and continues to be, considerable evidence that pay can be a particularly powerful incentive (Lawler 1981; Locke, et al. 1980). Studies show productivity increases of 15 to 35% when incentive pay systems are put into place; a Public Agenda Foundation survey (1983) reports that 73% of workers surveyed said that the lack of incentive pay decreases job effort.

Psychological research shows that pay is an effective motivator of performance when it has two fundamental properties: first, it is important to people; second, it is tied to their performance in ways that are visible, creditable, long-term, and perceived by them to be direct (see e.g. Lawler 1971, 1973). For most people, pay is important, so typically there is no problem in using pay as a motivator. The critical issue is whether a relationship is perceived to exist between pay and performance.

Despite the existence of widespread support for performance-based pay, there is considerable evidence that in most organizations pay systems fail to create a perceived relationship between pay and performance. For example, the 1983 study by the Public Agenda Foundation found that only 22% of American workers say there is a direct link between how hard they work and how much they are paid. As a result, it is likely that most pay-for-performance systems fail to produce the positive effects expected of them. In addition, there are some reasons to believe that in the future, it is going to be harder to have effective merit pay programs. But before we consider what the future holds, a brief review of the reasons why pay systems often do not produce the perception that pay and performance are related will serve to highlight the problems in using pay as a motivator of performance. First, we will review the experience with incentive pay plans, and then we will consider plans that rely on merit salary increases.

Incentive Pay

Incentive plans that pay employees bonuses based on the number of units produced are perhaps the most direct way to relate pay to performance. However, the literature on pay incentive plans is full of vivid descriptions of the counterproductive behaviors that piece-rate incentive plans produce (see e.g., Whyte 1955). In many respects, these behaviors are caused not so much by the concept itself, but by the way it has been employed in most organizations. Nevertheless, it is difficult to separate the practical problems with the plan from the general idea of incentive pay. Let us briefly review the major problems with piece-rate incentive plans.

Beating the System

Numerous studies have shown that when piece-rate plans are put into place an adversarial relationship develops between system designers and the employees who work on them (Lawler 1971). Employees engage in numerous behaviors in order to have rates set in such a way that they can maximize their financial gains relative to the amount of work that they have to do. They engage in behaviors such as working at slow rates in order to mislead the time study expert when he or she comes to study their job. They hide new work methods or new procedures from the time-study person so the job will not be restudied. In addition, informal norms develop within the organization about how productive people should be with the result that the workers themselves set limits on production. Anyone who goes beyond this limit may be ostracized or punished. Unfortunately for the organization, this limit is often set far below what people are capable of producing.

Another way of beating the system is producing at extremely low levels when employees consider established rate levels too difficult to reach, and using union grievance procedures to eliminate rates that are too difficult. Finally, it is often suggested that, in order to gain leverage in negotiating piece-rates, employees will organize unions so that they can deal from a more powerful base. Often, when unions exist in the work place, they are able to negotiate piece-rate plans that allow workers to work off standard, while being paid at a rate that represents a high level of performance. Thus, organizations end up with the undesirable combination of high pay and low performance.

In summary, piece-rate plans often result in an adversarial relationship between those on the plan, and those designing and administering the plan. The result is that both sides often engage in practices designed to win the game or war at the cost of organizational effectiveness.

Divided Work Force

Since many support jobs and nonproduction jobs do not lend themselves to piece-rate pay, the typical organization that has incentive pay has part of the work force on it and part of the work force not on it. This often leads to a we/they split that can be counterproductive and lead to noncooperative work relationships. This split, interestingly enough, is not a management-worker split, but a worker-worker split. In its most severe form, it can lead to incentive people complaining about materials-handling people, maintenance people, and others on whom they depend for support. This split can also lead to some dysfunctions in the kind of career paths people choose. Often, individuals will bid for and stay on incentive jobs even though such jobs do not fit their skills and interests because of the higher pay. The higher pay of established incentive jobs may also cause individuals to be inflexible when asked to change jobs temporarily or to resist new technology that calls for a rate change.

Maintenance Costs

Because incentive plans by themselves are relatively complicated and need to be constantly updated, a significant investment needs to be made in the people whose job it is to maintain them. The problem of maintaining the incentive systems is further complicated by the adversarial relationship that develops between employees and management. Since employees try to hide new work methods and avoid changes in their rates (unless, of course, it is to their advantage), management needs to be extremely vigilant in determining when new rates are needed. In addition, every time a technological change is made or a new product is introduced, new rates need to be set.

Finally, there is the ongoing cost of computing peoples' wages relative to the amount of work and the kind of work they have done during a particular performance period. This requires the work of engineers, accountants, and payroll clerks, making the support costs of an incentive system significantly greater than those of a straight hourly pay, or a traditional pay-for-performance salary increase plan.

Organization Culture

The combined effects of dividing the work force into those who are and are not on incentive pay and of rate-setting (an adversarial process) can create a hostile organization climate resulting in low trust, lack of information-sharing, poor support for joint problem-solving, and inflexibility because individuals want to protect their rates. Overall, incentive pay works against creating a climate of openness, trust, joint problem-solving, and commitment to organizational objectives.

In summary, the above analysis should make it clear that the installation of incentive pay is, at best, a mixed blessing. Although it may improve work performance, the counterproductive behaviors, the maintenance costs, the division of the work force, and the poor climate it leads to may make it a poor investment. Many organizations have dropped it or decided against it simply because they feel the possible negative effects and increased maintenance costs outweigh the potential advantages.

Merit Salary Systems

Merit salary systems are the most common form of pay for performance. There are, however, a number of problems with them.

Poor Performance Measures

Fundamental to an effective merit pay system are creditable comprehensive measures of performance. Without these, it is impossible to relate pay to performance in a way that is motivating. There is a great deal of evidence that, in most organizations, performance appraisal is not done well and that, as a result, no good measures of individual performance exist (see e.g. Meyer, Kay, and French 1965; Derives, Morrison, Shullman, and Gerlach 1981). Sometimes good measures of plant or group performance exist, but similar measures are not available for individuals. In the absence of good objective measures of individual performance, most organizations rely on the judgments of managers. To subordinates, these judgments often seem to be invalid, unfair, and discriminatory. For these reasons, little is done to create the perception that pay is based on performance (Lawler 1981). Indeed, in the eyes of many employees, merit pay is a fiction that managers try to perpetuate.

Poor Communication

In many organizations, salaries have traditionally been kept secret; in addition, so have pay practices. For example, it is common for organizations not to disclose the amounts of salary increases or bonuses, or the highest and lowest raises. Thus, the typical employee must often accept, as an article of faith, that pay and performance are related because it is simply impossible to determine actual criteria.

In situations of high trust, employees may accept the organization's statement that merit pay exists. However, trust depends on the open exchange of information; thus, with secrecy, it is not surprising that many individuals are skeptical. In a significant number of organizations, communication is worsened because the organizations either don't spend the time and energy needed to explain their system, or they communicate in ways that lead people to doubt the system. For example, organizations often state that all pay increases are based on merit, even though virtually everyone gets an increase because of inflation and changes in the labor market. It is hardly surprising that individuals often question how much merit had to do with their "merit increase."

Poor Delivery System

The actual policies and procedures that make up a merit pay system often lead to actions that do little to relate pay to performance. In addition, the policies and procedures often are so complex that they do more to obfuscate than to clarify the relationship between pay and performance. The typical merit salary increase is particularly poor at actually relating pay and performance, because it allows only small changes in total pay to occur in one year. All too often, only a few percentage points separate the raises given the good performers and those given the poor performers. Thus, the differences are often both unimportant and invisible. Salary increase systems further compound the problem by making past "merit payments" part of the individual's base salary. This means that an individual can be a poor performer for several years after having been a good performer, and still be highly paid. Bonus plans are typically better at relating pay to performance, but they are sometimes flawed by policies that fund them at insignificant levels and by procedures that pay everyone the same bonus.

Poor Managerial Behavior

Managers do a number of things that adversely affect the perceived connection between pay and performance. Perhaps the most serious is the failure to recommend widely different pay increases or bonuses for their subordinates when large performance differences exist. Some managers are unwilling to recommend very large and very small pay actions, even when they are warranted. One reason for this seems to be the unpleasant task of explaining why someone got a low raise or bonus.

The difficulty of explaining low raises or bonuses often leads to a second destructive behavior on the part of managers: disowning the pay decision. Despite the fact that they may have recommended a small raise and believe it was appropriately given, supervisors sometimes deny or discount their role in determining their subordinates' pay. They may, for example, say that they fought hard for the subordinate to get a good raise but lost out. This clearly communicates to the subordinate that pay increases are beyond their control, and thus not based on performance.

Conclusion

The existence in most corporations of any one of the common problems that plague the administration of merit pay programs is usually enough to destroy the belief that pay is related to performance in the eyes of most employees. In reality, the merit pay systems of most organizations typically suffer from all or most of these problems. At best, the resulting merit pay policy fails to achieve its intended objective; at worst it becomes an embarrassment that undermines management's credibility.

The New Scene

The United States has changed dramatically since the first installations of incentive and merit pay. The society, the work force, and nature of work have all changed. Let us look at each of these and how they relate to the ways that pay-for-performance can be effectively delivered.

Nature of the Work

In the early 1900s, many jobs in the United States were in manufacturing and agriculture, and involved the production of relatively simple, high volume products. Today, the United States is moving rapidly toward work that is service-sector-, knowledge, information-processing-, and/or high-technology-based. Many simple repetitive jobs in manufacturing have left the United States for less developed countries, or they have been automated. Instead of simple stand-alone jobs that an individual can do alone, many jobs now involve the operation of complex machines, continuous process plants, or the delivery of services that require the integrated work of many individuals.

The type of work that exists in the United States today, therefore, is less amenable to individual measurement and to the specification of a normal level of individual production. Instead, performance can only be measured reliably and validly when a group of workers or even an entire plant is viewed. In many knowledge-based jobs, it is difficult even to specify what the desired product is until it has been produced. Work of this nature simply does not lend itself to traditional incentive pay. High-tech jobs are subject to rapid change, which conflicts directly with an incentive pay system that requires stability to set rates and to justify the initial costs.

Finally, even in situations where there are simple, repetitive, stable jobs that lend themselves to piece-rate pay, work on individual job enrichment has led organizations to try to make those jobs more complex and to create conditions under which employees will be intrinsically motivated to perform well. For example, in some cases, self-managing teams have been given responsibility for whole pieces of work (Hackman and Oldham 1980). In many cases however, the process of enriching jobs has made them less likely candidates for incentive pay, first, because a different kind of motivation is present, and second, because the enrichment process has made the simple, measurable, repetitive, individual nature of the jobs disappear. In summary, the nature of work, at least in the United States, has become less and less amenable to an individual pay-for-performance system.

Nature of the Work Force

When incentive pay was introduced in the United States, the work force was primarily composed of poorly educated immigrant workers who were, for the first time, entering factories and manufacturing environments. Today, the work force is more highly educated, and there is evidence to indicate that its members have different values and different orientations toward work. For example, over 20% of the current work force has a college education; this, combined with a number of other changes, has produced a different work force, one that is interested in influencing work place decisions, desires challenging and interesting work, and hopes to develop its skills and abilities. Incentive pay plans, because of their top-down nature and the kind of work they are typically associated with, do not fit this kind of work force. Indeed, it is this change in the nature of the work force that is often used to support the call for more enriched jobs and for the elimination of standardized, specialized, highly repetitive work (Hackman and Oldham 1980).

Nature of the Society

The rate of social change in the United States has been accelerating in recent years. Particularly in the last ten years, the United States has seen an expansion in employee rights, employee entitlements, and the kind of legal avenues open to employees when they feel unfairly treated. This has made incentive pay plans and merit salary increase plans subject to grievances and to the kind of challenges that make them difficult and expensive to maintain.

In addition, our society has seen increased international competition and the loss of jobs to other countries. The net effect of these and other changes seems to have been to push the society toward pay practices that are more egalitarian and have less money at risk. Today we have high fringe benefits and high base wages. In many respects, this is not consistent with the increasing national awareness that the United States needs to be more productive, but it does complement the idea of increased entitlements and the elimination of incentive pay plans. Interestingly, the fear of job loss also can lead to production restriction on incentive jobs. Individuals reduce production because they are afraid that if they produce too much they will work themselves or their co-workers out of a job. The macro issue of international competitiveness is overlooked because of the short-term need for a job.

Overall, the United States has become a society in which the profits of companies are at risk as a function of performance, but the pay of individuals is affected only at the extremes of performance. That is, an employee only loses when the company is in such poor shape that it has to lay the individual off, and the employee only gains when growth is such that the employee has the opportunity to be promoted. The society seems to have evolved to a state where individuals consider that they are entitled to a fair wage and extensive fringe benefits simply because they are employed by the organization. This kind of thinking is represented in the union contracts that have eliminated piece-rate pay and in companies that, in order to stay nonunion, have simply given high base wages to all employees.

Future Developments

There are no indications that changes are occurring that are likely to tip the scales in favor of traditional incentive pay or merit salary increase plans. Indeed, if anything, the trends that have led to the abandonment of incentive pay seem to be continuing so that, within the next ten years, we will probably see a continuing decline in the use of incentive pay plans. In the case of merit increases, the approach itself is so flawed that it is hard to imagine a set of conditions that would make it effective. There is, however, one important trend that seems to call for the increased use of pay as a motivator—the lack of growth in national productivity and the strong international competitive situation with respect to productivity and economic growth.

Given the competitive situation, it seems foolish for any organization to abandon such a potentially powerful incentive for performance as pay. Just this point was made by the 1984 White House Conference on Productivity; it recommended the increased use of pay as a motivator. The Public Agenda Foundation study also supports pay for performance; it found that 61% of the workers it surveyed want pay tied to performance. On the other hand, the analysis so far has suggested that incentive pay plans and merit increase plans are not a good strategy. Simply stated, they fail to create the perception that significant amounts of pay are tied to performance and so fail to motivate performance. What then is the answer? To the degree there is *an* answer, it rests not in a new form of pay for performance, but in a new pay that fits the new approaches to management emerging in the United States.

Pay in Organizations

Reward systems are an important part of the very fabric of organizations. As such, they must fit with the overall design of an organization and must reinforce and support the kind of behavior and culture that is desired. Thus, changes in the way an organization is managed demand a change in the reward system. Indeed, one of the things that is so fascinating and interesting about the exploration of alternative management styles is the discovery that they typically do include different reward system practices. For example, the Japanese emphasize lifetime employment and large bonuses for everyone in the organization. Although we can learn from the practices of other countries, it is unlikely that their pay practices can be adopted simply. Rather, what is needed is the development of a new structure that fits the new approaches to management being tried in the United States. These approaches stress such things as greater employee involvement in the business; leaner, flatter organizations; and developing cultures that support business strategies.

Reward systems in organizations are made up of core values, structures, and processes. Often, in organizations, the emphasis is on the structures, which are tangible and easy to manipulate. They include such things as merit pay systems, job evaluation systems, and pay ranges. In short, these structures or mechanics are the nuts and bolts of the reward system. Associated with the various structures are a number of process issues that concern communication and decision-making. At the heart of the reward system though, are the core values; thus this discussion of new approaches will begin by considering them.

Core Values

Organizations have core values with respect to their pay systems. These may be explicitly stated, as they are in some corporations, or they may simply develop over time and be generally shared as part of the culture. Core values usually concern key process issues (e.g. communication) and key structural issues (e.g. pay-for-performance). They guide what is done in these areas.

The realization that values are something that can be consciously planned has important implications for compensation. Specifically, it means that pay needs to be driven by a clearly articulated, well accepted set of core values. These core values should not be simply a passing emphasis in the organization; rather, they should be fundamental beliefs that remain unchanged for decades. There is no right set of core values. What *is* right is placing a strong emphasis upon them, matching them to the desired culture of the organization, adhering to them, and being sure that people are aware of them.

There are a set of important core issues that the values ought to address. These include:

1) Job security.
2) A comparison of pay levels with those of other organizations.
3) The major determinants of an individual's pay; that is, performance or seniority.
4) The individual's rights concerning access to information and involvement.
5) The relationship of pay levels to business success.
6) The degree to which the system will be egalitarian.
7) The degree of support for learning, personal growth, and involvement.

Although there are no "right" values, it is possible to make some statements about the general orientation that is congruent with some of the major changes in American management. In particular, the core values in the new pay need to emphasize the relationship of pay to the success of the business, individual rights, due process, egalitarian approaches, pay rates that are competitive with similar businesses, and greater emphasis on rewarding individual growth and skill development. These core values support a management style in which the organization depends upon people both to think and do, and stresses broad scale business involvement on the part of all employees.

Process Issues

The new approaches to management suggest some very important changes on the process side of pay administration. In particular, they suggest greater openness of communication about pay practices and broader involvement on the part of all organizational members in the development of pay and reward systems practices. Greater openness, of course, is a prerequisite for broader involvement and participation in the development and administration of pay practices. Openness and participation are congruent with the emphasis on egalitarian reward structures, individual rights, and having individuals involved in both the thinking and doing sides of the business. They acknowledge that for a reward system to be effective it has to be both understood and designed in ways that individuals accept. Participation in the design and administration process helps assure this, as well as that the system will fit the situation because it allows the people who will be affected by the system to influence its designs.

With openness and participation, widespread ownership of the reward system develops so that it is not simply the responsibility of the compensation or personnel department. Instead, it becomes the responsibility of everyone in the organization to see that it operates effectively and fairly. This is a particularly important point, since in traditional management structures, the reward system too often becomes the property of the personnel department, and as a result, it ends up being ineffectively and poorly supported by line management. It almost goes without saying that in the absence of broad support in the organization the reward system cannot support particular business objectives and strategies.

Pay System Structure

The structure of pay must flow directly from core values and management style. There are some structural mechanisms that fit particularly well with the way management thinking is changing. Many of them represent important changes in the way pay is currently administered in organizations.

The following structural approaches to rewards are particularly appropriate for organizations practicing employee involvement oriented management.

1. Pay for Performance. A widely applicable approach to pay-for-performance is the use of a combination of profit-sharing, gain-sharing, and stock ownership. As a combination, they can riddle an organization with pay for performance plans and dramatically increase the business involvement of everyone in the organization. At the same time, they avoid many of the problems associated with individual pay-for-performance plans. Not surprisingly, the use of these plans is showing a dramatic increase in the United States and every indication is that they will continue to grow in popularity. Let us therefore turn to a brief discussion of them and a consideration of why they seem to be an appropriate method at this point in time.

   A. Gainsharing Plans. The Scanlon Plan is perhaps the oldest and best known gainsharing plan (Moore and Ross 1978). More recently, a number of companies have adopted the Improshare Plan, while many others have developed their own plans. The idea in all of these plans is to define a business unit, typically a plant or major department, and to relate pay to the overall performance of that business unit. Bonuses are paid to all employees in that unit on a monthly basis. A formula is used to decide the size of the bonus. Typically, bonuses are paid when the formula indicates a decrease in such costs as labor, materials, and supplies.

      The Scanlon Plan was first formulated by Joe Scanlon, a union leader in the 1930s, and has been in place in some companies for over 30 years. Until recently, it was used primarily in small family-owned manufacturing organizations. During the 1970s, however, an interesting and important trend developed. Large companies such as General Electric, TRW, Dana, and Owens-

Illinois began installing gainsharing plans in some of their manufacturing plants. The tendency of large corporations to define
organizational units that have their own bonus plans seems to be
spreading. The reasons for this are many and relate directly to
the kinds of changes that have been going on in the work force in
the society in general. In many respects, the work situation in the
United States today is more in tune with the idea of plantwide or
organizationwide bonuses, such as those that are typically generated by gainsharing plans, than they are in tune with the idea of
piece-rate or merit pay. Let us briefly review why gainsharing
plans seem to fit better in the current situation.

First, gainsharing plans do not rely on individual performance
measurement. This is important in several respects. First, it fits
many work places because performance in them can only be
measured in an objective manner at the group or plantwide level.
The technology in them does not lend itself to the identification
of individual output.

Typically, gainsharing plans are participatively developed and
administered. That is, employees have a say in the design of the
plan and are able to participate in the ongoing maintenance and
administration of the plan. This tends to significantly decrease
the adversarial relationship between employees and management and to fit better in a society in which people want to
influence work-place discussions and be involved in business
decisions.

Gainsharing plans also affect everyone in the work force—
managers, production employees, and support people—so they
encourage cooperation and teamwork and thus produce an
increase in organizational performance. This contrasts with incentive plans, which affect only a limited number of employees
and increase competition within organizations.

Finally, to a degree, gainsharing plans meet the needs of
organizations for increased productivity. There is considerable
evidence that indeed they do produce performance improvements (Lawler 1981, Bullock and Lawler 1984). On the other
hand, it is important to note that they may not produce as great
an increase in the performance of individual production workers
as will piece-rate plans. They produce a much less direct connection between individual performance and reward, and therefore
are a less powerful motivator than are individual piece-rate
incentives. Clearly then, there is a loss here in comparison to
piece-rate incentive plans, but the expectation is that the loss will
be made up.

First, extra cooperation should lead to better performance

particularly in work places where cooperation is key to performance (e.g. process production technologies). Second, the ability to
include everyone in a plan can be an important advantage in
most work places since it means that the performance of many
can be increased, not just the performance of a few. Third,
gainsharing plans do not seem to produce as many negative side
effects, because rather than leading to an adversarial relationship, they typically lead to a cooperative problem-solving relationship between management and workers since managers and
employees are on the same incentive plan. Fourth, most plans
include a problem-solving group process intended to develop
and implement individuals' ideas about how the work process
can be improved. Fifth, gainsharing improves organizational
performance, and this produces a greater correlation between
an organization's profits and individual financial reward. Situations where a bonus is paid and the organization performs
poorly are unlikely to develop. Finally, gainsharing plans often
take less administrative support than do individual piece-rate
plans. While they still require administrative support, they do
not require the setting of individual standards for each job nor
the calculation of pay for each individual based upon performance.

So far, the installation of gainsharing plans has largely been
limited to manufacturing situations. Recently some service organizations such as banks and hospitals have begun to experiment
with gainsharing plans. A good guess is that over the next five to
ten years there will be increased use of gainsharing plans in
nonmanufacturing situations. Although a great deal remains to
be learned about how such plans should be installed in nonmanufacturing environments, gainsharing is one approach for
linking pay to performance that fits the conditions in today's
work places.

B. Profit-Sharing and Stock Ownership. Profit-sharing and employee stock ownership are better known, older, and more
prevalent than gainsharing. By themselves, they are typically less
effective motivators, however. This is particularly true in large
organizations where the line of sight from individual performance to corporate performance is poor and the connection
between individual performance and stock price is virtually
nonexistent. Thus, particularly in large organizations, these approaches are desirable primarily because of their symbolic value.
They effectively point out to everyone that they are part of one
organization and that joint effort is needed. Stock ownership in
particular can serve to emphasize the importance of long-term

organizational performance. In very small organizations, profit-sharing and stock ownership may make gainsharing unnecessary because they have the same effect. In most organizations, however, these plans, important symbolically and as balancers, should be thought of as supplements to gainsharing. The one exception is top management for whom profit-sharing and stock ownership plans should be thought of as the major motivators of performance.

At the management level, pay needs to place emphasis upon long-term performance. Particularly in the case of executive compensation, this suggests the importance of replacing or supplementing many of the current short-term profit-driven incentive plans with five- to ten-year incentive plans. It also argues for paying managers based on the performance units they have managed in the past as well as on the performance of their current units. This can help to assure that when managers leave a position, they cannot simply walk away from their past performance.

In summary, more emphasis needs to be placed on rewarding performance. The emphasis needs to change from individual performance-based rewards to business-based rewards and from short-term rewards to longer-term rewards for performance. Overall, organizations need to be riddled with pay-for-performance systems.

2. Decentralized. In a large corporation, a centralized compensation approach is incongruent with the ideas of business involvement, and targeting organization structure and reward system practices to the business strategy. By their very nature, most large corporations are engaged in multiple businesses that have quite different needs and compete with organizations that pay differently. Having a single approach to pay, which emphasizes a corporate-wide approach to market position, to merit pay, to performance measurement, and so forth, makes it impossible for particular business units to structure their rewards system effectively. Business units end up being forced to adopt a corporate structure that often is not congruent with what is needed to compete in the particular environment in which they operate. Smaller organizations tend not to have this problem because they often face a single external environment. Some large, single business organizations may not need to decentralize since they also face a single external market. In most cases, however, organizations with multiple businesses need to decentralize compensation practice.

3. Choice-Oriented. Traditional compensation provides the individual with a fixed package of benefits, cash, and perquisites. This approach is inconsistent with the substantial individual differences in the

workforce, and with the idea that individuals can and should be able to make decisions concerning their own lives.

Some organizations are already giving individuals greater choice. Initially, this was evident in the popularity of flexible working hours, and more recently by the growing popularity of flexible benefit systems. In flexible benefit systems, individuals are allowed to choose the mixture of benefits they wish. Individual choice, however, does not need to be limited simply to fringe benefits and hours of work.

Ultimately, individuals could have tremendous flexibility in determining their own reward package. It could extend, for example, to the kind of perquisites and benefits they receive, and to the mixture of cash, stock, and bonuses that they receive. This has the potential of benefiting both the individual and the organization because it will help individuals to get the rewards they value and assure the organization that the money they are spending on pay is being spent in ways that produce the maximum impact on individuals.

4. Skill-Based. Traditional pay emphasizes paying people for the jobs they do rather than the skills they have. The new pay suggests paying individuals for the skills they have. This has already been done in a number of high-participation manufacturing settings (see e.g. Lawler 1981, Ledford and Lawler 1985). In these settings, individuals are put into self-managing work teams and are cross-trained so they can perform all the functions within the team's area of responsibility. It is particularly useful in this situation to have individuals who understand the whole manufacturing operation; thus, paying individuals more to learn additional jobs fits with the general management style and business strategy. Paying for skills in manufacturing situations reinforces psychological participation. It creates a situation where individuals are able to understand the total operating situation and feel responsible for the overall performance of the organization.

Changing demographics also suggest that skill-based pay should be increasingly popular. "Baby boomers" are rapidly approaching the age when they will be in middle management at a time when flatter organizational structures and leaner staff groups are indicated. This means that the number of positions in middle management will be limited, and there will be less upward mobility for the larger group of individuals in the age group that typically staffs middle management. In traditional management, this would simply mean individuals staying at a particular level or dead-end position for a long period of time. If skill-based pay were put into place, employees could be rewarded for making lateral moves and, as a result, continue to learn and develop. They also might become more valuable to their organizations since they would have a better overall understanding of the business, and not be subject to the negative impact of topping out in pay.

In summary, a number of forces suggest the increasing use of skill-based pay, which fits the changing nature of the workforce, and the type of work being done in the United States. If widely accepted, a skill-based pay system would represent a truly revolutionary change in compensation practice. For instance, individuals at lower levels of the organizational hierarchy could be paid more than people at higher levels. With an emphasis on skills, it is quite possible that a highly skilled production worker or a highly skilled specialist might make considerably more than a middle level manager. In this way, pay would become unhinged from the hierarchical nature of the organization and could then be used to reinforce skills rather than hierarchy.

5. Egalitarian. There are several respects in which the pay system can be made more egalitarian in order to match this emphasis in the new management. A number of organizations already designate all employees "salaried" employees and treat them in the same way by eliminating time clocks and putting all individuals on the same benefit package. Sometimes, many of the perquisites that are usually allocated according to management level (e.g., parking spaces, office size) are more broadly applied. An egalitarian approach can be combined with flexible benefits so that, although individuals have different total compensation levels, they have access to all benefits in the organization.

Summarizing Pay Changes

New management practices and strategies evolving in the United States require new pay practices. Table 3.1 shows that pay needs to be characterized by egalitarianism, local control of decision-making, individual

---

TABLE 3.1 The New Pay

	FROM	TO
Communication	Secret	Open
Decison-making	Top down	Wide involvement
Structure	Centralized	Decentralized
Pay for performance	Merit pay	Business success-based
Reward mix	Standardized	Individual choice
Base pay	Job-based	Skill-based
Degree of heirarchy	Steep level effect	Egalitarian
Design strategy	Tradition-driven	Congruence, strategy-driven

---

choice, and most importantly, a strong performance-based system that ties into the business itself. The strategy of installing multiple pay systems that reward organizational performance represents a potentially effective approach to improving organizational performance by using pay as an incentive. The alternative of essentially abandoning pay as a motivator is always there, but it represents the abandonment of a very important potential incentive, something that most organizations cannot afford to do. If anything, it is surprising how slow most organizations have been to move to the use of multiple bonus plans. Particularly in large organizations, it has been noted for decades that people often lose a sense of the business and a sense of involvement in the ongoing operation of the organization. As a result, they become bureaucrats routinely carrying out tasks with little appreciation or concern for how their performance relates to the overall success of the business. Indeed, it has often been suggested that it is this type of relationship between individuals and organizations that has led to stagnation in national productivity growth in the United States, and in many cases, to the production of poor quality products.

Gainsharing, profit-sharing, and stock ownership, when combined with a number of other organization design features, are ways of increasing the involvement of employees in their organizations (Lawler 1982). Other strategies such as quality circles, self-managing work teams, and individual job enrichment can also be effective, but in the absence of any relationship between the success of the organization and the pay of individuals, an important part of the business experience for the individual is missing. Everything known about motivation clearly points out that it is greatest when people have both a psychological and a financial stake in the organization's success. Instituting concomitantly a variety of pay-for-performance plans is a significant means of increasing employees' motivation and involvement.

References

Bullock, R. J. and E. E. Lawler. "Gainsharing: A Few Questions, and Fewer Answers." *Human Resource Management* 23 1984: 23–40.

Devries, D. L., A. M. Morrison, S. L. Shullman, and M. L. Gerlach. *Performance Appraisal on the Line*. New York: Wiley-Interscience, 1981.

Hackman, J. R. and G. R. Oldham. *Work Redesign*. Reading, Mass.: Addison-Wesley, 1980.

Lawler, E. E. "Increasing Worker Involvement to Enhance Organizational Effectiveness." In *Change in Organizations*, P. Goodman, ed. San Francisco, Calif.: Jossey-Bass, 1982, pp. 280–315.

———. *Pay and Organizational Effectiveness*. New York: McGraw-Hill, 1971.

———. *Motivation in Work Organizations*. Monterey, Calif.: Brooks-Kole, 1973.

———. *Pay and Organization Development*. Reading, Mass.: Addison-Wesley, 1981.

Ledford, G. E. and E. E. Lawler. 1985. "Skill-Based Pay." *Personnel* 62: 30–37.

Locke, E. A., D. B. Feren, V. M. McCaleb, K. N. Shaw, and A. T. Denny. 1980. "The Relative Effectiveness of Four Methods of Motivating Employee Performance." In *Changes in Work Life*, K. D. Duncan, M. M. Gruneberg, and D. Wallis, eds. Chichester, England: Wiley, pp. 363–88.

Meyer, H. H., E. Kay, and J. R. R. French. "Split Roles in Performance Appraisal." *Harvard Business Review* vol. 43, no. 1 (1965): 123–29.

Moore, B. E. and T. L. Ross. *The Scanlon Way to Improved Productivity*. New York: Wiley-Interscience, 1978.

Peck, C. "Pay and Performance: The Interaction of Compensation and Performance Appraisal." New York: The Conference Board, No. 155, 1984.

Whyte, W. F., ed. *Money and Motivation: An Analysis of Incentives in Industry*. New York: Harper, 1955.

4

The Economics of Supervision

Guillermo A. R. Calvo

This chapter concerns the economics of situations in which the firm cannot directly and costlessly observe the product or effort of each one of its workers. As a result, the firm will normally find it advantageous to resort to devices like direct supervision accompanied by layoffs if workers are discovered cheating, or offering higher-than-competitive salaries, profit-sharing programs, promotions, or vested pensions. As a matter of fact, our discussion will demonstrate that the above-mentioned type of imperfect information could be an important fundamental reason for the existence of the many commonly observed incentive packages in modern organizations.

The chapter is organized around a very simple example of imperfect information where, in order to elicit effective labor services, it is mandatory for the firm to give more incentives than would be sufficient in a perfect-information environment. Section 1 explores the case where the firm offers a wage, and subjects workers to random supervision; workers are advised that they will be layed off if they are found performing their duties below certain pre-specified levels ("shirking"). Our main conclusion is that the optimal wage is very sensitive to the costs of supervision and the potential damage that a worker can inflict by his shirking. There is also an example showing where it would be optimal for the firm to offer a wage higher than the best alternative offer that the worker can get.

Section 2 shows that the basic model can be extended to allow for hierarchical supervision structures. Despite the bureaucratic cost and complications of a hierarchical organization, it is shown that such an organization may be more profitable than the alternative (boss + production workers.) This is a significant finding because it suggests that

I am very thankful to Haig Nalbantian for helpful comments. Partial funding from the National Science Foundation is gratefully acknowledged.

87

large, complex organizations may partly reflect an optimal response to imperfect information in the labor market. In addition, in an optimal arrangement, supervisors will normally receive a higher salary than regular workers, even when their quality is not significantly different from that of their supervisees. Section 2 also explores the implications of the supervision model for income distribution and unemployment theory; it is demonstrated that abnormal income inequality and downward price rigidity (usually associated with unemployment situations) may be natural consequences of the type of imperfect information postulated in our examples.

Section 3 departs from the simple model in that more "creative" wage schemes are allowed for. In this connection, the advantages and disadvantages of charging "entrance fees," of offering promotions and pension plans, and, finally, of profit-sharing are discussed. The general conclusion is that these alternative schemes normally offer effective ways to improve a worker's performance, but they do so at the "cost" of sometimes inoptimally strengthening the hand of the supervisor: a very strong whip may simply scare away potential workers!

Section 4 provides a brief tour of relevant literature.

1. A Basic Framework

To start our discussion, consider the case of a perfectly competitive firm that has to decide the number of workers to employ (for the time being we will assume that their quality has already been chosen, and that there exists no information problem in that respect). If the firm is in the position to determine the exact contribution to output of each extra worker (i.e., the "marginal productivity of labor"), then the profit-maximizing strategy would be to expand employment to the point where the value marginal productivity (i.e., marginal productivity *times* the price of output) equals the wage rate. This analysis, which is the traditional one in text-book microeconomics, assumes that the firm is a perfect competitor in product and labor markets, and that the wage rate is the only important dimension of a labor contract.

The proof of the above statement is straightforward; if it did not hold and, for instance, the value marginal productivity of labor exceeded the wage rate, it would be profitable to expand employment beyond the previous level. Notice that a crucial element in this reasoning is that employing one more laborer leaves the wage rate unchanged. If this were not the case, say, the employment of an extra worker increased the wage for the entire crew, then the "profit at the margin" (given by the difference between the value marginal productivity and the wage) has to be weighed against the extra cost of the higher labor cost for the entire crew. Hence, in this case—called the "monopsony case" in microeconomics—profit maximization implies that the value marginal productivity of labor exceeds the wage rate. We will show below that imperfect information may give rise to a situation similar to monopsony in the labor market, even when the firm is actually a perfect competitor for labor services.

Let us return to perfect competition, but add a bit of realism to the model by assuming that, in order to ascertain the amount of services provided by an individual worker, the firm has to incur "supervision" costs, and that labor contracts are such that a worker receives his wage and is, under normal circumstances, reemployed if he is either (1) checked and found to be performing according to preset standards, or (2) he is not checked. Otherwise (i.e., if he is checked and is not performing according to the standards), he is fired. Condition 2 is crucial for our ensuing results, because it implies that a worker cannot be laid off unless he is caught holding a "smoking gun," even when indirect evidence may point to him, or to the team to which he belongs as having shirked. This undoubtedly strong assumption is made here in order to highlight some of the new implications associated with the existence of imperfect and asymmetric information in the labor market.

Let us first examine the strategic problem faced by a worker who knows that he is going to be monitored with probability P. For the sake of definiteness, imagine that this is a one-period job (extensions to more than one period are discussed below), and that after he is hired he has to decide between "doing the job," which would be equivalent to working according to the preset standards, or simply "shirking," staying idle. We assume that if he does the job his income is just his wage, w; but if he decides to shirk his income is increased to $w + k$; k can be interpreted as the value of on-the-job leisure, the extra income that he could earn by doing side jobs, taking bribes, or stealing equipment. According to the rules of the game, if he decides to do the job his expected income would be

$$w \qquad (1)$$

i.e., the contracted wage; otherwise, if he shirks and is not caught, he will get $w + k$; according to our previous assumptions this will happen with probability $(1 - P)$; on the other hand, if he is caught shirking he will earn his expected wage in alternative employments, h; by assumption this event occurs with probability P. Consequently, his expected income would be

$$(1 - P)(w + k) + Ph \qquad (2)$$

Assuming that workers' decisions are made on the basis of expected income, a firm will have to make sure that (1) is larger than or equal to (2), which implies

$$w \geq h + (q - 1)k \tag{3}$$

where $q = 1/P$. If, in addition, we make the innocuous assumption that in case of equality in (3) the worker has a preference for doing the job, we obtain that the wage to be offered by a profit-maximizing (thus, cost-minimizing) firm will be

$$w = h + (g - 1)k \tag{3'}$$

A comparison with the perfect information case is now in order. To simplify the exposition, let us further assume that h is the wage at the alternative employment *before* joining the firm. In the full-information case $q = 1$ and hence the wage paid by the firm will be just h; this is confirmed by setting $q = 1$ in (3′). However, if information is less than perfect (i.e., $q > 1$), w will have to exceed h. The intuition behind this result is clear. Imagine that, to the contrary, the firm offers a wage w equal to h; in such a case there would be no loss to the worker if he is fired (remember: $w = h$); so shirking always dominates doing the job, because, by previous reasoning, if he is found shirking, there will be no punishment, and there is a positive probability that he will be able to get away with it (if he is not checked) and grab the extra income k.

Hence, in a way, imperfect information has transformed the wage-taker into a wage-*maker* firm; the "wage premium" $(w\text{-}h)$ is a function of conditions prevailing *within* the firm: by (3′), it increases with the extra income associated with shirking, k, and with the probability of *not* being checked, $(1 - P)$; in fact, when P goes to zero, and, hence, q goes to infinity, it follows that the wage premium goes to infinity. This suggests that in a competitive economy we could find individuals with comparable qualities earning substantially different wages. This is an important topic to which we shall return below.

If the probability of detection, P, is exogenous, then the profit-maximizing level of employment is found, as in the traditional analysis, by equating the value marginal productivity of labor to the wage (the latter being determined by (3′)). For our ensuing discussion, however, it will be helpful to have a theory for the determination of P (or q, its inverse).

Imagine a firm owned by an individual (or very cohesive family) who can supervise a maximum of n workers during the "job period." If supervision is random, and N workers are employed by the firm (and $N \geq n$), we have

$$P = n/N \tag{4}$$

Hence, recalling (3′) and that $q = 1/P$, we get

$$w = h + [N/n - 1]k \tag{5}$$

Consequently, we have found that (for $N \geq n$) the wage that the firm is willing to pay is an increasing function of total employment at the firm. This is formally similar to the monopsonistic situation that was discussed at the beginning, and has, therefore, identical consequences. In particular, it follows that at the profit maximizing point the value marginal productivity of labor will exceed the wage rate. Notice that, recalling (5), in this example the wage rate increases without bound as N goes to infinity. An interesting implication of the latter is that even in the case where the marginal productivity of labor is a constant—where, therefore, a perfectly competitive firm could expand without bound if there was perfect information in the labor market—, the existence of supervision problems may (in our example actually *does*) impose a limit (due to skyrocketing wages) to the size of the firm.

This is perhaps an appropriate time to pause and summarize our analysis in a more intuitive, less example-specific, way. In order to understand the new vistas provided by introducing imperfect information in the labor market, we have focused our attention on the realistic case where the firm has less information than the worker on the intensity of his effort. So we have a situation where piece-rates, in particular, would be simply nonviable. The worker is the owner of his labor services, and it is to his advantage to (normally) provide less than he is supposed to deliver. Thus, to ensure the actual deliverance of those services the firm has to find a way to give the right incentives. The alternative that we have explored thus far consists of offering a (flat) wage and the threat of termination of the contract if the worker does not comply with preset standards. Clearly, in order for this sort of contract to have any "teeth," there has to be a positive probability of supervision, and the wage should generally exceed the worker's expected income in case of being fired. We have, therefore, a rationale for the often-heard statement that certain firms "overpay" their workers in order to ensure top performance. In addition, it is natural to expect that the smaller the degree of supervision (i.e., the smaller the chances that an individual worker be actually supervised), the higher will have to be the wage offered by the firm to guarantee top performance. This observation lies at the basis of our last result in the previous paragraph; for if, as seems natural to expect, the quality of supervision deteriorates (given the same number of supervisors and associated devices for monitoring effort) as the number of workers is increased, then it follows by our earlier observation that the required wage for top performance should also increase. Although, formally, this gives rise to a positive association between employment and the wage, there remains an important conceptual difference between this case and that of monopsony: in the latter, the wage rises because workers' opportunity costs increase with more employment (which requires the firm not to be insignificant in the labor market), or because workers at the firm have succeeded in putting barriers to the entry of new workers (unions, etc.); here, instead, it is the firm itself that finds it profitable to increase the wage as it expands the level of employment (no party is exercising any kind of monopoly power).

Before closing this Section, I would like to point out some new insights contributed by these kinds of models. In the traditional framework with perfect information, there is no essential distinction between capital and labor services. Factors of production are hired by the firm and their quantities are predetermined or, more generally, determined up to a random variable not controllable by any of the parties. In reality, however, there is a fundamental difference between capital and labor as factors of production. The fact is that while his capital is at work in New Jersey, the owner could be playing golf in Palm Beach. In contrast, the owner of labor services is stuck to his wares wherever they are put to productive use. Yet this distinction plays no significant role in models with perfect information: by assumption, the flow of services can be ascertained independently of how close or how far they are from their owners. This scenario changes dramatically when information in the labor market is less than perfect. Even when the firm could perfectly determine the quantity and quality of services that could potentially be extracted from a machine and a worker, the services-owner inseparability poses a new set of complications in the hiring of labor. Our example has illustrated the possibility that, as a consequence of those complications, the employment of labor in certain firms can be severely limited.

2. Applications and Extensions of the Basic Model

There are two central applications of the previous framework that are particularly significant. The first one is essentially microeconomic and deals with the theory of hierarchies within a firm; the second is a theory of involuntary unemployment and income distribution.

2.1 Hierarchies

We will confine our discussion to implications that follow rather directly from the example of Section I; no attempt will be made to summarize the many other aspects of this field. (For a wider perspective see Williamson 1975).

A central finding of section I is that the size of a firm composed by owners and productive workers may be severely limited by supervision considerations. Could the situation be remedied by hiring supervisors that would stand between the owners and the production workers, and who themselves would be supervised by the owners? *Prima facie*, the answer seems to be "no," because the new setup appears to essentially add more bureaucratic "fat" to the system. However, as will be shown next, this answer is not generally correct, thus showing that imperfect information in the labor market could provide us with a totally independent rationale for the existence of hierarchies.

To keep matters as simple as possible, imagine that the value of marginal labor productivity is constant, independent of the size of the workforce, and equal to unity. Let us consider the 1-layer organization examined before. Let w^* and N^* indicate, respectively, the profit-maximizing wage and employment level; thus, profit of a 1-layer organization is given by

$$\text{Revenue} - W^* N^* = (1 - w^*) N^* \tag{6}$$

(Remember that, by assumption, the value of marginal productivity = 1).

On the other hand, if the owner (we assume there is only one) were to work for himself without hiring any workers, his profit would be just 1, his marginal productivity. Thus, a necessary condition for the 1-layer organization to dominate self-employment is that the expression in (6) be larger than unity, i.e.,

$$(1 - w^*) N^* > 1 \tag{7}$$

Consider now a 2-layer organization, where, perhaps inoptimally, the owner hires N^* supervisors, and places N^* workers under each one of them. Assuming that each supervisor is identical to the owner in terms of his supervision abilities, and that supervisors and workers are indistinguishable in terms of shirking preferences and opportunities outside the firm, it follows that w^* is the minimum wage that ensures appropriate performance of workers and supervisors. Hence, remembering that this arrangement implies the existence of $(N^*)^2$ productive workers, the associated profit would be

$$N^{*2} - w^* (N^* + N^{*2}) \tag{8}$$

We show now that if (7) holds, then profit of a 2-layer organization is higher than that of a 1-layer organization. By subtracting w^* from both sides of (7), and then multiplying (again, both sides) by N^*, we get

$$N^{*2} - w^* (N^* + N^{*2}) > (1 - w^*) N^* \tag{9}$$

This implies that the associated profit of a 2-layer organization is larger than the *maximum* profit of the 1-layer structure (recall (6)). Consequently, a 2-layer form is shown to be more profitable, despite involving the use of a group of supervisors that do not supply directly productive services. In fact, in our simple world, a profit-maximizing firm employs supervisors to help identify the shirkers; but the optimal arrangement is such that no "crime" will be committed. To the casual observer, the net productivity of supervisors will appear to be nil.

Imagine that 2 layers is more profitable than 1 layer, the next question of considerable interest is: what is the optimal wage structure of a 2-layer firm? Should, for instance, wages differ across supervisors and supervisees?

Let us denote

S = number of supervisors
N_s = number of workers *per* supervisor
w_s = wage of a supervisor
w = wage of a production worker

With this notation, the total number of production workers is (SN_s), and profit becomes

$$[N_s (1 - w) - w_s]S \qquad (10)$$

The firm is assumed to maximize profit by choosing the number of supervisors, S, the number of supervisees per supervisor, N_s, and the wages of supervisors, w_s, and supervisees, w. Again, assuming that the owner can supervise a maximum of n supervisors, and that each of the latter can, in turn, monitor a maximum of n workers during the "job period", and in addition that supervisors and production workers are identical in all respects, we get, as in the previous section (remember (5)) that

$$w = h + [N_s/n - 1]k \qquad (11)$$

$$w_s = h + [S/n - 1]k \qquad (12)$$

are the minimum levels of wages that are required to stave off shirking.

It is important to keep in mind that the profit of a 1-layer organization is

$$N_s (1 - w) \qquad (13)$$

given that there would be only one supervisor (the owner). Therefore, the profit-maximization problem of a 1-layer firm would be to maximize (13) by choosing N_s and w, subject to (11). But a brief perusal of (10) indicates that, for a 2-layer firm, the optimal choice of N_s and w also involves maximizing (13) subject to (11). Therefore, we have shown that *the optimal wage for production workers, and the supervisor/production worker ratio are, respectively, equal in a a 1- and in a 2-layer organization.*

Put differently, imagine that it is optimal, in a 1-layer organization, to employ 100 workers at $10 an hour; then according to the previous result, if the same firm were to expand to a 2-level form, it would be optimal to employ 100 production workers per supervisor at $10 an hour. Hence, the optimal organization under each one of the supervisors is identical to that of a 1-layer organization. An interesting implication of this framework is that the existence of firms with different hierarchical complexity does not necessarily imply the existence of wage differentials across their production workers.

Denoting, as above, the optimal level of N_s and w by N^* and w^*, respectively, expression (10) becomes (when N_s and w are chosen at their optimal levels)

$$[N^* (1 - w^*) - w_s]S. \qquad (14)$$

The only remaining task, therefore, is to optimally choose the levels of S and w_s subject to (12). But a brief examination of this problem shows that this task is formally similar to the one encountered in the 1-layer case (See equation (13).), except that in (14) the (indirect) value marginal productivity of a supervisor is

$$N^* (1 - w^*) > 1 \qquad (15)$$

(the inequality is due to (7).)

In other words, we have shown that the problem of choosing the optimal number and wage of supervisors in a 2-layer organization is formally equivalent to that of choosing the profit-maximizing number and wage of production workers in a 1-layer organization; the difference lies in the fact that while the value marginal productivity of a production worker is, by assumption, unity, that of supervisors (given by (15)) is greater than unity. By previous analysis, the larger value marginal productivity of a supervisor with respect to that of a production worker is due to the fact that whenever there are returns to organization and team production, i.e., when condition (7) holds, a 2-layer organization is more profitable than a 1-layer organization. Now, since, as argued before, the wage of a production worker in a 2-layer firm is equal to that in a 1-layer firm, we would be able to determine the relation between the wages of supervisors and supervisees if we could give an answer to the following simple question: In a 1-layer organization, how does the optimal wage vary as we increase the value marginal productivity of labor? Given that we have shown the formal equivalence between our case of imperfect information in the labor market, and the one where the firm acts as a monopsonist in that market, the above question is equivalent to asking: Assume there is perfect information in the labor market, but the firm faces an upward-sloping supply of labor—how does the optimal wage vary as we increase the value marginal productivity of labor?

The intuitive answer, which in this case is also the correct one, is that the optimal wage goes up as the value marginal productivity of labor is increased. (For a formal proof, see any intermediate microeconomics textbook.) In terms of our original problem, this implies that at the optimum

$$w_s > w. \tag{16}$$

Hence, the profit-maximizing solution calls for offering a higher wage to supervisors than to production workers. Notice that wage differentials occur even when we assume that there exists no noticeable difference between supervisors and supervisees, except for their role in the hierarchical structure. Therefore, the example is able to offer an explanation for the existence of a wage progression as we move up in the hierarchical structure, which is completely independent of sociological or conventional considerations.

Another interesting result is that since, at the optimum, equations (11) and (12) must hold, (16) implies that supervisors are monitored less frequently than production workers. (There are more supervisors per owner than workers per supervisors.)

2.2 Income distribution and Unemployment

The example of section 2.1 can be easily extended to allow for labor heterogeneity. Calvo and Wellisz (1979) have explored the implications of assuming that an employee's productivity and alternative wage (h in our notation) is an increasing function of some objective quality parameter (like years of schooling). Not too surprisingly, it is found that quality tends to improve as we move towards the top of the hierarchical structure. Also the wage increases; however, and in line with the results of section 2.1, the increment in the wage is more than proportional to the productivity differentials. This result helps resolve the puzzle that income appears to be more unequally distributed than "ability"; more able people tend to receive a higher income than seems to be accounted for by their extra ability.

Another implication of the theory is that, within certain limits, the imposition of a minimum wage (i.e. for production workers) may result in a higher level of employment and labor quality at the lower level. This at first appears odd if one is thinking about the perfect information case, where a wage increase always lowers the level of employment; the puzzle tends to disappear, however, when one recalls that imperfect information makes the firm a virtual monopsonist in the labor market. It is well known that, under monopsony, employment would rise (again, within certain limits), if a higher-than-equilibrium minimum wage were to be imposed. Calvo and Wellisz (1979) also show (in a static framework) that the number and quality of supervisors fall with the imposition of the minimum wage for production workers. This result is also intuitively plausible, because the imposition of a (binding) minimum wage will tend to reduce the (indirect) value marginal productivity of supervisors.

Another area where this kind of framework has been applied is to the theory of structural or long-run unemployment. To see how this could be done, let us revert to the simple model of section 1. We will interpret h as the wage in the self-employment sector. Imagine, for the sake of concreteness, that there exists only one firm that requires labor monitoring (the firm is assumed to behave in a competitive manner). Profit maximization implies maximizing (13) subject to (11). This determines a level of employment, indicated by N^*, and a wage level, w^*, that exceeds the one in self-employment, h; this means that if total population is greater than N^*, some workers will be forced to remain in the self-employment sector with a wage lower than the one offered by the firm to its workers. Normally, therefore, those who remain in the self-employment sector will try to get a job at the firm; they may even spend resources (time, for instance) looking for a job at the firm. Thus, the wage disparity may give rise to open unemployment (usually called search unemployment).

Notice that the type of unemployment described above would be incompatible with perfect information, because it would be to the advantage of the firm not to pay more than the opportunity wage. In such a case, one would not be able to find wage differentials across sectors. In contrast, however, with our kind of imperfect information, the firm has no incentive to employ anybody at a wage less than w^*, since, if $w < w^*$, the worker will find it to his advantage to shirk (because inequality (3) will not be satisfied). The firm knows that, and there are no promises on the part of the workers knocking at its doors for a job that will make the firm change its mind, since unemployed (or self-employed) workers can make no credible nonshirking commitments when $w < w^*$. Imperfect information is thus able to provide us with a story of wage rigidity in the presence of unemployment (or, more generally, excess supply of labor), which does not depend on the existence of trade unions or any other exogenous distortion. Contrary to the trade union-type of explanation for unemployment, where the union's leaders set a wage higher than that of full employment, wage rigidity is a feature of the optimal strategy of the firm; workers obviously contribute to that kind of decision, given their tendency to shirk, but it is firm owners, not workers, who prefer to pay a wage differential over the opportunity wage.

3. Extensions of the Basic Framework

Our analysis has shown that the introduction of imperfect information in the labor market gives new insights into familiar forms of organization and wage differentials within a hierarchical structure. Up to this point, however, we have explored a rather simple form of labor contract by which the worker is layed off only if he is found breaking some preset rule; otherwise he keeps his job and is paid the full salary. Given these constraints, the optimal strategy for the firm is to pay a wage differential above the workers' opportunity wage. This suggests that the firm may try to devise new ways to extract the wage-differential "rent" away from its employees. This section will discuss a few of the devices that have been subject to analysis in the literature.

3.1 Entrance Fees.

This is the simplest device. Let f denote the entrance fee; then, if the worker does not shirk, his expected utility is (recall (1))

$$w - f \tag{1'}$$

Furthermore, recalling (2), if he shirks, his expected utility is

$$(1 - P)(w + k) + Ph - f \tag{2'}$$

Consequently, a worker is given incentives not to shirk if inequality (3) above is satisfied. This implies that, given P (i.e., the probability of detection), the profit-maximizing value of w, w^*, is the same whether or not entrance fees are charged.

By (3') above and our previous discussion, we have $w^* > h$ = expected utility in the self-employment sector. Consequently, the firm will be able to attract workers insofar as

$$w^* - f \geq h$$

Clearly, then a profit-maximizing firm will set $f = w^* - h$ = "rent" of workers who join the firm, which equalizes expected utility across sectors.

A potential problem with such an arrangement is that now workers would be, so to say, at the mercy of the owner. The latter may be tempted to employ an inordinate number of workers just to collect the entrance fee. So we see here an example of a particular sort of tension that is hard to eliminate in imperfect information markets: devices that tend to discipline one of the parties, also tend to strengthen the hand of the other party, making the former more vulnerable to cheating by the latter.

In our example, there exists an even more basic reason why the entrance fee solution may not be viable: workers may not have the funds required for such a fee (however, see the next section).

A closely related "solution" that has been discussed in the literature is "bonding." Under this arrangement the worker puts up a bond when he enters the firm; at the end of the "job period," he recovers the bond if he is not found to be shirking. If the funds for the bond have to be obtained by the worker before he enters the firm, there are two polar cases: in case no. 1, the bond is bought by means of the worker's own funds; and in case no. 2, the funds are borrowed from a bank. Case no. 1 is practically identical to an entrance fee, the only difference being that the worker's performance is ensured by the threat that his funds will not be returned if he shirks. This solution may be impaired by the moral hazard and budget constraint considerations discussed in connection with the entrance-fee scheme. Case no. 2 has the added complication that the threat of not returning funds is virtually eliminated, because it is the bank, and not the worker, who would stand the risk of losing the funds in case the worker is found shirking.

3.2 Promotions and Pension Plans.

When the worker-firm relationship lasts for a considerable length of time, there are new ways for the firm to ensure the worker's performance. One possibility that will be explored in this section is for the firm to manipulate the wage paths, such as offering higher future wages under the condition that the worker performs his duties according to predetermined standards. This type of scheme would call for paying relatively "low" wages at the start of the contract, together with "high" wages at the time the contract is terminated.

It is interesting to note that although wages would increase with seniority, this does not necessarily reflect the fact that the worker improves (i.e., his marginal productivity increases) as he gains experience. The outward form that the contract may take could be a system of "promotions" and unvested "pension plans". Lazear (1979) argues that these schemes may involve, at the time of retirement, a wage that vastly exceeds the worker's marginal productivity. He goes on to show that what might look like arbitrary mandatory retirement rules (because the worker normally takes up a lower-paid job after retirement), may, in fact, be the outcome of an optimal contract, where shirking incentives are minimized at the time that the worker first entered the firm.

From a formal point of view, the upward time profile of the wage rate is just a more subtle form of entrance fee; it is paid by the worker during his earlier years at the job. Its advantage over a straight entrance fee is that it is less likely to be larger than the worker's budget constraint. On the other hand, it shares with entrance fees the problem that whether or not an employee is promoted or given the "end-of-game" prize is a decision that would now be left in the hands of the owner who, for obvious reasons, would have the incentive to claim that the worker does not deserve any of them.

A relevant question is whether the above-mentioned type of wage profiles could eliminate altogether the need for direct supervision and associated distortions (wage differentials across identical individuals, supervision hierarchies, etc.). I do not think economists speak with one voice on this question. Lazear (1979) appears to think that distortions might be eliminated. I, for one, tend to be pessimistic. In the first place, direct supervision cannot be eliminated if compensation is going to be made a function of individual, not group (for this, see below), performance. In the simple model of section 1 (especially equation (3′), the wage differential, $(w - h)$, increases without bound as the probability of detection goes to zero; this phenomenon, in the present dynamic framework, would take the form of the wage differential between the wage when old and when young, becoming unboundedly large as the probability of detection goes to zero. So, it seems that moral hazard and related considerations may prevent the wage-steepness kind of scheme to fully preempt the usefulness of the supervision schemes discussed in earlier sections.

3.3 Profit Sharing: the Principal-Agent Literature

So far we have assumed that the labor contracts specify wages and punishments on the basis of individual performance. In practice, however, it is normally possible to observe some aggregate variables as output and profit, so it is interesting to study the implications of the situation where, in polar opposition with our assumptions, the owner can observe output, but not actual effort. This is one of the central cases studied by the so-called Principal-Agent literature.

Since it is far from our objective to review the Principal-Agent literature, we will confine our attention to the example of section 1 (where, among other things, there is no production uncertainty, and everybody is risk neutral). Again, let h denote the worker's opportunity wage in self-employment (his "acceptance" wage), and imagine that the firm can observe total output or revenue. If we further assume that the value marginal productivity of labor equals unity, then, if every worker works full time, total output would be N, the number of workers. Thus, the owner can offer the following contract to each one of the N workers:

$$w = h \quad \text{if revenue} = N \tag{17a}$$

$$w = 0 \quad \text{if revenue} < N \tag{17b}$$

Assume, as before, that the only options for the individual worker are to shirk or to work full time. If he shirks, his income is just k, the income derived from shirking. Thus, if $h > k$, and he believes that none of the other workers are shirking, his optimal decision will be to work. Thus, there exists a possible solution where every worker is induced to work full time even when neither the owner, nor, for that matter, the other fellow workers are able to monitor individual actions. Notice that this kind of solution will dominate supervision, because in equilibrium the firm does not pay a wage above h.

There are several difficulties with this kind of arrangement. The first is that there exists another equilibrium where nobody works because laborers expect somebody to shirk. (In that kind of equilibrium, it would be to the advantage of *everybody* to shirk, thus validating the hypothesis.) Therefore, the expected income of working at the firm would be $k < h$, the acceptance wage, and, thus, no worker will accept employment at the firm (neither will the owner have any incentive to operate it!) This is the serious difficulty of this type of contract: the existence of multiple solutions. Unfortunately, the multiplicity of solutions is a typical feature of principal-agent type of contracts, and does not tend to disappear (in fact, the opposite appears to be the rule) in more dynamic scenarios (where, for example, compensation is made a function of accumulated past performance; see Radner (1981)).

An arrangement like (17) requires the existence of an agent who gets the residual income (profit), for otherwise the threat of zero income if *someone* shirks would not be credible. If only one shirks, for example, revenue would be $(N - 1)$; it would be hard to believe that, ex post no one will receive any income (implying that total revenue is dumped or given away by the group) if some unidentified individual shirked. The existence of a residual income earner (the owner, in our example) tends to resolve the problem, because he pockets or disburses the difference. (See Holmstrom 1982 for a very clear discussion of this and related issues.) However, we are here again faced with another instance where, in order to give cheating disincentives to one group, we have to strengthen the hand of the other side. A scheme like (17) is, in principle, a credible one if we make the strong assumption that the owner has no participation whatsoever in the production process; to the extent that this is not so, workers will start being concerned about the owner's actions because, with a contract like (17), it would be to his advantage to prevent output from reaching its full potential, N. In fact, as can be shown, the incentives to do so will increase with the size of the workforce.

Another independent reason for a principal-agent sort of contract not to fully substitute for supervision is given by Holstrom (1979) and Shavell (1979) who show that more information about individual action (which supervision will help provide) may be beneficial to both the owner and the workers when agents are risk averse.

Our discussion strongly suggests that, although the principal-agent type of contract may be optimal in certain special circumstances, its applicability appears to be seriously limited, particularly when we are dealing with a relatively large workforce. However, one could very well imagine situations where the optimal contract has elements of output-, revenue-, or profit-sharing for the top rungs of an organization (where numbers are few, and there may be better possibilities for mutual monitoring), giving way to the more rigid wages-cum-supervision forms as one descends towards the bottom of the hierarchical structure.

4. Guided Tour of the Literature

These notes are aimed at helping the uninitiated find his/her way around the literature. No attempt will be made to provide a complete listing of relevant material. Hopefully, however, the reader should be able to have a rather complete set of references by combining the list here provided with the bibliography of the cited papers.*

The model of section 1 is based on the work of Becker and Stigler (1974) who also suggested the "bonds" solution of section 3.1. Calvo (1977) suggested making the probability of detection an increasing function of the supervisor/supervisee ratio. Lazear (1979) extended the Becker-Stigler model to allow for nonstationary wage profiles (discussed in section 3.2), and to allow for cheating by the owner. A seminal paper, which stresses the kind of imperfect information discussed in this paper, is Alchian and Demsetz (1972).

Application of the above-mentioned framework to hierarchical organizations can be found in Calvo and Wellisz (1978, 1979). In this connection, an important paper emphasizing risk considerations is Stiglitz (1975). For a more general discussion about hierarchical organizations, I would strongly recommend Williamson (1975).

For the unemployment application (section 2.2), see Calvo (1979, 1985); Shapiro and Stiglitz (1984); and Yellen (1984); and references cited therein. Weiss (1980) offers an interesting explanation of unemployment, and, more generally, downward wage rigidity in terms of a model where the quality of each individual job applicant is unknown to the firm, although it is fully aware of the type of workers that a given wage offer will attract.

The literature on the principal-agent problem is rather extensive. Particularly relevant for the present discussion is Holmstrom (1982).

References

Alchian, A. and H. Demetz. 1972. "Production, Information Costs, and Economic Organization." *American Economic Review* 62: 777–95.

Becker, G. S. and G. J. Stigler. 1974. "Law Enforcement and Compensation of Enforcers." *Journal of Legal Studies* 3 (January): 1–18.

Calvo, G. C. 1977. "Supervision, and Utility and Wage Differentials across Firms." Mimeo. Columbia University Economics Workshops (April 1977, revised July 1977).

*Editor's note: see also the extensive bibliographies included in chaps. 1 and 2 of this volume.

————. 1979. "Quasi-Walrasian Theories of Unemployment." *American Economic Review, Proceedings of the American Economic Association* (May): 102–7.

————. 1985. "The Inefficiency of Unemployment: The Supervision Perspective." *Quarterly Journal of Economics* (May): 373–87.

Calvo, G. C. and S. Wellisz. 1978. "Supervision, Loss of Control, and the Optimum Size of the Firm." *Journal of Political Economy* 86 (August): 943–52.

————. 1979. "Hierarchy, Ability, and Income Distribution." *Journal of Political Economy* 87 (August): 991–1010.

Holmstrom, B. 1979. "Moral Hazard and Observability." *The Bell Journal of Economics* (Spring): 74–91.

————. 1982. "Moral Hazard in Teams." *The Bell Journal of Economics* (Autumn): 324–41.

Lazear, E. P. 1979. "Why Is There Mandatory Retirement?," *Journal of Political Economy* 87 (December): 1261–84.

Radner, R. 1981. "Monitoring Cooperative Agreements in a Repeated Principal-Agent Relationship," *Econometrica* 49 (September): 1127–48.

Shapiro, C., and J. E. Stiglitz. 1984. "Equilibrium Unemployment as a Worker Discipline Device." *American Economic Review* (June): 433–44.

Shavell, S. 1979. "Risk Sharing and Incentives in the Principal and Agent Relationship." *The Bell Journal of Economics* (Spring): 55–73.

Stiglitz, J. 1975. "Incentives, Risk and Information: Notes Towards a Theory of Hierarchy." *The Bell Journal of Economics* (Autumn): 552–79.

Weiss, A. 1980. "Job Queues and Layoffs in Labor Markets with Flexible Wages." *Journal of Political Economy* 3 (June): 526–38.

Williamson, O. E. 1975. *Markets and Hierarchies: Analysis and Antitrust Implications.* New York. The Free Press.

Yellen, J. L. 1984. "Efficiency Wage Models of Unemployment." *American Economic Review* (May): 200–205.

Part II

EMPIRICAL EVIDENCE

5

Effects of Economic Incentives on Productivity: A Psychological View

Richard A. Guzzo and Raymond A. Katzell

This chapter discusses the impact of economic incentives on performance of individuals and small groups at work. The first part of the
chapter gives a brief review of the nature of psychological research on
pay. Then, recently cumulated evidence of the impact of incentives on
workplace productivity is presented. Included in that presentation are
data comparing the impact of financial incentives to that of other means
of raising productivity and an analysis of how the effects of incentives
vary for different aspects of productivity. This chapter also considers the
effects of incentives in terms of existing psychological theories of work
motivation and guidelines for the effective use of money as a motivator.
Discussed last are methods of estimating the economic impact of gains in
worker productivity.

Early Psychological Research on Pay

Now surprisingly, the role of pay in affecting behavior at work has
received attention from psychologists for many years. Early studies of
pay compared the importance of money relative to other outcomes
obtained through working, such as job security or prestige. The pattern
of results that emerged from these studies showed that pay was infrequently cited as the most important outcome from work but did, on
average, rank highly in most assessments (Lawler 1971). Further, the
importance of pay to individuals has been found to be directly related to
the level of their jobs in an organization: the higher the level, the *less*
important is pay (Lawler 1971).

Although data on the relative importance of pay are interesting, they
relate in only a limited way to the use of pay to motivate high levels of
work productivity for two reasons. First, pay is one of several consequences of work, and there is no reason to believe that pay must be the

107

only—or the most important—outcome from working for pay to be an effective inducement to increased productivity. Second, *how* pay is used as an incentive may be as important as the mere fact that it is used. There are many ways of using financial incentives to stimulate high work performance. Individual commissions are one form of pay used to stimulate performance, profit-sharing plans another. Such different forms of the use of money as an incentive may have quite different effects on employee productivity according to how those plans distribute incentive pay.

Other early research was directed at understanding how employees' responses to monetary incentives were shaped by the social context at work. For example, numerous cases were discovered in which financial incentives failed to spur higher levels of performance because of prevailing work group norms against increased production (Whyte 1955). That is, employees restricted their productive output even though the amount of pay they earned was directly tied to output through a piece-rate incentive pay plan. Not all individuals were equally inclined to be influenced by group norms, however.

More recent psychological research has taken two directions, one concerning the theoretical interpretation of the effects of financial incentives and the other concerning assessments of the frequency or magnitude of productivity gains resulting from the use of various forms of financial incentives. In the following section, we present a summarization of theoretically based conclusions about the principles of work motivation, highlighting the role of pay in relation to these principles. Following this section, recent evidence on the magnitude of productivity gains associated with the use of financial incentives is addressed.

Understanding the Impact of Financial Incentives

Psychological theories of work motivation provide a means of understanding the impact of financial incentives on the productivity of a workforce. In particular, the theories and their supporting research identify those factors that, if present, make financial incentives powerful in motivating high levels of constructive effort on the part of employees. Several such factors have been identified, eight of which are reviewed in this section.

1. Opportunity to gain a valued reward. The chance to gain a reward such as money is an important ingredient in human motivation, though it is not valued in the same way by people. Consequently, financial incentives may motivate some people more strongly than others. The differences reported in this paper regarding the relative impact of financial incentives on the productivity of various types of workers may reflect this. From a psychological point of view, the importance of

money is subjective. That is, the "worth" of money to an individual is determined not by its actual value but by its perceived value. The psychological value of money may be related to the background and organizational level of workers. For example, professional employees may be motivated by money to a different degree than blue-collar employees because these two types of workers tend to place a different value on money. Recall the findings reported earlier that higher-level employees attach relatively less importance to money. The psychological value of money is also affected by the presence of other rewards to be gained by working; money is only one of numerous outcomes that may be realized. Other outcomes include job security, prestige, interesting work, and friendships, among others. When numerous other valued outcomes are attainable by working, money may be only a weak incentive for effective work performance because the pursuit of these other outcomes may be dominant.

2. Satisfaction with the job. Satisfaction with pay is an important component of overall satisfaction with one's job. Although job satisfaction is not strongly related to the level of worker output on a job (Iaffaldano and Muchinsky 1985), it is related to employees' tendencies to remain with an organization. The greater the satisfaction, the stronger the tendency to remain in an organization (Mowday et al. 1982).

3. Involvement. Pay plans can be used to increase worker involvement in planning and decision-making at work. The Scanlon Plan, for example, combines financial incentives with a process of eliciting suggestions from workers and engaging them in planning and decision-making. Worker involvement may have little direct influence on day-to-day productivity but, like satisfaction, it appears to be related to the propensity of workers to remain in an organization.

4. Clear and challenging performance goals. Pay can play a role in motivation by clarifying goals for workers. That is, if pay is linked to performance, financial incentives help communicate to people what is expected of them and what it means to be successful.

5. The social environment. To the extent that high performance depends on teamwork, linking pay to performance may help generate social norms that favor high productivity. However, pay that is contingent on performance may "backfire" if it increases competition among workers or feelings of insecurity that can be expressed in terms of protective social norms such as those that favor restricted productivity. Rarely are the effects of pay not shaped by the social environment at work.

6. Adequacy of resources. Part of what motivates people to perform effectively at work is having superior resources to do their jobs. Leaders can provide resources needed for effective performance, such as infor-

mation, guidance, and materials. Similarly, practices and policies that ensure the availability of tools, equipment, and the like all can enhance motivation because with adequate resources employees are more likely to feel that their own effort will pay off in high performance. In contrast, poor resources discourage employee efforts. Pay plans that encourage communication and sharing knowledge of improvements in work methods (such as Scanlon gainsharing plans) can enhance motivation by increasing the availability of resources.

7. Contingency between rewards and performance. Perhaps the most important determinant of the motivational impact of financial incentives is the degree to which they are contingent on performance (Lawler 1971). The more closely pay is tied to performance the more powerful its motivational effect. Piece-rate and commission pay plans represent attempts to link directly the level of pay to job performance. Annual merit increases in salary based on performance evaluation also link pay to job performance but do so less directly than other pay plans. Pay based solely on tenure or seniority in an organization makes for an even weaker link between job performance and financial rewards. The successful use of financial incentives to stimulate productivity, then, depends heavily on how closely pay is tied to job performance.

Not only must pay be closely tied to performance to be effective, the link between pay and performance must also be perceived by employees in order for the pay to be motivating. That is, without the belief that one's efforts will result in performance that provides monetary rewards, the use of money as an incentive will be ineffective. Complicated and long-range incentive pay plans are those that obscure the linkage between pay and performance. Some profit-sharing plans, for example, have these characteristics and may fail to instill in employees a strong belief that high performance leads to financial rewards.

8. Equitable rewards. Pay equity concerns judgments of fairness, and judgments of fairness have at least two components to them (Adams 1963). One is an assessment of the balance between what a worker puts into a job (time, effort, skills) and outcomes gained through performing the job (pay, prestige, satisfaction). The other component involves a social comparison. That is, people compare the balance of inputs and outcomes as perceived for themselves to that which they perceive to exist for others. Fairness is perceived to exist when the ratio of inputs to outcomes for self is in line with the ratio perceived to exist for others. Unequal ratios give rise to perceptions of inequity.

Note that considerations of equity do not concern issues of equality: an individual receiving smaller outcomes than another may see this as fair as long as the other's inputs are perceived to be proportional to those outcomes. Further, equity determinations are made on the basis of subjective perceptions of the inputs and outcomes of others, not objective measures of them. This is relevant to understanding perceptions of pay equity: often there is secretiveness in organizations regarding pay. Consequently, perceptions of others' salary may not be accurate since secrecy prevents workers from learning the actual amount of pay received by co-workers. Under these circumstances individuals may tend to overestimate the pay received by others.

To be effective in motivating higher productivity, financial incentives must be distributed in a way that prevents perceptions of pay inequity. Perceptions of inequitable underpayment can lead individuals to decrease the amount of effort they put into their work. A reduction of effort is a "logical" response to perceived inequitable underpayment. Reducing one's inputs is a way of "justifying" the (under)payment one receives from working. Thus, the effective use of financial incentives to motivate higher productivity demands that the incentive pay plan not bring about perceptions of inequitable pay.

Interestingly, inequity can exist because of perceptions of overpayment. Not surprisingly, people tend to be much more tolerant of overpayment than underpayment, although there is evidence that overpayment can induce people to increase the effort they put into their work, especially with regard to the quality (rather than quantity) of their output (Miner 1980).

Recent Evidence on the Effects of Pay

The evidence on which this paper draws was first examined in literature reviews conducted by Katzell, Bienstock, and Faerstein (1977), and Guzzo and Bondy (1983). Those reviews reported the nature and results of over two hundred "experiments" involving changes in managerial and organizational practices designed to bring about some increase in productivity. One type of change examined in those reviews was the adoption of financial incentives in settings where they had not previously been used.

These two reviews provided a narrative account of the studies and their results (supplemented by tabulations of the frequency with which each type of experiment had a positive, negative, or nonexistent effect on productivity). They reported a majority of instances in which financial incentives were found to have a positive effect on productivity. Because the reviews were restricted to simple indicators of the rate of success, however, the reviews could not provide quantitative estimates of the *magnitude* of the impact of a productivity program implemented in an organization, nor could the reviews precisely compare the impact of financial incentives as a stimulus to increased productivity relative to the strength of other routes to increased productivity. Since the time of those reviews, however, quantitative techniques have been developed for summarizing and integrating the results of large numbers of studies. These techniques are variants of *meta-analysis* (e.g. Glass, McGaw, and Smith 1981; Hunter, Schmidt, and Jackson 1982; Rosenthal 1984).

Meta-analysis permits the integration and comparison of findings from numerous studies through the calculation of *effect sizes*. Effect sizes are indices of the magnitude of the relationship between two variables, such as incentive pay and productivity. Effect sizes are expressed in terms of the measured difference between the productivity of workers subject to financial incentives and those not subject to incentives. A basic formula for calculating effect size estimates is $ES = (M_i - M_c)/SD$, where ES is effect size, M_i is the mean productivity of employees working under an incentive, M_c is the mean productivity of employees not working under an incentive, and SD is the standard deviation (a measure of variation) of employee productivity. Thus, an effect size can be regarded as a measure of the difference between the average productivity of workers, some of whom are exposed to a "treatment" such as incentive pay and some of whom are not, relative to the typical variation in productivity. As such, effect sizes calculated from data obtained in one work setting can be meaningfully compared to those calculated on the basis of data obtained in other work settings.

The sign of the effect size (positive or negative) indicates a favorable or unfavorable effect on productivity and the magnitude of the effect size indicates the strength of that effect. Effect sizes range from zero (no effect) to any number, though typically the value of effect sizes falls between 0 and 1.5. (For a further discussion of effect sizes and the merits of meta-analysis as a tool for integrating data from different studies, see Glass et al. 1981; Guzzo, Jackson and Katzell 1987; Hunter et al. 1982; and Rosenthal 1984.)

Meta-analysis was used by Guzzo, Jette, and Katzell (1985) to reexamine the literature initially reviewed in narrative form by Katzell et al. (1977) and Guzzo and Bondy (1983). A primary objective of the meta-analysis was to furnish more precise information about the relative magnitude of the impact of programs implemented to raise productivity. Data from the Guzzo et al. (1985) report are used in this paper to discuss the impact of financial incentives on productivity.

Sources of Data

The studies analyzed through the meta-analysis shared several characteristics. All were reports of an experiment intended to affect worker productivity. By experiment, we mean a planned change in organizational practices that was systematically implemented and monitored over time for its impact, as assessed through objective indicators, on some aspect of productivity. All of the studies were carried out in organizations in the United States, and all reports appeared in a publicly available form during the period 1971–1981. Further, all experiments took place in organizations with missions to provide goods or services and in which workers were gainfully employed. A wide variety of public and private organizations of varying sizes were represented in the sample. Similarly, the experiments involved many types of employees: managerial, professional, clerical, and blue-collar.

Meaning of Productivity

Productivity refers to the relationship between outputs and the cost of inputs required to yield those outputs. Consequently, the term is applicable to many levels of analysis. It is meaningful, for example, to speak of the productivity of a nation, a firm, or an individual within an organization, although the measures and indicators of productivity differ according to level of analysis: some measures of productivity at the level of the firm may not be useful for assessing the productivity of individual employees, for example. The concern in this chapter is with the productivity of individual workers and small groups of workers and the extent to which their productivity can be improved by the use of financial incentives and other practices.

Improvements in worker productivity are evidenced by changes in worker outputs or inputs. Improvements in outputs are expressed in terms such as gains in the quantity, quality, or rate of output. Improvements in input are indicated by reduction in the costs of labor as indicated by reductions in turnover, absenteeism, and employee-based disruptions such as accidents. Thus, the data reported by Guzzo et al. (1985) and summarized here concern the impact of financial incentives on these specific measures of productivity-related inputs and outputs.

Evidence: The Impact of Financial Incentives

The findings reported by Guzzo et al. (1985) are summarized here in the following way. First, evidence concerning the average impact of financial incentives on productivity is presented and discussed. Second, the difference of the impact of financial incentives on output and withdrawal is considered. Third, the impact of financial incentive on productivity is compared to that of other practices.

Substantial but Variable

The eleven different practices and programs examined by Guzzo et al. were found to have, on average, a positive, statistically significant impact on productivity. The average effect size of the eleven programs was +.44. Assuming that worker productivity is normally distributed (that is, similar numbers of workers have above average and below average productivity, and the differences between average and above average performers are about the same as the differences between average and below average performers), an effect size of .44 indicates that the productivity of the average worker exposed to the programs is greater than the productivity of about 67% of the workers not exposed to the programs.

In particular, financial incentives were observed to have a positive impact on productivity (the average effect size for financial incentives was + .57). This is a substantial effect. However, the effects of financial incentives were found to be more variable than the effects of any of the other ten programs and practices. The effects of financial incentives were so variable that, statistically speaking, the average effect size of + .57 was not significantly different from zero. In some of the experiments reviewed, financial incentives had a pronounced positive effect on the productivity of employees in an organization, but in other cases there was evidence of negligible or unwanted negative effects. Thus, it appears that financial incentives can have substantial postive effects on worker productivity but that those effects are quite variable. It should be noted that most of the studies included in this analysis made use of individual, rather than group or organization-wide incentives.

Aspects of Productivity

Three major aspects of productivity—output, withdrawal, and disruptions—were examined in the Guzzo et al. analysis. Is it possible that the effects of financial incentives differ for each of these three aspects? The evidence indicates this to be so. The average effect of financial incentives on output was found to be much greater than their effect on withdrawal (no studies investigated the effects of incentives on costly disruptions at work such as accidents). Output, especially in terms of quality or quantity of work produced, was particularly responsive to the use of money as an incentive. In contrast, productivity-related behaviors such as absenteeism or quitting seem little affected by monetary incentives. Considering productivity as a relationship between outputs and inputs, financial incentives appear effective in raising worker outputs but less effective in reducing labor costs associated with withdrawal from the workplace.

Relative Impact of Financial Incentives

Attempts to raise worker productivity can take many forms. Several practices are used to raise productivity by increasing motivation, for example, financial incentives, goal setting, and work redesign. *Goal setting* involves the specification of difficult but attainable objectives for targeted aspects of job performance. Goals might be set for rate of output, for example, or quality of work. *Work redesign* seeks to enrich jobs with motivating qualities such as the exercise of many rather than few skills in a job and the opportunity to make decisions and experience personal responsibility for one's work. Other practices seek to raise productivity by altering the conditions in which people work. The adoption of *flexible working hours*, for example, is a practice meant to raise productivity by allowing workers the opportunity to work at those times they most prefer and find most convenient. Still other practices seek to raise productivity by developing the skills and abilities of workers relevant to the performance of their jobs. *Training* programs are used in this way.

Compared to these other programs and practices for raising worker productivity, what is the relative impact of financial incentives? The data reported by Guzzo et al. show that training had the greatest average impact on productivity (average effect size of .78). Two motivational strategies, goal setting and work redesign, have a different impact. Goal setting was found to have a comparatively strong effect on worker productivity (average effect size of .75) while work redesign had a smaller though notable average effect (.42). Systematically providing feedback to workers, such as might be done through the use of performance appraisal practices, was also found to raise productivity (average effect size of .35). The use of flexible working hours was found to have even smaller average effects (.21). Thus, the impact of financial incentives on worker productivity is weaker than the impact of some practices but stronger than that of others.

Information about the comparative impact of financial incentives versus other practices for raising worker productivity is useful in many ways, including cost-benefit determinations. Some organizations may find the cost of implementing work redesign programs so small relative to the cost of implementing an incentive pay plan that the net benefit to the organization may be greatest if job redesign is carried out, even though job redesign has been shown to have smaller average effects on productivity improvement than incentive pay. Similarly, the cost of mounting a training program may make it a less beneficial route to productivity improvement than the use of financial incentives, even though training programs, on average, have been found to yield greater increments in productivity than financial incentive programs. Cost-benefit considerations are not the same in all organizations and thus must be determined on a case-by-case basis when considering productivity improvement programs.

Contextual Factors

The report by Guzzo et al. (1985) also found that the impact of productivity improvement programs tended to vary according to contextual factors. For example, it was found that the effect of productivity improvement programs tended to be stronger the smaller the organization in which the programs were implemented. Further, productivity gains in government organizations tended to surpass those in private organizations. Also, differences were observed according to type of worker: sales and managerial workers showed greater evidence of productivity gains in response to the programs than did, for example, clerical workers. Although the number of cases analyzed was not large enough to permit clear conclusions to be made about the impact on productivity of financial incentives as they might vary with organization size, type, or kind of employee subject to them, it does appear that further investigation along these lines is warranted.

Evaluating Productivity Improvement Programs in Economic Terms

The effects of programs and practices such as goal setting, job redesign, flexible work schedules, and the use of financial incentives are often evaluated in statistical terms. An effect size estimate of the magnitude of these practices' impact on productivity is an example of such a statistical expression. However, there is often a need to evaluate such programs and practices in economic terms. Although there is no single, generally accepted accounting procedure for estimating the economic impact of human resource practices and programs, a few alternative methods exist (Cascio 1982). In this section these methods are briefly reviewed. Particular attention is given to a method useful to estimating the economic benefits of productivity improvements expressed as effect size estimates.

Human Resource Accounting Models

Asset Model. One approach to assessing the dollar value to an organization of its members treats employees as assets. This approach concerns itself with measures of an organization's investment in its employees. Investment in employees can take many forms, including recruitment and training costs. While this approach has the advantage of facilitating comparisons of human resource costs among units in an organization, it suffers from the disadvantage that its focus is on past costs and provides no information about the present value of an employee to an organization (Cascio 1982).

Replacement Cost. An alternative approach to assessing the economic value of employees to a firm focuses on the cost of replacing an employee. Replacement costs arise from recruitment, selection, training; loss of income to a company occurs during the absence of the employee replaced and, assuming that a new employee is not immediately as effective as a former employee, during the period of time the new employee rises to the level of the replaced employee. Both the replacement cost and asset model of assessing the economic value may be difficult to put into practice because estimating component costs (of training, etc.) may be difficult. Further, neither provides estimates of the economic value of gains in the productivity of employees.

Utility Models. Utility analyses are concerned with the economic gain or loss to an organization that results from various programs or practices designed to affect employees. Although the concept of utility analysis has been in existence for some time, a problem in its use has been the difficulty in obtaining an accurate estimate of the economic value of current employee performance. This estimate is crucial to the determination of the expected economic gains accruing from a new practice or program designed to affect employee performance.

Recently, though, new methods have been developed for estimating the economic value of employee performance. These concern the estimation of the standard deviation of dollar-valued job performance (SD_y). Rather than pursuing the arduous and often inaccurate path of using cost accounting procedures to estimate the dollar value of each job behavior of each employee and then computing a standard deviation of these values, Schmidt, Hunter, McKenzie, and Muldrow (1979) devised a judgmental procedure for determining SD_y. Their procedure asks people knowledgeable about a particular job (such as the supervisors of employees in that job) to estimate SD_y using their best judgment. More specifically, the procedure asks the experts to consider the output of the average employee in the job and place a dollar value on it, recognizing that the dollar value is but a "best guess." Then, an estimate of the dollar value of the "superior" employee in that job, defined as one who performs better than 85% of his or her peers, is obtained, and a similar estimate is obtained for the jobholder who outperforms only 15% of peers.

At this point the properties of a normal distribution are helpful in interpreting the dollar value estimates. If job performance in terms of dollar value is normally distributed, then the difference between the dollar value of the employee performing better than 85% of peers and the employee performing better than 50% of peers is an estimate of SD_y, since 35% of the cases in a normal distribution are within one standard deviation above the mean. Likewise, the difference between the dollar value of the average worker and the worker who performs better than only 15% of peers also is an estimate of SD_y since another 35% of the cases in a normal distribution are within one standard deviation below the mean. Schmidt et al. (1979) recommend using the average of these two estimates, if, in fact, the assumption of normally distributed performance is tenable. An alternative, more detailed approach to the same problem (estimating SD_y) is given by Cascio (1982, pp. 163–73). These approaches appear to give reasonable accurate estimates of SD_y without the problems inherent to cost accounting methods of estimating SD_y.

Productivity Gains in Economic Terms

The estimation of SD_y through Schmidt et al.'s (1979) and Cascio's (1982) methods make it possible to calculate economic gains due to productivity improvement practices. Effect sizes as estimated by Guzzo et al. (1985) are interpretable in terms of standard deviations of performance. Assuming that worker performance is normally distributed, an effect size of $+1.0$ would indicate that a productivity improvement program had the effect of raising the average level of productivity among workers subject to the program one standard deviation above the average level of productivity of workers not subject to the program. With an estimate of SD_y in hand, the dollar value of the gains in performance due to the program can be easily calculated. These calculations are potentially useful either for assessing the economic impact of a program already implemented or projecting the expected economic impact from implementing a program.

Summary

Recent evidence shows that financial incentives can be used as a means to improve worker productivity. However, financial incentives are quite variable in their effects. Comparatively speaking, the average impact of financial incentives on productivity is greater than that of some human resource management practices (e.g., flexible working hours) but less than that of others (e.g., goal setting). Theories of work motivation suggest that financial incentives have their most powerful effects when the incentive is sufficiently valued, contingent on performance, and perceived to be equitable. Further, the impact of productivity improvement programs (such as the use of financial incentives) can be estimated in economic terms.

References

Adams, J. S. 1963. "Toward an Understanding of Inequity." *Journal of Abnormal and Social Psychology* 67: 422–36.

Cascio, W. F. 1982. *Costing Human Resources: The Financial Impact of Behavior in Organizations.* Boston: Kent.

Glass, G. V., B. McGaw and M. L. Smith. 1981. *Meta-Analysis in Social Research.* Beverly Hills, Calif.: Sage.

Guzzo, R. A. and J. S. Bondy. 1983. *A Guide to Worker Productivity Experiments in the United States 1976–81.* New York: Pergamon.

Guzzo, R. A., S. J. Jackson and R. A. Katzell. 1987. "Meta-analysis Analysis." In B. M. Staw and L. L. Cummings, eds., *Research in Organizational Behavior* (Vol. 9). Greenwich, Conn.: JAI Press, pp. 407–42.

Guzzo, R. A., R. D. Jette and R. A. Katzell. 1985. "The Effects of Psychologically Based

Intervention Programs on Worker Productivity: A Meta-analysis." *Personnel Psychology* 38: 275–91.

Hunter, J. E., F. L. Schmidt and G. B. Jackson. 1982. *Meta-Analysis: Cumulating Research Findings Across Studies.* Beverly Hills, Calif.: Sage.

Iaffaldano, M. Y. and P. M. Muchinsky. 1985. "Job Satisfaction and Job Performance: A Meta-Analysis." *Psychological Bulletin* 97: 251–273.

Katzell, R. A., P. Bienstock, and P. H. Faerstein, 1977. *A Guide to Worker Productivity Experiments in the United States 1971–75.* New York: New York University Press.

Lawler, E. E. 1971. *Pay and Organizational Effectiveness: A Psychological View.* New York: McGraw-Hill.

Miner, J. B. 1980. *Theories of Organizational Behavior.* Hinsdale, Ill.: Dryden Press.

Mowday, R. T., L. W. Porter and R. M. Steers. 1982. *Employee-Organization Linkages.* New York: Academic Press.

Rosenthal, R. 1984. *Meta-Analytic Procedures for Social Research.* Beverly Hills, Calif.: Sage.

Schmidt, F. L., J. E. Hunter, R. C. McKenzie and T. W. Muldrow. 1979. "Impact of Valid Selection Procedures on Work-Force Productivity." *Journal of Applied Psychology* 64: 609–26.

Whyte, W. F., ed. 1955. *Money and Motivation: An Analysis of Incentives to Industry: New York: Harper.*

6

Group Financial Incentives: An Evaluation

John W. Kendrick

There are two major types of group financial incentives discussed in this chapter: profit-sharing (PS) programs, and productivity gainsharing (PG) plans. The latter can be further divided into plans based on "economic productivity" formulae involving current value ratios and represented chiefly by Scanlon-type plans; and plans based on physical productivity ratios and calculated savings in labor hours as in the case of Improshare.

I shall summarize the results of empirical evidence on the effectiveness of these types of group incentives. Since the quantitative evaluations are scarcely definitive, I shall also give my qualitative appraisal based on analysis of the main features of the several types of plans. Both quantitative and qualitative evaluations are useful in further improving existing plans, or in creating new types of programs that can build on the strengths and avoid the weaknesses of older schemes.

Brief Analysis of Main Types

Most readers will be acquainted with the main features of the several types of group financial incentives, and there is an extensive literature describing the different plans.[1] So I shall only summarize briefly the chief elements of each, and provide some commentary on how the formulas relate to productivity, which they are designed to promote.

Group financial incentives may be contrasted with individual incentives such as piecework and sales commissions. Both recognize the principle that if pay is related to performance it will be more effective in stimulating higher productivity. But in a large and increasing proportion of jobs, individual financial incentives are hardly feasible, and group

1. For a good general summary and discussion of the various gainsharing plans, see O'Dell, 1981.

financial incentives are being used more frequently. While less immediately related to the efficiency of any single worker, they encourage cooperation and even peer pressures among members of production units to increase productivity.

Group financial incentives are also to be distinguished from productivity improvement programs such as quality control circles and joint labor-management productivity teams that do not provide financial incentives over and above the normal pay schedules. The productivity gainsharing plans generally have mechanisms such as periodic group meetings that seek to channel worker energy, intelligence, and knowledge into raising productivity. And sometimes the nonfinancial programs are coupled with incentives such as profit sharing. Proponents of group financial incentives believe strongly that by sharing productivity gains employees are more likely to identify with the interests and objectives of managers and owners, and be more strongly motivated to try to reduce unit costs through higher productivity.

Profit Sharing

There are three forms of profit sharing. A predetermined percentage of profits (sometimes after a specified minimum return) is put into a pool that may be (1) distributed to eligible employees in cash, or (2) deferred and made part of a retirement program, in which case the profit contributions and income on the funds are not taxed to the employee until paid out, or (3) distributed through a combination cash or deferred arrangement (CODA) such as provided for in the January 1983 G.M.-U.A.W. labor contract.

Profit sharing is the most prevalent form of group financial incentive used in the United States. According to the Profit Sharing Research Foundation, there are more than 320,000 plans,* plus almost five thousand stock bonus and employee stock ownership plans (ESOPs) that also give employees a stake in profits. According to a New York Stock Exchange study (described later), about a quarter of companies with 500 or more employees have profit sharing, compared with 7 percent having group PG plans. The latter have been growing more rapidly in the past 5 years, however.

Relative changes in profitability of firms in the same industry depend not only on total factor productivity (output in relation to all associated inputs, in real terms) but equally on "price recovery" (changes in prices of output relative to prices of inputs). (See Kendrick 1984; pp. 57–64.) One objection frequently raised with regard to profit sharing is that it provides weaker motivation than incentives tied more directly to pro-

---

*Editor's note: this estimate is based on 1981–1982 data. Since that time, there has been substantial growth in the number of qualified deferred profit-sharing plans recorded by the United States Department of the Treasury. See Chap. 1, p. 5.

ductivity performance. Annual bonuses are considered to have less incentive value than more frequent rewards, but some profit-sharing plans do make semi-annual or quarterly payments. Within the profit-sharing approach, cash bonuses are considered to provide more incentive than deferred plans, although the latter provide more tax advantages for employees. Finally, it seems clear that profit sharing can be more effective when combined with some form of employee involvement system (although empirical studies have not discriminated among plans on that basis).

Economic Productivity Gainsharing

As initially formulated by Joseph Scanlon to reinforce his philosophy of employee involvement, the single ratio formula to determine bonus payments had the virtue of simplicity. It takes as a base for "allowed" payroll the average ratio of payroll costs to the sales value of production over the prior 3 to 5 years. The monthly difference between actual and allowed payroll costs is put into a bonus pool to be distributed 25% to the company and 75% to workers, of which 25% is put into a reserve and 75% distributed as a bonus. The bonus is distributed in proportion to the compensation of each employee who has been on the payroll for a minimum period ranging from one to six months.

Because changes in composition of output among products with differing proportions of labor costs can cause changes in labor ratios, "split ratios" were developed to correct for this. A problem with both the single and split ratios is that changes in the proportions of purchased materials, supplies, and services could affect the labor ratio independent of changes in labor productivity. One way out of this problem was to base the bonus calculations on the ratio of payroll costs to value added. This is the basis of the Rucker plan, which may be considered one variant of the Scanlon plan. Another variant is the multicost formula, by which base-period and actual ratios of *all* expenses to the sales value of production are compared. This is very close to profit sharing.

As with profit sharing, Scanlon bonuses are affected by changes in the relative prices of outputs and of inputs in addition to changes in productivity of labor, or of total inputs. Such changes, if expected to continue, can be compensated for by adjusting the base-period allowance ratio. Frequent adjustments do not breed confidence, yet the formula can (and has) become unworkable if not adjusted. Also, like all group financial incentives, the bonuses are affected by volume, and so tend to be cyclical—but this can be a virtue, as discussed later.

Scanlon plans have a fairly elaborate structure of production and screening committee that provide channels of communication between management and workers; elicit, screen, and help effectuate employee suggestions; and provide a forum for discussion and analysis of problems. Rucker committee structures are somewhat less elaborate, but also focus on ways to improve the economic productivity ratio. Mitchell Fein considers the Scanlon plan to be overly structured.

Performance PG: Improshare

Mitchell Fein introduced Improshare in 1964 as a means of combining work measurement techniques with organization-wide incentives. His formula is based on the ratio of actual labor hours worked each week or month to the labor hours that would have been required to produce the various products in the base period (a recent historical period), which is called the "Accepted Productivity Level." The value of the hours saved is split 50–50 between covered employees and the firm. The ratio of half of the saved hours to the hours worked gives the percentage of bonus added to each employee's pay for the period.

If investments in new plant and equipment are the cause of productivity increases, the gains are shared 80–20. Recently Fein has introduced new versions of his plan that provide bonuses for savings in materials, energy, and other expendables (measured in constant prices) per unit of output as measured in base period labor hours. This version comes close to a total- or multi-factor productivity approach.

A ceiling on productivity improvement is generally set at 60% in Improshare plans, after which management can buy back measurement standards.

Fein explains the plan fully to employees in small groups before activation so it can have its full incentive effect in promoting cooperation. He also advocates subsequent use of labor-management committees, suggestion systems, and other means of tapping employees' creative ideas and keeping them involved.

Empirical Evidence

Proponents of the several types of financial incentive programs have assembled evidence regarding their efficacy. Although it is fragmentary and selective, except in the case of Improshare, I shall summarize it before looking at presumably more objective, third party studies.

Profit Sharing

In an early study that he co-authored, Bert Metzger, President of the Profit Sharing Research Foundation compared the financial performance of a group of department store chains using profit sharing with a similar group without financial incentives. (Metzger and Colletti; 1971). Over a 17-year period, the first group increased sales by 35% more than the control, net worth by 47%, net income per employee by 80%, and earnings per share by 88% more. In a 1975 study Metzger found that, as measured by profit ratios to both sales and equity, 23 profit-sharing manufacturing firms outperformed Fortune's 500 largest industrials, and 10 profit-sharing retailers outperformed Fortune's 41 retailers (Metzger 1975). Presumably five in his sample of 38 profit-sharing firms did not do as well as the control groups.

Bion B. Howard (1979) of Northwestern University compared 16 operating ratios and growth rates for profit-sharing companies in 6 industries for a 20-year period ending in 1977. He found that the *levels* of the measures (not the trends) were higher for two-thirds of the firms than the average of nonprofit sharing firms, and significantly lower for only one-fifth. Another study of 83 profit-sharing firms in 1980 found labor turnover rates to be lower than industry averages for 64% of the firms, and significantly higher for only 6% (Nightingale, 1980). Financial measures were not compared, but responses to a questionnaire indicated executives rate profit sharing as most effective in attracting and holding desirable employees, providing employee security, increasing productivity, and improving cooperation.

Other studies cited by Metzger show favorable results from employee ownership, and from employee stock ownership plans. The studies appear to be less than definitive, however.

Empirical analysis of the results of profit-based bonus systems should be relatively simple to carry out at moderate cost using financial data bases such as that of DRI, Inc. This would involve comparisons of levels and rates of change in profit ratios of firms before and after PS plans, and after the plan was installed with firms without such plans. The records of firms with plans should be broken down into those with significant Employee Involvement (EI) programs and those without. The same type of analysis could, of course, be carried out for firms with ESOPs, or a combination of PS and ESOP, or for other types of financial incentive programs. The control group of firms without financial incentive plans could, in turn, be broken down into those with significant EI programs, and those without. Various combinations and permutations of those variables could be tried if the sample of firms in each industry were large enough.

Scanlon Plans

There have been quite a few case studies of company experience with Scanlon plans, most of them qualitative since most companies require confidentiality of financial data. The literature has been summarized by Brian E. Moore in a document for the Work in America Institute (1982). His findings relate to both positive and negative aspects of company experiences with the plan. One bit of empirical evidence he cites indicates that the percentage of employees who make suggestions ranges from 46 to 95% annually, compared with around 26% under suggestion systems not a part of Scanlon plans.

A few case studies do contain more quantitative information on plan results. For example, Moore and Ross (1978, p. 145) tracked the annual bonus paid by one firm over a 10-year period. They found it averaged almost 10%, and did not fall below 7% in any one year. Bonuses were paid in about three-quarters of all months, and year-end bonuses were paid in 7 of the 10 years. In a recent study of DeSoto, Inc., Graham-Moore and Ross found the average bonus percentage of annual pay from 1971 through 1981 to be 7.8%, with a range from 2 to 21%. Productivity increases cumulated to 78% by 1979, but dropped during the subsequent recession.

A compilation of the results of studies of plans in 44 firms, done by the National Commission on Productivity and Work Quality in 1975, is summarized in table 6.1.

Improshare

The most comprehensive quantitative analysis of experience with a PG plan was that done of Improshare by its creator, Mitchell Fein, in 1982. It was based on data from 72 of the almost 100 firms who had adopted the plan since 1974. Of that number, 57 were still in operation in early 1972. The 73 companies had 1600 or fewer workers; 22 had under 100. Over half of the companies were nonunion. About three-quarters combined the group financial incentive with labor-management productivity committees, a practice that Fein favors.

Table 6.2. prepared by Mitchell Fein, shows that the companies continuing the plan increased productivity by 10.3% in the first 12 weeks, and by 24.4% over the first year. Fein is extending his survey to include most of the 150 or so companies that have now adopted Improshare (in Canada as well as in the United States). He recently told me that preliminary results indicate at least as good performance in the first year for the others as for the 72 in the tabulation shown here when due allowance is made for the 1982 recession. He is also collecting data on experience beyond the first year of plan operation.

In table 6.2, the companies are identified only by number and chief line of business. Graham-Moore and Ross present a summary tabulation of the evidence of 19 firms that adopted Improshare between 1975 and 1980, inclusive, identified by name. This summary also shows distinctly positive results with respect both to productivity gains and bonus payments.

National Productivity Center

In 1975 the National Commission on Productivity and Work Quality tabulated the results of 22 studies of 44 companies with group PG, mainly of the Scanlon type (See table 6.2.) The plans had been in operation for an average of nearly ten years, one dating back to 1947.

Table 6.1 Breakdown of Plan Studies by Key Characteristics

Company, Author, Year	Type of Industry	Employ-ment	Years of Plan	Bonus Range	Coopera-tion	Outcome	Comments
1. Adamson/Scanlon/47	steel fabrication	125	10 plus	0–50%	very good	success	few bonuses complex formula, and management changes
2. American Optical/ Johnson/59	optical equipment	150	18 plus	0–11%	no change	failure	
3. Anderson Bro. Johnson/59	machine tools	150	6 plus	"quite good"	very good	success	
4. Atwood/Lesieur & Puckett/69	automotive hardware	2000	17	5–20%	very good	success	
5. Canfield/Sweeney/54	rubber specialties	300	3 plus	9.5 ave.	apparently good	success	
6. Dalton/Dreyer/52	steel fabrication	200	2 plus	0–3.6%	poor	failure	poor formula and management attitudes
7. DeSoto/Moore & Goodman/72	chemical coatings	180	2	0–12%	very good	success	
8. Embossing Co./ Morris/54	wood games	75	2 plus	0–40%	very good	success	
9. Lapointe/Schultz & Crisara/52	broaches	1000	25	0–52%	very good	success	
10. Linwood/Gray/71	auto bodies	6000	3	0–?	poor	failure	large inequities in pay, rapid changes in product mix
11. Market Forge/ Goodman/64	steel fabrication	300	3	"regular & good"	significant increase	partial success	

Study	Product					Result	Notes
12. Michigan Wheel/*Production*/69	propellers	250	24	9–72%	very good	success	
13. Parker Pen/Lesieur & Puckett/69	writing instruments	1000	17 plus	6–20%	very good	success	
14. Pfaudler/Lesieur & Puckett/69	glassed steel equipment	750	17 plus	3–18%	very good	success	
15. Stromberg-Carlson/Tait/51	electronic products	—	—	"12% ave."	apparently good	success	
16. Towle/Humphries/52	silver flatware	500	3 plus	0–25%	very good	success	
17. Anonymous/Gilson & Lefcowitz/57	ceramics	80	1	0–6%	very poor	failure	formula poorly constructed, individual incentives better, changes in product mix
18. Anonymous/Helfgott/62	survey across 6 manufacturing firms	—	—	0–?	no change to good	4 successes	2 failures; no bonuses ever paid
19. Anonymous/Jehring/67	household fixtures	200	6	0–11%	apparently good	partial success	
20. Anonymous/Preston/51	manufacturing	1000	2	—	—	success	
21. Anonymous/Ross/69	raw material processor	250	15	—	apparently good	success	
22. Anonymous/Ruh, et al./72	survey across 18 manufacturing firms	—	—	—	no change to very good	10 successes	8 failures; no reasons given
Total = 22 studies (44 firms)					30 successes	14 failures	

Source: National Commission on Productivity and Work Quality, 1975.

Table 6.2 Productivity Improvement Obtained in Improshare® Companies

Company	Manufacturing	Total empl.	Union	Year estab.	Percent gain Start(1)	Percent gain After 1 yr.	Still oper.(2)	Prod. team
1	metal stampings	75	IUE	1974	12	32	yes	no
2	automotive parts	200	AIW	1976	22	70	yes	yes
3	steel fabrication	375	Teamsters	1980	8	8	yes	yes
4	steel products	500	IAM	1978	11	40	yes	yes
5	mobile trucks	100		1980	6	11	yes	no
6	consumer plastics	125		1978	23	65	yes	no
7	pleasure boats	125		1978	23	42	yes	no
8	outdoor products	350		1979	20	32	yes	no
9	machine shop	300	UK	1977	8	15	NV	yes
10	metal stampings	150		1979	7	18	yes	yes
11	machine shop	85		1978	13	36	yes	yes
12	metal treating	40		1978	8	16	yes	yes
13	automotive	1550	Rubber	1980	3	8	yes	yes
14	electrical products	800		1981	8	16	yes	yes
15	photocopy products	500		1980	9	15	yes	yes
16	heavy machinery	1600	IUE	1979	12	52	yes	yes
17	foundry	275	Moulders	1979	11	52	sus	yes
18	auto parts	750	UAW	1979	15	32	yes	yes
19	trucks	250		1976	13	32	yes	yes
20	automotive	200		1978	7	16	NPC	yes
21	automotive	800	UAW	1980	3	8	yes	yes
22	electrical	250	UAW	1980	3	6	yes	yes
23	consumer	35		1979	10	30	yes	yes
24	consumer	120		1981	7	(3)	yes	yes
25	industrial	125		1979	8	42	NPR	yes

26	chemical	675	OCAW	1980	9	16	yes	yes
27	chemical	650		1980	6	12	yes	yes
28	appliances	400	IUE	1979	20	32	NPC	yes
29	electrical	75		1981	5	10	yes	yes
30	chemicals	375		1979	3	10	NV	no
31	paper	150	Paper Wkrs	1978	8	44	yes	yes
32	paper	1000	USW	1980	2	3	NL	no
33	chemical	450		1980	9	15	NV	yes
34	lumber	40	Woodwkrs	1980	10	18	yes	yes
35	clay products	65	USW	1981	30	30	yes	yes
36	lumber products	85	Woodwkrs	1981	24	34	yes	yes
37	concrete	20		1976	8	22	yes	no
38	plastics	250		1981	6	18	yes	yes
39	steel wire	250	USW	1981	11	26	yes	yes
40	machine shop	125		1981	8	26	yes	yes
41	machine shop	250		1981	9	16	yes	yes
42	sheet metal	50		1979	8	22	yes	yes
43	wood products	175		1979	4	22	yes	yes
44	furniture	300		1977	8	19	yes	no
45	upholstered furn.	200		1979	11	15	yes	no
46	furniture	35	Brick Clay	1978	12	70	yes	yes
47	upholstered furn.	100	Furn Wkrs	1979	12	16	yes	no
48	upholstered furn.	125		1979	9	20	yes	no
49	wood furniture	450		1981	16	31	yes	no
50	leather	55	AMC	1976	12	25	yes	yes
51	fabric	100	Textile	1980	12	44	yes	yes
52	warehouse	50	Textile	1980	18	75	yes	yes
53	consumer	65		1977	18	35	yes	yes
54	consumer	250		1978	12	18	yes	yes
55	electrical	65		1978	35	55	yes	yes
56	metal stampings	90		1978	16	35	yes	yes
57	metal products	35		1978	10	25	yes	yes

No.	Product	Total plants	Union	Year			12 wks.	1 yr.
58	metal furniture	550	Teamsters	1981	10	55(4)	yes	yes
59	chemical	300	Teamsters	1979	0	0	no	no
60	automotive parts	110	Independ.	1980	11	28	yes	no
61	consumer	140		1978	12	22	yes	yes
62	trucking	75		1975	5	0	no	no
63	consumer	550	IUE	1979	6	8	no	no
64	fabric	15	UAW	1981	15	(3)	yes	no
65	machine shop	65	UE	1981	9	(3)	yes	yes
66	electrical	155		1981	21	(3)	yes	yes
67	electrical	160	IUE	1981	19	(3)	yes	yes
68	oil equipment	600		1977	6	0	NL	no
69	machine shop	110	Teamsters	1980	8	10	yes	yes
70	sheet metal	85	Teamsters	1978	30	58	NPC	yes
71	plastics	220	Teamsters	1977	11	8	no	no
72	construction	200		1978	7	0	no	no

Summary increase percent

	12 wks.	1 yr.
Average all companies	9.4	22.2
Average companies continued plan	10.3	24.4

	Total plants
Notes:	
(1) first 6 weeks	5
(2) as of 2/10/82	1
(3) less than one year	
(4) expected year end	
Plans not operating:	
Sus suspended, will restart	1
N No, discontinued	5
NPC No, plant closed	3
NPR No, plant rebuilt	1
NV No, volume reduced	3
NL No, labor problems	2

Source: Mitchell Fein, 1982.

Employment in these companies ranged from less than 100 to 6,000. Almost one-third of the plans ended in failure for reasons indicated on the table. Sixteen firms were identified by name. Most of the authors of the studies are named. Over two-thirds of the plans were successful. Bonuses averaged around 12% in the firms for which means or ranges (from which the mid-point was taken) were given.

The GAO Study

A study of 36 firms using group PG plans of both the economic and performance productivity types was published in 1981 by the General Accounting Office (GAO). In addition to interviewing both management and labor representatives of the three dozen firms using PG, GAO staff also interviewed another nine which had productivity improvement plans without financial incentives, and nine others who were considering or had rejected plan installations.

The two dozen companies that provided financial data reported average annual labor savings that averaged 16.9%. The thirteen firms with annual sales of less than $100 million had about one percentage point greater labor savings than the larger firms. Labor savings increased over time; they averaged 8.5% in firms whose plans have been in effect less than five years, but almost 29% in those more than five years old. One of the latter firms had annual savings of around 77%.

Respondents mentioned various benefits of the plans, particularly better labor-management relationships and improved worker performance. The GAO report (1981) concluded: "The results of productivity sharing plans suggest that these plans offer a viable method of enhancing productivity at the firm level" (p. 28). It cautions that management dedication and careful design, installation, and monitoring of a program are required for a high probability of success.

The New York Stock Exchange Survey

The most comprehensive survey of "human resource" programs of various types was conducted by the New York Stock Exchange in 1982. A sample of 4,372 separate corporations was drawn from the universe of around 49,000 corporations employing one hundred or more employees. The number of separate companies responding was 1,158, more than one-quarter.

Of the survey respondents from corporations with 500 or more employees, 76% evaluated their group PG plans to have been successful in raising productivity, 58% were "somewhat successful"; and 18% were "very successful." Only 2% considered the PG plans unsuccessful. The remainder either had no response, or said it was too early to evaluate the plans (16%), which reflects the rapid growth of PG plans in the preceding couple of years. The favorable response on group PG plans was almost the same as for piecework and other individual financial incentives.

With regard to profit-sharing plans, 73% judged them to be successful (26% "very"). In that connection, it should be noted that about half of the profit-sharing plans were in firms also using quality circles, which had a 57% successful rating but only 1% unsuccessful since their very rapid recent growth caused 36% of respondents to consider it too early to evaluate. Profit-sharing plans were considered unsuccessful by 5% of respondents.

Sixty-one percent of stock purchase plans were considered successful, but, of the financial incentive programs, this type had the smallest percentage of "very successful" ratings (4%), and the highest percentage of unsuccessful (15%).

Need for Further Study

The studies cited present impressive evidence that group financial incentives have had distinctly favorable effects on productivity growth in the majority of firms, probably in at least two-thirds, in which they have been tried. The studies made by authors or proponents of the plans might have been suspected of possible bias. The government studies were based on a relatively small number of cases. But the New York Stock Exchange study, based on a large and representative sample of corporations, confirmed the positive effects on productivity of the major types of financial incentives in the companies using them at the time of the survey.

Although the NYSE study is the most systematic and comprehensive study so far, there are a number of areas in which it could be improved. In any case, follow-up on empirical studies will be needed in view of the recent rapid growth of productivity improvement programs both with and without financial incentives. It will be recalled that a substantial proportion of the firms responding to the NYSE study indicated that it was too early to evaluate their programs.

Related to this is the fact that the NYSE study related to human resource programs and activities in effect at the time of the survey. It does not pick up the abandonment of programs, which presumably indicates lack of success. Yet we know that a significant proportion of group financial incentive programs failed. Surveys could be structured to try to get at this phenomenon, and possibly the major reasons for discontinuances. We know from the case studies that failures were often ascribed to inadequate preparation for installation of the programs, including their explanation to employees; insufficient backing from management, poor economic conditions and few bonuses; and problems with the formulas, particularly in the Scanlon-type programs. Study of the failures as well as the successful programs can help in devising improvements.

The meaning of the term "success" in evaluating the productivity impact of various programs should be specified. Does it mean an increase at least a certain percentage greater than that of the industries in which the firm is classified, and/or greater than the firm's own past trend-rate of productivity growth? Or is it based on indirect evidence, such as the widening of profit margins? How does the respondent abstract from the effect of changes in economic conditions generally?

The sample size should be large enough to permit further breakdown of categories and cross-classification of responses. In the NYSE survey, for example, it would be helpful to know if there is a difference in evaluation of quality circles and production teams depending on whether or not they are combined with group financial incentives. Conversely, it would help to know the difference in evaluation of financial incentive plans depending on whether they were linked to employee involvement programs or not. It would be useful to break down the group productivity programs into the Improshare and Scanlon categories, and possibly the latter into its major subdivisions, particularly the Rucker variant. Similarly, the profit-sharing plans could be broken into their three component types.

Finally, it is always desirable to have control groups, so that the results of the various productivity programs can be compared not only with each other, but also with a group of similar firms without such programs.

In the last analysis, however, no empirical study of these matters can be entirely definitive. It is not possible to hold other things equal, particularly in human affairs. Each company adapts each of the various plans, programs, or activities to its own circumstances. They are sometimes combined (e.g., the Improshare formula with the Scanlon committee structure) in different ways. Managers and workers will add their own distinctive features to the programs. Perhaps most importantly, the degree of success or failure of any program will depend on the quality of management. Certainly there will always be a need for detailed case studies, as well as for broad surveys. And since the empirical studies cannot provide all the answers, there is always room for qualitative appraisals, theoretical analysis, and creative insights as a basis for innovative new programs or modifications of old programs to promote better productivity performance.

Concluding Observations

What about the claim of the economic productivity proponents, particularly of the Rucker plan, that their measures take account of ability to pay as well as of productivity enhancement? That is true under usual circumstances, but it is possible for the ratio of labor compensation to value of production and also to value added to decline even in the face of falling profits if other costs are rising enough. Actually, only profit sharing fully addresses the ability-to-pay question.

The problem with profit sharing is that workers do not see the immediate relationship of their efforts and ideas to productivity gains. It is important in both profit-sharing and Scanlon-type plans that workers understand that productivity is half the picture, but that economic results are also affected by the relative movements of prices charged by the firm and the prices it pays for labor and other inputs. The relative price movements may be either favorable or unfavorable to the interests of the owners and employees of firms, but productivity improvement always is beneficial.

Another advantage of profit sharing is that profits reflect improvements in total factor productivity. This gives workers an incentive to save on materials, energy, and capital as well as labor. The Scanlon plans using labor ratios do not have a built-in incentive to economize on other cost elements. The Rucker plan, while reflecting materials as well as labor saving, does not promote more efficient use of capital. But the multi-cost Scanlon plan is quite close to profit sharing in promoting efficiency generally.

The advantage of profit sharing is that the "formula" emerges from normal accounting practices. To be most effective, however, profit sharing should be linked to formal employee involvement structures and activities such as are an integral part of Scanlon plans, or quality control circles. This is necessary to take full advantage of and channel the greater motivation of workers to cooperate in reducing costs.

The chief attraction of Improshare or possible alternative physical productivity approaches is that they are directly linked to the objective of the programs. In its original form, however, Improshare bonuses were based on improvements in labor productivity, plus a small share of improvements from innovations requiring investment. Recently, Mitchell Fein has devised a variant of Improshare that would reward workers for savings in energy, materials, and "expendables." This comes close to a multi- or total-factor productivity (TFP) approach.

Indeed one wonders if the ideal formula would not be one based on TFP, subject to some profit constraint—i.e., that bonuses would not be paid even with requisite increases in TFP if profits fell below some minimum percentage of sales receipts. This would combine ability to pay with a direct link of bonuses to productivity performance. Measurement of TFP has spread to many firms, as courses and literature devoted to the subject have increased (see Kendrick 1984, pp. 1–5).

In some industries, particularly in the growing services sector, output and productivity cannot be measured well enough to serve as the basis for gainsharing formulas. In those industries, profit-sharing or other economic-productivity-based plans are indicated. But my earlier injunctions should be underlined: explain carefully to employees the close link of productivity to profits, and meld the profit sharing with an EI structure.

The time pattern of bonuses under all of the group financial incentive plans reflect both structural and cyclical forces. By structural, I mean that the increases will usually be greatest in the first year or two as greater employee involvement reduces costs over which workers have direct control and influence—attendance, punctuality, turnover, care in use of equipment and materials, diligence and efficiency with the given technology, and so on. This is bound to result in bonuses under the performance-based PG plans unless volume is dropping. It probably will do so in the economic PG and profit-sharing programs unless volume and relative movements of prices received and paid are unusually unfavorable. If the unfavorable circumstances are cyclical or otherwise temporary, bonuses will emerge eventually.

After the initial pickup in productivity, bonuses in subsequent years will tend to increase under the profit-sharing and economic-productivity PG plans only if the company increases its productivity faster than that of its competitors. This is so since the relative changes in the ratio of prices received to prices paid tend to reflect industry productivity growth. The company productivity trend depends importantly on the quality of management, and the financial incentive programs can help if they can tap innovative ideas of the work force, and not just elicit more efficient performance under given technology.

Under Improshare, continuing productivity gains tend to increase the bonus even if the gains are not better than those in the industry. I suspect this is one reason why Mitchell Fein devised his buy-back arrangement once bonuses reach 30% of base pay.

Even if bonuses don't increase much from the levels reached after the first year or two, the additional pay is beneficial to the company in helping it attract, develop, and retain employees of above-average ability and/or performance levels. This assumes the initial relative gains in productivity are not subsequently dissipated. Paradoxically, however, once all or most firms of an industry have incentive and/or EI systems, the advantage to the individual firm will largely be competed away unless it can stay ahead of the pack. But the economy as a whole continues to benefit from the greater increases in productivity and real income per head than would have occurred without the plans.

Another advantage of group financial incentives from a macro-economic viewpoint is the cyclical flexibility they lend to labor compensation. In boom periods, one reason for a downturn is a slowing in productivity gains that raises unit labor costs, often squeezing profits. If the incentives can keep productivity growth on a stronger trend, that helps prolong expansions. Conversely, the decline in bonuses due to falling volume in a recession helps to bring the increase in unit labor costs down below price increases, helping to widen profit margins, which is a prerequisite for recovery. Also, during recessions, payments to workers out of reserves accumulated from past contributions help stabilize demand, without adding to current costs. As Ouchi (1981) has pointed out, greater stability of employment in firms conduces to greater investment in human capital by managements. This upgrading of the work force will raise productivity and real income per capita over and above the direct effects of group incentives.

References

ESOP Association of America. "The Performance of ESOP Companies." Association *Newsletter,* San Francisco, September, 1979.

Fein, Mitchell. "Improved Productivity Through Worker Involvement." Mimeo. Hillsdale, N.J.: Mitchell Fein, Inc., 1982.

General Accounting Office. *Productivity Sharing Programs: Can they Contribute to Productivity Improvement?* Washington: General Accounting Office, 1981.

Graham-Moore, E. Brian, and Timothy L. Ross. *Productivity Gainsharing: How Employee Incentive Programs Can Improve Business Performance.* Englewood Cliffs, N.J.: Prentice-Hall, Inc., 1983.

Howard, Bion B. *A Study of the Financial Significance of Profit Sharing, 1958–1977.* Chicago: Profit Sharing Council of America, 1979.

Kendrick, John W. (in collaboration with the American Productivity Center). *Improving Company Productivity: Handbook With Case Studies.* Baltimore: Johns Hopkins University Press, 1984.

Metzger, Bert L. "Evidence of Superior Performance." In *Profit Sharing in 38 Large Companies.* Evanston, Ill.: Profit Sharing Research Foundation, 1975.

Metzger, Bert L. and Jerome A. Colletti. *Does Profit Sharing Pay?* Evanston, Ill.: Profit Sharing Research Foundation, 1971.

Moore, Brian E. *Sharing the Gains of Productivity.* Work in America Institute Studies in Productivity 24. Elmsford, N.Y.: Pergamon Press, Inc., 1982.

Moore, Brian E. and Timothy L. Ross. *The Scanlon Way to Improved Productivity: A Practical Guide.* New York: John Wiley & Sons, Inc., 1978.

National Commission on Productivity and Work Quality. *A National Policy for Productivity Improvement.* Washington, D.C.: Government Printing Office, 1975.

New York Stock Exchange Office of Economic Research. *People and Productivity: A Challenge to Corporate America.* New York: New York Stock Exchange, 1982.

Nightingale, Donald V. "Does Profit Sharing Really Make Any Difference?" Ottawa: The Conference Board in Canada, January 17, 1980.

O'Dell, Carla S. *Gainsharing: Involvement, Incentives and Productivity,* an AMA Management Briefing. New York: Amacom, 1981.

Ouchi, William G. *Theory Z: How American Business Can Meet the Japanese Challenge.* Reading, Mass.: Addison-Wesley, 1981.

7

Incentives and Worker Behavior: Some Evidence

Andrew Weiss

This chapter is concerned with three types of incentive programs: first, individual wage incentives that cause a worker's efforts to have a major effect on his pay; second, group incentives in which the pay of an individual is determined by the output of a group of workers (a group can be as small as a four member work team or as large as the whole firm); finally, seniority based payment schemes in which the pay of a worker rises rapidly with his tenure with the firm. We shall examine whether these payment schemes have the effects in practice that we would predict from optimizing behavior by workers.

1. Aims of Incentive Programs

Individual incentives are chosen to motivate employees to work hard and to help the firm retain its most able workers. Because each employee is paid in accordance with his own output, a payment schedule can be chosen to induce the optimal level of effort on the part of employees. In addition, since this wage schedule typically results in substantial pay differences between the top and bottom deciles of workers by ability, the more able workers are less likely to quit and the less able workers more likely to quit than if each received the same wage. Unfortunately, individual wage incentives also have significant drawbacks. Workers are not motivated to cooperate with one another, and serious morale problems (and grievance procedures in unionized plants) can result from inequalities in the payment schedules across jobs. Consequently, considerable resources must be allocated to evaluating jobs.

Often, workers spend time waiting for parts or have their output otherwise hindered by faulty equipment. Under individual wage incentives, managerial decisions about the impact of these "special conditions" on worker performance may cause friction and result in grievances.

137

Finally, and perhaps most important, workers may think that technological innovations provide management with an opportunity to tighten
wage rates. The threat posed to an individual worker by any single
innovation is greatest if that worker is paid piece-rate and the technology
affects his job. Hence, resistance to new technology is likely to be greatest
in firms using individual wage incentives.

Group incentives avoid many of these drawbacks, but at the expense
of less motivation for high effort and lower rewards to high performance workers. For any payment schedule, the larger the group, the lower
is the motivation for an individual worker to exert himself: if the
average worker in a 100 member group were to double his output, the
output of the group would rise by only 1%, and for any reasonable pay
schedule the individual's earnings would not be significantly affected.
Similarly, because the most and least able workers within each group
receive the same wages, those pay differences that help firms retain their
most able workers are effectively eliminated. On the other hand, group
incentives encourage co-operation among members of the same group
(especially if groups are small) and reduce friction over perceived
inequities in rates (tight rates for any one job have only a trivial effect on
the group wage incentive of workers assigned to that job).

Although wage incentives are generally thought of as payment systems that link the output of workers to their pay, wages can have
incentive effects even when pay is unaffected by output. For example,
pay schedules in which earnings or the vallue of pensions increase
rapidly with seniority provide strong incentives for workers to stay with
the firm. In this case, the behavior that is being affected by the incentive
mechanism is the quit rate of workers.

We shall examine the effect of piece-rate, group wage incentives, and
seniority based wages on the output and quit rates of workers.

2. Group vs. Individual Incentives

The evidence in this section comes from three plants of a large electronics manufacturer based in the United States. Because the same patterns
were observed at all three locations, we only present data from the
largest of the three plants.

The firm pays its workers on a nonlinear individual piece-rate schedule when they are first hired, and uses a group incentive pay system for
its experienced workers. The initial piece-rate schedule provides significant financial incentives for workers to exert themselves. For a worker
performing at 60% of the expected output on his job, a 1% increase in
his output increases his pay by .7%. For a worker performing at 115% of
expected output, a 1% increase in output increases his pay by 1.2%.
Once a worker achieves 83.5% of the expected output for his job he is

placed in a pay group in which his pay is proportional to the output of the group. The vast majority of workers are on group incentives by their 3rd month with this firm. The average pay group has 126 members. Thus, for experienced workers there is almost no direct financial reward for high output.

By examining the change in the output of workers as they switch from individual to group incentives we can obtain a measure of the relative impact of individual and group incentives on performance. By comparing group incentives with individual incentives in the same plant, we avoid many of the drawbacks of previous studies of the effects of incentives on worker behavior. In particular we ensure: a) that changes in payment schedules are not associated with radically different supervision (few of the workers changed supervisors when they went from individual to group incentives), and b) that the observed effects of individual incentives are not due to better monitoring of output under

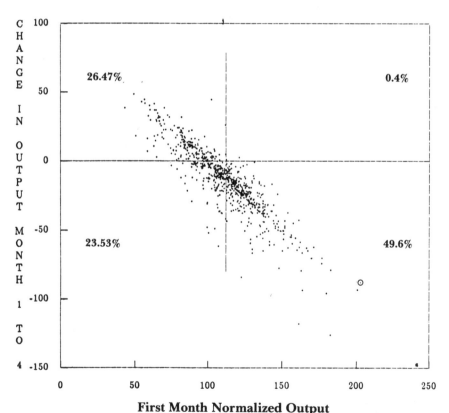

First Month Normalized Output

**Figure 7.1   Effects of Piece-rate vs. Time-rate on Productivity
(752 observations, nonlearners in month 4)**

individual incentives. (Output under a measured daywork system can be as much as 20% greater than the output under the same time-rate pay system but without careful records of individual output.)

As was mentioned, in the firm we're studying all newly hired production workers are paid on individual incentives. By their fourth month on the job almost all of these workers are on group incentives.

In figure 7.1 we plot the change in output from their first to fourth month on the job for newly hired production workers. These workers were ordered on the horizontal axis according to their normalized output in the first month.[1] Thus the circled dot denotes a worker whose normalized output in the first month was approximately 205% of the expected level for his job and whose output in month 4 was approximately 120% of the level expected for a fully trained worker on his job. (All the workers in figure 7.1 had jobs requiring fewer than 4 months experience in order to be fully trained. After the fourth month we did not discern any increase in physical output on these jobs.)

Almost all the workers whose first month performance was above the median decreased their output between months 1 and 4. On the other hand, only half of the low performing workers decreased their output between months 1 and 4. This effect is accentuated if we focus on workers whose first month output was more than 10% above or below the median. Among workers whose first month output was more than 10% below the median, 79% increased their output. Out of the 208 workers whose first month output was more than 10% above the median only one worker increased his output.

These effects are unlikely to be due to random noise or measurement error causing convergence toward the mean. As we see in figures 7.2a and 7.2c, among workers who completed their training within four months the variance of output is much lower during their 4th month on the job than during their first month. This same pattern held at the two other locations of the firm that we studied.

It is of course possible that the industrial engineers miscalculated the difficulty of learning different tasks. These errors would be likely to increase the variance of recorded normalized first month output. When we estimated the effect of the reported time needed to learn a job on normalized first month output, we found that, after correcting for the personal characteristics of the workers, the workers that were assigned to jobs that took longer to learn reported higher levels of normalized first month output.[2]

In figure 7.2b we first removed the effects on normalized output of our estimates of the industrial engineer's overassessments of the difficulty of learning complex tasks. We then recorded these adjusted output levels as a percentage of the mean of the recalculated output levels. (Thus we forced the mean of the renormalized output levels to be equal

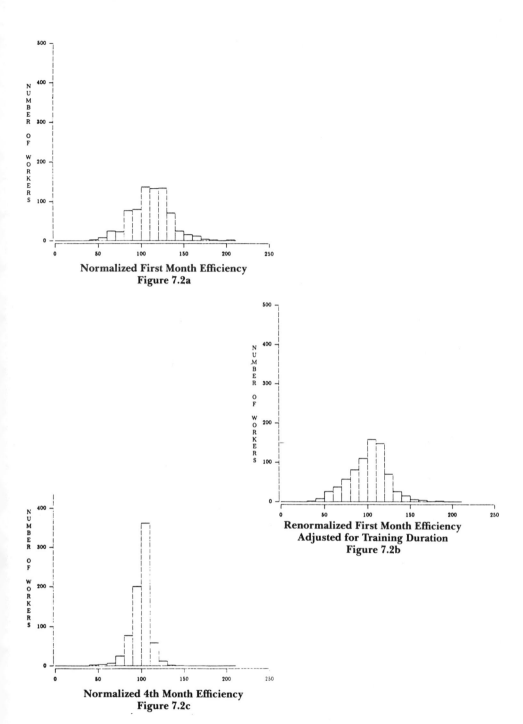

Figure 7.2   Effect of Piece-rate vs. Time-rate on the Productivity
Distribution (752 observations, nonlearners in month 4)

to 100. For experienced workers who are off the learning curves for their jobs the mean normalized output level as computed by the industrial engineering force is 100.2.)

Comparing figure 7.2b with figure 7.2a it is apparent that our renormalization decreases the variance in the first month output of workers. However, comparing figure 7.2b with figure 7.2c it is also apparent that, even after the renormalization, the variance of the first month output of newly hired workers is still far higher than the variance of the output of those same workers during their fourth month on the job.

The data described in figure 7.1 retains its same qualitative features if renormalized output is used as the measure of first month performance rather than the normalized output reported by the industrial engineering force.

Of course, even after performing this renormalization, it is still possible that the wide distribution of the output of newly hired workers relative to the distribution of their output after four months of employment is due to larger measurement errors in calculating the output of the newly hired workers than in calculating the output of experienced workers.[3]

It is also possible that the collapse in the distribution of the output of experienced workers relative to new hires is due to convergence to some "natural" level of performance.

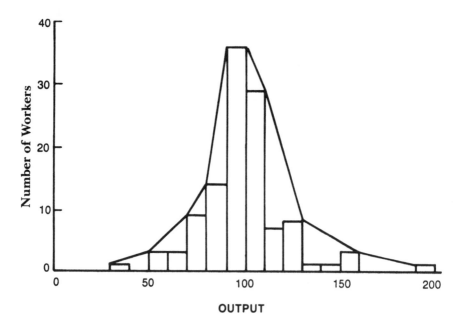

Figure 7.3 Output Distribution for Experienced Piece-rate Workers

The data presented in figure 7.3 casts doubt on these explanations. figure 7.3 uses English data from the Industrial Health Research Board to construct the distribution of the output of piece-rate workers on production jobs as a percentage of the mean output of workers on their jobs. This distribution is much wider than the normalized output of experienced workers at any of the plants we studied, a phenomenon that appears inconsistent with either the measurement error for newly hired workers or convergence hypotheses.

This English data, along with the data presented in figures 7.1 and 7.2, suggest that it is the movement of workers from individual to group wage incentives, coupled with the socialization process within the plants we studied, that caused the output of workers to converge to some (artifical?) standard.

Workers whose output is low are exhorted by their supervisors and threatened with dismissal unless they reach a satisfactory output level for their job. Those workers either quit or push themselves to reach the standards. The more able workers, on the other hand, have only trivial financial incentives to achieve high levels of output, and often their co-workers exhort them not to "break the rates." Workers correctly anticipate that exceptionally high performance by one worker will cause management to reevaluate the expected output for that worker's job. Hence, the most able workers are likely to work less hard than they would under piece-rate pay.

Because of pressures to shirk, the high ability workers may even work at lower levels than they would under an unmonitored wage system where there is no peer pressure not to "break the rates." In another location of this firm, in which there were no wage incentives and little use was made of individual output records, the top decile of workers on a job often performed at more than twice the expected output for their job, while the bottom decile was at 70–80% of expected output. Thus it would appear likely that at least some workers on group wage incentives might be working more slowly than the pace at which they would be most comfortable.

The firm is accustomed to having few high performance workers and so does not penalize a supervisor for not having any superstars among his workers. Consequently, supervisors concentrate on either pushing the low performance workers to work harder or to quit, rather than encouraging their most able workers to achieve the high levels of output of which they are capable.

Because group incentives do not reward high performance, and because promotional opportunities in this plant were nil, we would expect the most able workers to be more likely to quit to work for a firm in which their performance is rewarded either directly through higher pay or indirectly through more rapid promotions.

As we can see in figure 7.4b those workers whose output was highest (the 5th quintile) are the most likely to quit within their first 18 months on the job. These quits may be due to the attraction of better alternative opportunities at firms where individual output is rewarded, or alternatively, these quits could be due to discomfort on their present job caused by pressures from their co-workers not to achieve high levels of output.

The least able workers also have higher quit rates than the average workers. For those low ability workers, pressures by their supervisors to achieve an "acceptable" output level make their jobs unpleasant. They may also be pressured to quit by supervisors, whose own performance evaluations are strongly affected by low output workers. These effects seem strongest for newly hired workers, so the relatively high quit rates of low ability workers are most noticeable for quits within the first 6 months of employment. The factors inducing the high ability workers to quit seem to take longer to have their full effect. The impact of relatively high quit rates of the most able workers is thus most noticeable for quits within the first 18 months of employment. This general pattern that the best performing and the worst performing workers were most likely to quit was also present in the other plants we studied.

In figure 7.5 we see the total effect of the switch from individual to

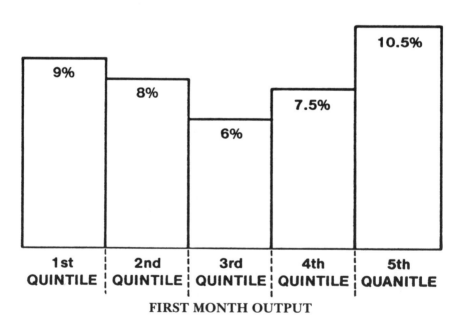

Figure 7.4a   Percentage of Each Quintile Who Left During Their First Six Months of Employment

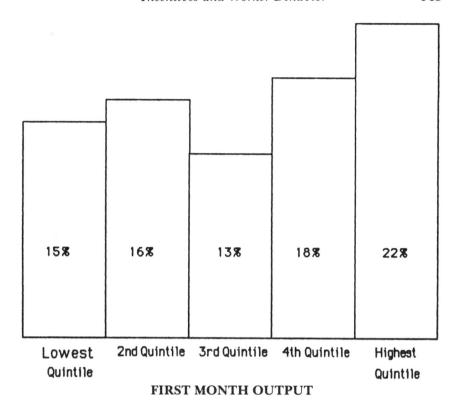

FIRST MONTH OUTPUT

Figure 7.4b   Percentage of Each Quintile Who Quit within Their First 18 Months of Employment

group incentives on the distribution of performance. The distribution has collapsed. By their sixth month on the job there are few workers performing either 10% above or below the median level. This collapse of the output distribution is due to attrition at both ends of the output distribution and to a slackening of the effort of the more able workers relative to the effort of the less able workers.

Most of the literature on wage incentives has focused on the effects of piece-rate type payment schemes on the behavior of workers. However, wages can be linked to aspects of behavior other than output to provide incentives in those areas.

3. *Seniority Based Wages*

As mentioned in section 1, a firm that wishes to discourage quits could pay wages that rise steeply with seniority. Employees of that firm are

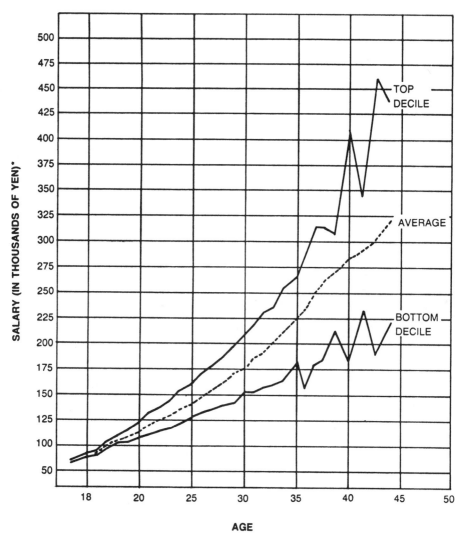

SALARY (IN THOUSANDS OF YEN)*

AGE

*To get salary in dollars, divide by 235

Figure 7.6a   **1981 Monthly Basic Salary Distribution in One Japanese Firm for White Collar, Male High School Graduates by Age**

146

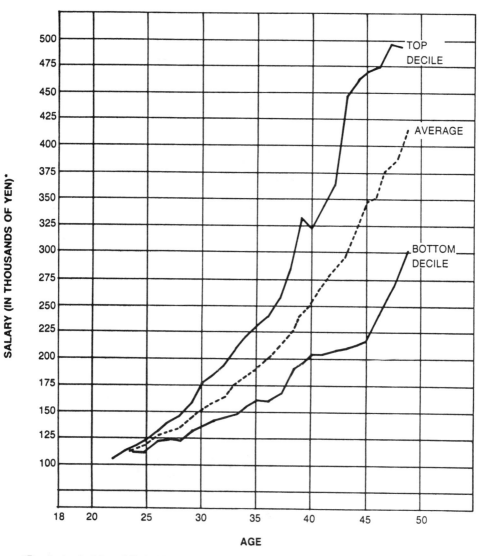

*To get salary in dollars, divide by 235

**Figure 7.6b   1981 Monthly Basic Salary Distribution in One
Japanese Firm for Male University Graduates by Age**

147

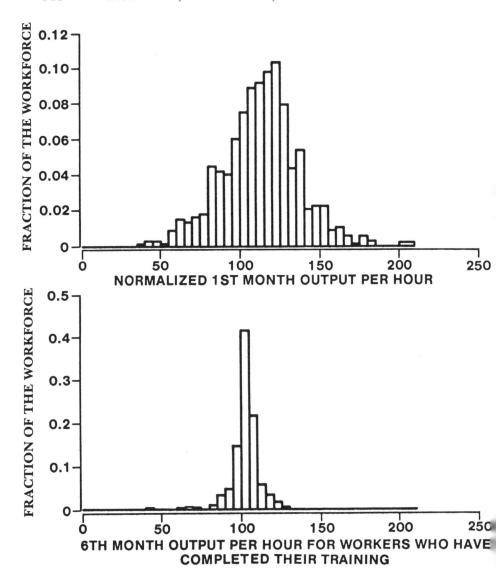

Figure 7.5   Combined Effect of Quits and Changes in Performance on the Productivity Distribution

paid less than the value of their contribution to output when they are young and more when they are old. Hence, after a few years of employment the worker has a strong incentive to stay with the firm. In effect, the employee has made a loan to the firm that is only fully repaid if the employee remains with the firm until retirement. The size of that loan initially increases as the worker stays longer with the firm. A firm

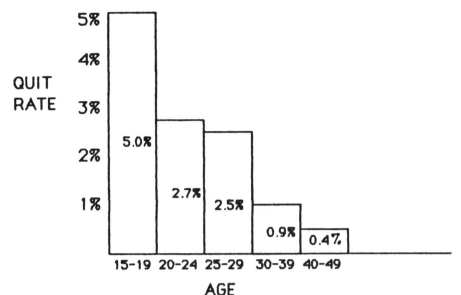

AGE

Figure 7.7   Male Workers at a Large Japanese Manufacturer

offering wages that rise steeply with seniority would expect to find that its more senior employees are much less likely to quit than are its new hires.

We shall test this hypothesis with data from a large Japanese electronics manufacturer. In that firm the average 50-year-old male high school graduate earns 4½ times as much as the average 20-year-old male high school graduate. Graphs of the average wage as a function of tenure are presented in figure 7.6.

In figure 7.7, we plot the quit rates for different age (tenure) groups. Quits fall rapidly with age and seniority. This decline in quits is much more dramatic than in the United States and is also much greater than in medium-sized or small Japanese firms. U.S. and smaller Japanese firms also offer wages that rise less rapidly with seniority than do the wages illustrated in figure 7.6. Hence, it would seem that the decline in quits is due to the incentive effect of the steep wage-tenure profiles, rather than to worker heterogeneity that would cause quitters to quit early and give a similarly rapid decline of quits with seniority.

By reducing quit rates, these steep wage-tenure profiles have indirect effects on other managerial decisions of the firm. In particular, we would expect firms that offer steeper wage-tenure profiles to invest more in recruiting and training their workers—since those workers will on average stay longer with the firm whose investments are more profitable. The evidence supports this hypothesis. Large Japanese firms that offer wages that rise rapidly with seniority also invest heavily in training and recruiting an elite work force.

Summary

1. When pay groups are large, a group wage incentive program does not adequately motivate the most able workers, nor does it dissuade those workers from quitting.
2. Linking pay to seniority lowers quit rates and increases the pay-off from expenditures on hiring and training workers.

Notes

1. Recorded output was normalized by the industrial engineers to adjust for differences in the expected output of experienced workers on the different jobs and for differences in the difficulty of learning the different jobs.

2. In the output equation that we estimated, the coefficient of the logarithm of required training on normalized output was 5.6. It is this distortion that we sought to eliminate by the renormalization described below. Workers were randomly assigned to jobs so we did not need to correct for job assignment effects.

3. For example, the industrial engineers may be underestimating the difference between the expected output of experienced and inexperienced workers on some jobs while overestimating this difference for other jobs—on the other hand, their assessments of the relative difficulty of different jobs for experienced workers could be accurate.

8

Why Some Long-Term Incentives Fail

Jude T. Rich and John A. Larson

SURVEY METHODOLOGY

In late 1982, McKinsey & Company, Inc. conducted a survey of the current and proposed long-term compensation practices at major U.S. corporations. Seventy-four companies in either the *Fortune 200* or the *Fortune 50* financials were contacted and interviewed over the telephone. (Approximately 20 additional companies were contacted, but declined to be interviewed.) An additional 16 companies, whose programs were adequately described in proxy statements, were also included in the analysis.

Typically, interviewees were the most senior compensation executive at each company, as listed in the *American Compensation Association* membership directory. All discussions were confidential and normally lasted from 20 minutes to half an hour. Topics included present long-term plans, results from these plans to date, and any recent (or anticipated future) changes to these plans. Specific attention was paid to the target-setting process and the communication of these targets to plan participants (for companies with performance-based plans). In selected cases, interviews were supplemented by proxy analyses.

The most significant development in executive compensation in the past 50 years has been the head-long rush of U.S. companies to install long-term, performance-based incentive plans. These plans typically establish earnings goals to be achieved over a four- to five-year period and reward top management with a cash or stock bonus for obtaining these goals. Long-term plans are often used in combination with the more traditional stock options. While very few corporations had such plans in 1970, nearly 40 percent of the *Fortune 500* companies have now adopted some form of performance-based, long-term incentive. Aggregate pay-

Reprinted by permission of the publisher from *Compensation Review, First Quarter 1984* © 1984. Periodicals Division of American Management Associations. All rights reserved.

The authors gratefully acknowledge the contributions made to this article by Nancy B. Larr and Suzanne F. Thomas of McKinsey and Company's Los Angeles office.

ments to executives from these plans could exceed $1.5 billion over the next ten years.

While American business leaders are unanimously in favor of rewarding sustained long-term performance, many senior managers and board members are questioning whether these plans are really worth what they are costing shareholders. For instance, at a recent meeting of the board of directors of a diversified, $3 billion company, the chairman of the compensation committee reviewed with some skepticism a proposal for installing a new long-term cash performance bonus. The committee chairman, who headed several other compensation committees, reported to the board that at least two companies that he knew about had decided to scrap their long-term plans and return to using stock options as their sole long-term incentive plan. He went on to tell the board that one company had paid out $3 million in long-term bonuses at a time when the company's stock price was at a ten-year low, thus causing considerable criticism of management by shareholders and the press. The second company gave up on long-term bonuses because of the difficulty of setting meaningful four-year performance targets in the current unstable economic times.

The difficulty of setting long-range performance targets was also cited by the chief executive officer of a *Fortune 200* manufacturing company as the reason he and his management had decided to redesign their long-term performance incentive. "When we first put in the plan four years ago, we were all charged up about the idea of receiving substantial rewards for producing results five years in the future. But the introduction of a new product by a tough competitor required huge increases in advertising, sales, and research expenditures (during the third year of the plan). These costs, combined with foreign currency losses, made the chances of any payout at the end of the five years very unlikely. I still ike the idea of a long-term incentive plan, but we clearly need to make some changes."

These comments and similar ones from top management and board members led the authors to undertake an analysis of the long-term incentive practices in major U.S. companies. This research began with an analysis of the actual performance of those companies with long-term performance bonuses, compared with the performance of those using only stock options or other stock-based plans. This analysis was supplemented by interviews with managers responsible for administering the long-term incentive plans in 90 companies in either the *Fortune 200* industrials or the *Fortune 50* financials. About one-half of these companies had stock options only, and one-half had performance-based plans.

The conclusions of this research, described further later on, were as follows:

1. To date, returns to shareholders of companies with long-term cash performance incentives do not differ significantly from those companies with only stock-based incentive plans (that is, stock options, restricted stock, stock appreciation rights).

2. Choosing the wrong measures of performance and failure to set targets properly are the two greatest shortcomings of these plans.

3. Companies with long-term performance incentives or companies considering the implementation of a new program can increase their chances of success by choosing the right performance measures and goal-setting process.

Higher Pay Without Higher Performance

On average, shareholders of the 46 survey companies with long-term performance incentives received a return on their investment of about 6 percent per year from 1977 to 1982. That is, the stock price appreciation and dividends provided a 6 percent annual return on the initial purchase price of the stock. Ironically, shareholders in companies without long-term incentives averaged a 7.8 percent return. This finding is disappointing, since companies will spend an estimated $400 million on these incentive plans over the next 5 years.

Clearly, however, this analysis does not prove conclusively that long-term performance incentives have failed to improve company performance. Many of these plans have not been in place long enough to produce results. In fact, the threats these companies were facing at the beginning of the period may very well have resulted in poorer performance had they *not* implemented the performance incentive. On the other hand, we cannot conclude that performance among companies with long-term performance-based incentives was significantly different from performance in those without such plans.

Performance Measures and Goals

Our discussions with survey respondents indicate that a number of factors may account for the failure of long-term performance incentives to produce greater returns to shareholders. For one thing, these long-term incentives typically cover only the topmost executives. Surveys show that under 25 percent of the total management team typically participates in such plans. Another reason offered is that these plans pay out at the end of a four- to five-year period, but larger annual bonuses offer opportunities for substantial rewards in the near term, thus motivating managers to pay more attention to making annual performance goals as opposed to long-term goals. As one chief executive put it: "To paraphrase Omar Khayyam, most of my guys believe in taking the cash and letting the credit go."

While these and other reasons were offered as an explanation of the disappointing results of long-term performance incentives, two reasons stood out from the rest: selection of the wrong performance measures and improper goal setting.

Measures

More than 85 percent of the companies with long-term performance plans used earnings-per-share growth, either alone or in combination with some other measure, as the key determinant in paying out awards under their plans (see Figure 8.1). The assumption underlining the use of earnings per share (EPS) as the primary performance measure under these plans is that EPS increases will drive up stock price. But recent research shows that EPS does not correlate with stock price performance for most companies. This will not be a surprising conclusion to students of modern financial theory; such theory holds that the price of a share of stock is equal to the present value of the expected future cash flows (mainly dividends) that the stock provides the investor. This present value is sometimes referred to as "economic value." Shareholder wealth in the form of stock price appreciation is created when a company's economic value is increased, not its EPS. This occurs when a company earns more on its investment than the cost of that investment. Using

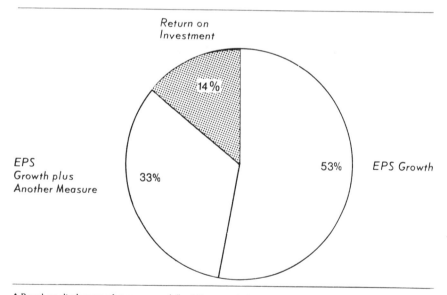

* Based on disclosures of measure used (by 37 companies).

Figure 8.1   Plan Performance Measures*

financial terms, this means that a company's return on equity exceeds its cost of equity (that is, the rate at which investors discount the stock's expected future cash flows).

During the comparatively stable environment of the 1960s and early 1970s, discount rates were relatively low and constant. During this period of stable discount rates, higher levels of EPS reflected increases in economic value (since rising EPS implied an increase in the corporate return on equity). The high correlation between EPS and share price deteriorated dramatically after 1972, when hyperinflation resulted in cost of equity capital increasing at a faster rate than earnings did. The increase in cost of equity offset the effect of rising EPS and resulted in a deterioration in the correlation between EPS and economic value and share price (see Figure 8.2). (In a previous article, Mr. Rich estimated that the cost of equity for the *Standard and Poor's 400* companies increased from slightly less than 10 percent in 1972 to nearly 19 percent in 1981. See the article, "Pay Executives to Create Wealth," *CEO Magazine,* Autumn 1982.)

The point is that EPS growth was never a valid measure of corporate performance. Hence, one possible reason for the failure of long-term incentives to produce shareholder gains greater than those in companies without such plans is that EPS growth, rather than economic value creation, has been used as the performance measure for the majority of these plans.

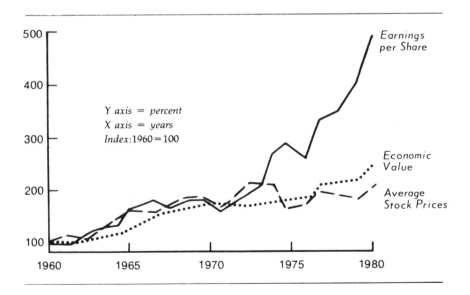

Figure 8.2   S & P 400 Companies

Target Setting

Our survey also indicates that the methods used to establish targets and communicate targets to plan participants reduce the effectiveness of long-term performance incentives (see Table 8.1). More than two-thirds of the companies surveyed felt that they have serious problems in deciding on the proper performance targets. Survey respondents raised questions about their ability to set sound long-term financial targets, given the status of their long-range planning efforts and the general uncertain economic conditions.

The survey produced another surprise. Only about one-half of the companies relate their performance target directly to company financial forecasts. Moreover, only a handful had been able to link the actions called for in their strategic plan (that is, actions aimed at gaining and sustaining an advantage over competitors) with their financial forecasts. In fact, nearly 20 percent of the survey respondents had no idea how targets were established. Typical comments were: "Our EPS target is set by the CEO and is based on his philosophy . . . there is no formula or rationale; we use a seat-of-the-pants approach to target setting." One manager said, "The plan provides little motivational value because the objectives are set arbitrarily by senior management." While the senior executives of some of these companies may have established the targets on the basis of sound analysis, the rationale behind the targets was clearly not communicated to plan participants.

Another problem was observed in the target-setting process. Only about one-half of the companies made any attempt to relate their incentive plan's targets to results obtained at other companies in their industry. This is a particular concern in companies buffeted by outside factors beyond the management group's control (for example, the impact on weapon manufacture of a government decision to cancel a planned new missile program). Such factors will have a comparable impact on many companies within an industry category. Without an external check, the credibility of the target in the eyes of line managers may be impaired, thus reducing the motivational value of the plan. The lack of such a check might also make the plan less acceptable to members

Table 8.1   Target-Setting Process

Problem	Percentage of companies
1. Unsure of proper performance measures.	68%
2. Targets based on long-term financial or strategic plan.	53
3. No provision for adjusting targets.	47
4. No comparison of competitors' performance in setting targets.	44

of the board's compensation committee, because large payouts could be made for results below industry levels.

Increasing Chances for Success

To see whether better designed long-term incentives performed better for shareholders, we identified six companies with plans that measured return on equity as well as growth (the key components of economic value) and used a systematic approach to setting and communicating plan targets. We found that these companies, unlike other companies using performance-based plans, actually did produce a return to shareholders well in excess of the 10 percent average obtained by the 90-company sample. In fact, the average return to shareholders among these companies was over 12 percent.

The results of our research suggest that these successful long-term incentive plans typically:

1. Use measures of performance that correlate with shareholder wealth creation (that is, return on equity and growth), not EPS growth.

2. Establish valid target levels and communicate them clearly to participants.

3. Provide for target adjustment under certain, well-defined circumstances. Each of these points deserves some elaboration.

Performance Measures

As noted earlier, EPS does not correlate with stock price appreciation, but economic value does. As Figure 8.3 shows, economic value is a function of four factors: the firm's return on equity, its cost of equity, the rate of equity growth and the duration over which spread and equity growth are maintained. Economic value is created when "spread" (the difference between the firm's return on equity (ROE) and its cost of equity) is positive. As long as spread is positive, economic value rises with growth in the equity base. The longer the duration over which positive spreads and equity growth can be maintained, the greater the increase in economic value.

Clearly, there are a number of ways to incorporate the determinants of economic value (that is, spread and equity growth) into a long-term incentive plan. One is simply to set targets for ROE and equity growth (or return on asset and asset, or imported equity, growth for a division). Another is to set discounted cash flow targets.

It should be noted that targets for spread may not mean positive spread. Take the example of Chrysler Corporation: It would not have been realistic during the early 1980's to expect a company in its position to generate ROE in excess of its cost of equity. For companies in such a turnaround mode, a reduction in negative spread may be a more

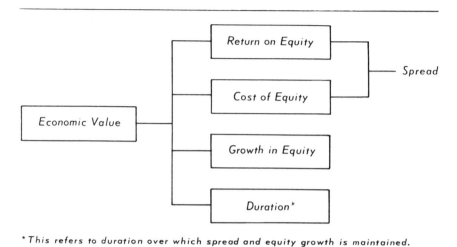

*This refers to duration over which spread and equity growth is maintained.

Figure 8.3   The Components of Economic Value

realistic target for management compensation. Reducing negative spread should result in wealth creation for shareholders. In fact, Chrysler's common stock performance in 1982 led the New York Stock Exchange with an increase of nearly 500 percent. Thus Chrysler shareholders benefited enormously from the company's performance improvement. The point is that the emphasis should be on increasing the differential between what a company earns on its equity and its cost of equity, either by creating a larger positive spread or by reducing negative spreads.

Establish Target Levels

Once an appropriate performance measure has been selected, the next step is to set a specific target level for a given award cycle. Careful target setting is essential to the success of a long-term incentive plan. Three guidelines on target setting emerged from our survey:

1. *Set the target to be consistent with the financial projections in the company's long-term plan.* Relating the target to the corporate plan will increase its validity in the eyes of participating managers and enhance its motivational value. Indeed, as one chief executive put it, "The greatest value that we've gotten out of our plan is to force us to think through what our strategy must be in order to attain our plan objectives. To set our targets, we have to do a better job of developing strategies and projecting financial results from those strategies."

2. *Determine whether the return to shareholders that is likely to result from target achievement is acceptable.* The economic value model or discounted cash flows can be used to project the stock price increase that will result from attaining certain levels of spread and equity growth or cash flow. Next, shareholder gains from the rising stock price can be compared with the total payout to executives that will be made if targets are attained. In this way, the percentage of shareholder gain to be shared with executives at each performance level can be estimated. Clearly, no model can accurately predict stock prices, but this approach provides a test against the company's internal plan and a more direct comparison of the executive gains with shareholder gains than simply dividing potential award payouts by planned earnings—the approach now used by many companies.

3. *Compare proposed performance targets with most comparable competitors.* Some companies with long-term incentives have found it useful to select a group of 10 to 20 comparable "peer companies" for target comparison purposes. This peer group can be used in one of two ways. First, the recent performance of the competitors can be used as one benchmark in setting the target, based on the two factors mentioned earlier (that is, the company's financial forecast and the return to shareholders compared with executive awards). For example, consider a company that had been earning a 5 percent positive spread and had a corporate forecast of 3 percent spread. Should the board's compensation committee adopt this 3 percent spread for the next performance award cycle, or should it insist that awards would be fully paid out only if the previous 5 percent spread is attained? Use of a competitive peer group can help resolve this issue. If committee members see that the performance of these peer companies is likely to be under 3 percent because of industrywide conditions, they might be more willing to adopt the lower spread target. In fact, they would realize that setting the target at unrealistically high levels would destroy the plan's motivational value.

The second approach under guideline 3 is to measure return and growth relative to these peer companies, as opposed to setting an absolute target. For example, one company's long-term performance plan provides that the full bonus payment to executives will be made only if the company's growth (and return) falls between the 40th and 60th percentile of its peer group. Performance above and below that level increases or decreases executive rewards under the program. Other companies have used a combination of an absolute target and a peer comparison. One oil company sets a return on equity threshold above which some award will be paid out. The actual extent of that award depends on the company's performance against a group of 16 comparable petroleum companies.

Constructing the group of peer companies for comparison is an easier task in such relatively homogeneous industries as utilities, petroleum, and insurance. In most diversified companies, developing a list of comparable companies is more difficult. In fact, some very diversified companies have chosen to compare themselves to the *Standard and Poor's 400*.

Provide for Target Adjustments

To keep executives motivated, performance targets should be reevaluated periodically. In the rapidly changing environment of the 1980s, expected performance can change radically in just a few months. For example, in late 1981 one respected source of earnings forecasts, *Value Line*, projected an average ROE for the 12 largest oil companies of 19.4 percent for the period 1981 through 1984. Less than a year later, projected ROE for the same companies for the same time period had been revised to 15.1 percent. Clearly, if an individual oil company had established an ROE target in 1981 based largely on expected competitive performance, the company would have run the risk that changing conditions would have resulted in low or no bonus payouts.

We concluded that at least five conditions should trigger a review, and possible adjustment of performance targets:

1. *Changes in the corporation's cost of equity.* If an ROE target rather than a spread target is set, this adjustment would be necessary in order to assure that the executive's rewards will correlate with economic value changes. Assume, for example, that a company sets an average ROE target of 15 percent over a four-year period and projects cost of equity at 12 percent. An increase in the cost of equity to 15 percent (driven by inflation) would eliminate the positive spread. Under these conditions, a review of the target would be appropriate.

2. *Changes in dividend policy.* Equity growth is very directly affected by a change in dividend payout ratio. In addition, an indirect effect on ROE is likely. One company, for example, had been paying out about 70 percent of its aftertax earnings in dividends. A new senior management team believed that prior management had been "milking" away too much of the profits. Thus the dividend policy was reduced to a 35 percent payout ratio over a four-year period. This resulted in a doubling of the forecast equity growth with no increase in earnings beyond forecast levels.

3. *Changes in the company's capital structure.* Major alterations in capital structure such as those brought about by a merger or acquisition will have a significant impact on the attainability of a company's spread and equity growth targets.

4. *Changes in tax or accounting methods.* Accounting changes can significantly affect the company's performance relative to its predetermined

targets. For example, it is estimated that if General Motors had adopted FIFO (first in, first out) inventory evaluation method in 1981, reported income for that year would have risen by more than 40 percent.

5. *Major changes in the company or industry environment that would render targets unrealistically high or low.* If performance is measured against a planned earnings target rather than against results of other companies, provision should be made for adjusting the target. However, such adjustments should be made only under unusual circumstances. For example, performance targets based on an assumed crude oil price of $11 per barrel and controls on domestic pricing may be totally inappropriate in a decontrolled pricing environment with oil selling for $33 per barrel. Careful adjustment of performance targets is clearly in order when industry conditions change this dramatically. Such adjustments may be necessary to protect shareholders against windfall payouts or to preserve the plan's motivational value if targets become totally unattainable as a result of conditions clearly beyond management's control.

While providing for target adjustments is essential, too frequent target modification tends to confuse plan participants and detract from the validity of the target-setting process. Similarly, maintaining an existing target long after it seems to be appropriate can act as a demotivating force. Target reexamination at specific points in the first half of a long-term incentive award (for example, at the end of the first or second year of a four-year cycle) based on changes in the environment of costs of equity should be sufficient. Adjustments during the second half of the cycle should be made only under the most unusual circumstances. Of course, adjustments for changes in accounting policies, capital structure, or dividend payout changes could be made at any point during an award cycle.

Communicate Targets

Our survey results show that many companies fail to communicate to participants how the performance targets were developed and how awards are calculated. Approximately 20 percent of the survey respondents did not know how performance targets were determined. Little motivation can develop under such circumstances.

Companies with effective plans have learned the value of educating plan participants on the nature of the measures selected and the level of performance demanded. Effective communications typically include an audiovisual presentation by a senior executive when the plan is introduced, a written description of the plan and how the targets are set, and one-to-one counseling of participants on plan mechanics by someone in the company's personnel department.

In addition to assuring that participants understand targets, greater motivation will result if companies let people know where they stand during the course of a four- to five-year award period. For example, the chief executive officer of one company with a long-term performance incentive issues a memorandum each quarter indicating what percentage of bonus awards would be earned out if current performance continued.

Summary

Our survey results suggest that long-term performance plans may not be as effective as they could be in improving company performance. This is not too surprising in view of the fact that these plans are quite recent additions to the executive pay program. Companies adopting performance plans have been "feeling their way" and making frequent changes to improve their plans. To improve plan effectiveness, we have suggested that the present emphasis on EPS as a performance measure be replaced with measures of economic value creation. We have also noted that more care should be taken in setting and communicating target levels.

We are convinced that the benefits to shareholders of a well-run plan can prove to be significant. To illustrate this point, we compared the payouts to executives with shareholder gains for one of the six companies that was identified earlier as having a well-designed plan. Since plan inception five years ago, total executive awards have amounted to $8.5 million. During the same time frame, the increase in the company's market value has been nearly $3.5 billion. Clearly, other factors aside from the compensation system contributed to this outstanding performance. However, senior executives at this company attribute a major role in achieving these results to the ability of their incentive plans to motivate managers and focus their attention on "what counts."

Part III

PRACTICAL DESIGN ISSUES

9

Incentive Compensation: Incentive Design and Management Implications

Sarah J. Armstrong

Employee pay is much more than a substantial cost of doing business, a fair exchange for workers' time and effort, and a means to attract and hold needed employees. Properly designed and managed, employee pay is a vehicle for management communication, an inducement to behavior change, and reinforcement and reward for accomplishment of desired results. For pay systems to operate effectively in these ways, a number of conditions must be present: the organization must have a clearly articulated strategy; the design of the pay system must be consistent with and support that strategy; and management must have the courage to use the pay system in a consistent way to reward results and to withhold reward for absence of results.

Incentive compensation is particularly suitable for communicating and reinforcing management strategy. While base pay and benefits are the conditions and reward for *membership* in the organization, an incentive pay element identifies the *behaviors and results* that management wants. If the incentive plan is properly designed, the demonstrating of those behaviors and accomplishment of those results will, in fact, drive forward the organization's strategy. Thus, the incentive plan communicates the actions needed from individuals and groups of employees at all levels, and then rewards those specific contributions and outcomes that will fulfill the organization's strategic objectives. Incentive compensation also provides a degree of flexibility that cannot be achieved with traditional base pay systems. It has the potential for sending various messages to various groups of employees at various times. It can be modified promptly in concert with changes of organizational direction or strategy. And it enables management to flex costs in direct relation to productivity or profitability.

This chapter will provide, from ITT's experience, an illustration of different approaches to employee pay that respond to changes in corporate strategy under different managements and market conditions. It will also describe the fundamental issues in sound incentive program design, and set forth some management prerequisites for the operation of successful incentive pay systems.

We begin with the ITT of the early 1960s to the late 1970s—Harold Geneen's ITT. This period was characterized by frequent acquisitions, rapid growth, and strong corporate and financial staffs charged with making sense of and controlling increasingly diverse field operations. The corporate strategy could be summarized as growth and diversification to minimize geographic and cyclical risk consistent with acceptable return on investment.

The pay system objectives of this period grew out of these characteristics and strategy and had to be:

- amenable to centralized administration,
- appropriate to diverse businesses without the need for customized design or application,
- able to be compared, contrasted, and summarized across total ITT.

Also affecting the pay system of this time were several prevailing assumptions about employees and their roles. To some extent, these may have been particular to ITT management, but in general they conformed to the prevalent American business culture of the period. These assumptions may be summarized as follows:

- Only a select few manage and control the business.
- These few—senior line executives—are responsible for results.
- This is the group that should have a portion of pay at risk.
- Other employees don't have a significant or visible impact on results.
- Lower paid employees can't afford variable pay. They need a fully competitive and consistent wage or salary to meet their personal needs.

ITT's pay program during this period reliably reflected these objectives and assumptions. The program emphasized a soundly designed base wage and salary system, with pay levels fully competitive with other major multi-national corporations. Incentives were limited to senior executives and sales where a commission or incentive bonus was a predominant competitive practice. Other employees did not participate in variable compensation. They had no gainsharing because they did not control results, and no loss-sharing because they could not afford significant variations in take-home pay.

From the late 1970s through today, ITT and its business environment have changed markedly from the earlier period. Acquisitions have been fewer and smaller. Asset deployment activity has focused instead on divestiture, on trimming those businesses and product lines that do not "fit" the newly streamlined ITT. Diversity has been contained in a management structure featuring four management companies with product line or process congruence. Administration has decentralized, focusing more on individual businesses or management companies, and less on the Corporation as a whole. This new strategy of contained diversity and leadership in selected product lines and services brought with it new objectives for ITT's pay programs. Centralized administration and corporate-wide reporting and comparability became less important. Instead, tailored approaches to pay system design were needed to enable each business to compete most effectively in its own industry and labor market. A strong linkage between each reward system and local business strategy was both possible and necessary.

Employee values and employer attitudes have also changed in recent years. Businesses increasingly recognize that the intelligence and personal effort of each employee are needed if the business is to compete successfully in a worldwide market. Each job is best known and understood by the person performing it, and that person is best positioned to identify improvements.

External events have also brought pay changes in the labor market. Variable compensation in several forms has become familiar at all levels of the work force. Short work weeks, job-sharing, temporary and permanent layoffs, wage cuts, plant relocations to compete with offshore manufacturing, elimination of layers of management, salary freezes, prolonged intervals between salary reviews, two-tier wage structures, and other cost-saving approaches have become commonplace as employers have intentionally varied compensation costs with profitability and productivity, paying less attention to competitive pay practices. Finally, labor agreements and minimum wage laws have continued to escalate wages of lower paid workers, while management restructuring and excess supply have slowed the growth of middle management salaries. The average wage and real income of lower paid workers has thus increased as a percentage of average management pay. The next logical step is more use of intentional forms of individualized variable compensation at all levels of the workforce.

ITT's current and developing pay programs reflect these changes in strategy, pay objectives, and employee values. Competitive base wages and salaries are now grounded on a flexible definition of "competitive." The industry in which the business unit participates, local labor market conditions, and local competitive needs determine local policy for setting base pay levels. Incentive and gainsharing systems are now seen as appropriate methods to motivate, reinforce, and reward desired employee contributions at all levels of the workforce. Such variable compensation involves sharing in both gains and losses, and results in compensation costs that vary directly with productivity and profitability.

Sales compensation has become more dynamic, rewarding both group and individual achievement, and changes to respond to market conditions and sales strategies. Margin contribution, new product introduction, national account management, and other factors are rewarded instead of or in addition to revenue. In short, in the past 25 years ITT has experienced two very different periods of corporate strategy, economic environment, and employee roles. As we have seen, two different approaches to employee pay have resulted. Now that ITT is using variable compensation below the executive level, standards have been developed for the design and administration of middle management and other incentive plans. These standards are not universal. That is, the specific decisions ITT has made with respect to the various design issues are not necessarily the ones that would be made by another organization. However, the design issues ITT has addressed are generic ones that must be addressed and resolved in any well thought out approach to incentives or variable compensation. The following sections will outline each of these key design issues and provide alternative approaches.

Objectives

A fundamental issue of incentive plan design is the objective or purpose of the plan. There are two principal possibilities, and subsequent design decisions will be in large part determined by which objective is chosen. The first objective is: *To offer a competitive total compensation package that includes a bonus or incentive element.* The industry in which you operate, or the organization itself, may have a tradition of paying a lump-sum bonus at the end of the calendar or fiscal year. If employees have come to expect a portion of their annual compensation to be paid in this way, or if the job is at a level where a year-end bonus is generally expected, you may choose to follow suit primarily to be competitive in the manner as well as level of the total compensation package. In this case you may be guided by industry practices regarding the amount or percentage of total cash compensation paid in the bonus portion. Two approaches to defining bonus levels are: (1) Competitive bonus, salary discounting method: Competitive Total Compensation less Competitive Bonus equals appropriate Base Salary; (2) Current salaries as a beginning point: Competitive Total Compensation less Current Average Base Salary equals appropriate Bonus. In practice, a combination of these methods is usually used when the principal objective is to offer a total compensation package that meets competitive or employee expectations both in structure and amount.

The second potential objective of incentive compensation is: *To manage employee behavior.* This objective needs further definition. To what end? What behaviors do we want? The following are some possibilities:

- Maximization of short term profitability.
- Steady growth in revenue and profitability.
- Increased market share.
- Consistent high levels of quality and customer service.
- Optimization of financial performance relative to other companies in the industry.
- Consistent long-term investment in research and development.
- Plant and people maintenance.

The specific objective of an incentive plan will strongly influence each of the design elements discussed below. Participation, performance criteria, and incentive fund formulae, in particular, should each be tailored to fit the plan's objective.

At ITT, our objective for incentive plans below the executive level is principally *to manage managerial behavior.* The specific goals of that behavior vary from business to business, and always focus on the key activities for which that group of managers are responsible.

Participation

Once the objective has been determined, the next key decision is: Who should participate in the plan? This question is a good one for illustrating the importance of the objective in all subsequent plan design decisions. If, for example, the objective is a competitive compensation package, then competitive industry practice will largely determine participation. Your plan will include those jobs and those levels of employees who typically receive bonus payments in other companies with whom you and your employees identify. If, on the other hand, your objective is to encourage specific employee behaviors, then participation will be determined by who must exhibit—or who primarily influences—those behaviors.

The relationship between design decisions and the plan's purpose is further illustrated by the third key design element.

Performance Criteria

In a behavior management plan, this is the most important element of plan design. The selected performance measurement will be the one that indicates whether the desired behavior has occurred. The following list of potential performance criteria matches the behavioral objectives listed above:

- Current year net income.
- Current year revenue and net income as compared to prior year, or to a rolling multiyear base period.
- Current year market share, absolutely or compared to prior year, or to a rolling base period.
- Scrap, rework, and return rates.
- Revenue growth, market share, earnings per share, or return on total capital as compared to a consistently defined group of industry participants.
- R&D investment as a percent of revenues.
- Safety record, employee turnover, etc.

Clearly, there are many other possibilities. The significant point is that *the performance criteria selected must indicate the presence or results of the desired behaviors and must be within the control or significant influence of the participants*. The plan's objectives, participants, and measurement criteria are thus integrally related. Appropriate participants are those who impact the criteria; appropriate criteria are those that can be controlled or significantly influenced by the participants.

In a plan designed principally to yield competitive compensation, the two most significantly related elements are Participation and Incentive Fund Formula. The participant group is that for which a competitive compensation package includes a bonus, and the formula must yield a bonus or total compensation amount that meets the desired competitive level.

In the ITT plans, the principal objective is to optimize current year profitability at each business and facility. The group of people who control or significantly influence most decisions that contribute to profitability is the management team of that facility. ITT's incentive plans thus include primarily management personnel, and select current year financial measurement criteria appropriate to each individual business or facility: net income (for a small business unit), expense control (for a manufacturing facility), gross operating profit.

Incentive Fund Formula

The two key aspects of an incentive fund formula are *how the fund is generated* and the *risk/reward orientation*. The fund may be generated directly from the performance criteria, e.g. a percentage of net income, costs saved. Or the fund may be created from a matrix or table relating measures of the performance criteria to specific funding levels or to percentages of participants' salaries.

Examples:
(1) Net income in excess of budget will be allocated as follows: 1/3 to incentive fund and 2/3 to the company.

(2) Cost savings (at budgeted production volume or after adjustment for higher-than-budgeted production) will be allocated 50% to the incentive fund and 50% to the company.

(3) Performance Criteria   Incentive Fund

Performance Criteria	Incentive Fund
Level A	$ 10,000
Level B	25,000
Level C	50,000
Level D	100,000

(4) Performance Criteria   Incentive Fund

Performance Criteria	Incentive Fund
100% of net income budget	3% of participants' base salaries.
105% of net income budget	8% of participants' base salaries.
110% of net income budget	15% of participants' base salaries.
120% of net income budget	25% of participants' base salaries.

The principal considerations in fund generation are the financial value of increased performance and the amount of money needed to create an adequate (i.e. competitive or motivating) incentive fund. Where there is a direct relationship between these two values, direct funding formulae (such as examples 1 and 2) are usually chosen. Where there is no direct relationship between these two values, or where the needed fund is a very high or very low proportion of the value of increased performance, indirect funding such as the table (3) or percent of salary (4) methods are usually chosen.

Concerning the risk/reward orientation, the question, simply put, is how high or low can the fund go? If there is a target funding level (x percent of net income or salaries at 100% budget, for example), how much should the fund vary from this target? With a high risk/reward orientation, the fund may drop to 0 at low levels of performance and reach 200% or more of the target fund at very high levels of performance. The same fund with a low risk/reward orientation may vary only from 75% to 125%. A plan designed principally to deliver a competitive total compensation package will typically have a lower risk/reward orientation, as wide swings in year-to-year payments would vary from competitive practice and introduce undesired instability in the employees' compensation package. A behavior-oriented plan, on the other hand, must have a higher risk/reward orientation in order to communicate and reinforce the desired behaviors and results. Formulae of these plans frequently vary the fund from 50% to 150% of target, or more.

Distribution of Earned Incentives

When year-end results have been measured against the plan's performance criteria, and an incentive fund created by application of the plan's incentive formula, how is the resulting fund distributed to individual participants? Again, there are essentially two approaches: each participant's share may be directly related to his or her job, without an independent assessment of the individual's contribution; or the plan may include an additional mechanism for evaluation of individual performance.

Each approach provides a number of possible methods of arriving at the individual's award. In the first approach, the fund may be divided:

- equally among participants,
- into equal shares or a target value for the participant's job or grade level,
- equally as a percentage of participants' base salaries.

In the last two methods, a senior level or highly paid individual will receive more incentive pay than a lower level or lower paid employee, but *these distinctions will be based on the individual's job, not on differences in individual performance.*

Methods of evaluating and recognizing individual performance and contribution also offer several variations. Individuals (or subgroups) may be ranked from highest to lowest; individual contribution may be rated on a normative scale; performance factors and standards may be provided to guide managerial judgment; individual performance objectives consistent with overall business objectives may be created at the beginning of the plan period and performance against them assessed; or a discretionary allocation may be made.

There are two distinct schools of thought on the value and utility of individual performance evaluation for incentive payments. One, perhaps the more traditional, holds that there are clear differences in individual performance and in contribution to the overall group or business unit performance, and that these differences should be recognized through differences in incentive award. Whatever means of evaluation are used—from purely subjective judgment to a predefined process of management by objectives—it is critical to individual motivation for these differences in individual contribution to be recognized. The other, perhaps newer school, holds that individual performance and reward distinctions are counterproductive. Business performance depends on effective teamwork, on efficient collaboration among groups of people and functional areas, not on individual stars. Performance recognition, therefore, should go to the group or team as a whole, without individual distinctions. Lesser contributors will then be subject to pressure from the rest of the group to improve their contribution.

Most ITT plans, being behavior oriented, have a fairly high risk/reward orientation; and all currently provide some mechanism for evaluation of individual contribution. The specific methods of evaluation vary among all the previously mentioned alternatives.

Communications

Essential to a behavior-oriented plan is thorough communication of plan objectives, performance criteria, and measurement methods *at the beginning of the plan period.* Only if these elements are communicated in the beginning will participants have an informed opportunity to optimize their influence on plan performance criteria and performance results. The motivational value of the plan—the key objective of this type of plan—is blunted or even negated if this communication does not take place in an open and timely manner. Absent, late, or misleading communication will frequently have a *demotivating* effect, as participants cannot knowingly control or influence plan results.

Interim Feedback on Performance

Closely allied with good initial communication is interim performance feedback. This simply means providing feedback on plan-to-date results periodically throughout the year. This is more difficult—and more important—than it sounds. It is difficult because performance on selected financial or nonfinancial criteria may not be a continuous curve throughout the year. Key decisions taken at year end, or other singular events, may have a disproportionate effect on results. Data, especially external industry comparative data, may not be available throughout the period. Business cycles may cause monthly or quarterly fluctuations in results, and external events may have unplanned and inconsistent effects. For all these reasons, interim communication of meaningful performance information may be difficult. It is, however, extremely important. If initial communication of plan criteria and design are essential to motivating appropriate behavior, then interim feedback is essential to inform participants of whether their chosen behaviors and efforts are working. If not, participants must know this as soon as possible so that new strategies and behaviors can be employed. Only in this way can participants have the opportunity to adjust their activities throughout the year in an attempt to continually improve on current performance and results.

In the ITT plans, announcement of all incentive plans is made at the beginning of the plan year, with sufficient information provided for each participant to estimate his/her own incentive payment under various operating conditions. Our most effective plans also use interim feedback on a monthly or quarterly basis.

At the beginning of this chapter, several conditions were enumerated that are essential if incentive systems are to deliver their promised benefits:

- the organization must have a clearly articulated strategy;

- the design of the pay system must be consistent with and support that strategy;
- management must have the courage to use the pay system in a consistent way to reward results and withhold reward for absence of results.

In addition to requiring good design and courage, variable compensation plans have further implications for management practices that must be understood at the outset. These involve sharing of information, consistent financial treatment, participative decision-making, and decentralization of control.

For an incentive plan to meet the standards of communication and feedback outlined above, the financial data on which performance will be measured must be shared with plan participants. This means the data must be available, current, accurate, and relevant to the plan, and that *management must be willing to reveal and discuss it with plan participants.* Management must also be willing to jointly consider changes in strategy or methods that may improve results. Further, the financial bases of the plan must be clear, fair, and free from inconsistent or irrelevant adjustments beyond the control of the participants. They must also be open to adjustment to reflect changes in product, production methods, or materials. Since participation in a behavior-based incentive plan implies significant influence on results, employee input must be encouraged, valued, and used. Participants must have the latitude to make changes in strategy or methods on the basis of interim performance information.

Finally, behavior-based incentives must be locally designed and managed. Performance criteria and incentive formulae must be based on specific business unit strategies and local plan participation. Communication and interim feedback must be based on local goals and results. The vital information is available only at the source, and cannot be anticipated or second-guessed by a distant corporate entity. This has powerful implications for the management and control structure of the company, and may explain why many organizations have, until recently, resisted widespread implementation of behavior-based incentives.

Many companies are concluding, like ITT, that the time has come for more informed employees, wider participation in decision-making, and decentralized control. Only in this environment can the benefits of behavior-based incentives be realized. Some of these benefits are illustrated in the following quotation from the general manager of an ITT manufacturing facility that implemented a group incentive plan for its middle management team.

> Results exceeded both budget and past performance, collectively, of the group of middle managers. The effect of this incentive plan was visible when the Industrial Relations Manager inquired aggressively and knowledgably into production scrap rates and the Materials Manager inquired

about controlling relocation costs. . . . Additionally, as a group it was easier for me to effectively focus their attention in weekly meetings on our collective financial progress. Reductions and control of salaried labor (including overtime costs) were made with significantly less parochial, defensive actions on their part, and there were numerous instances of planning to do the job with less resources.

10

Incentive Compensation: Practical Design from a Theory Point of View

Bengt Holmstrom

It is rare that economic theorists (at least micro theorists) become excited about the same subject at the same time as "practitioners." It could be a happy coincidence, but the fact is that incentive issues are presently high on the agenda both in economic theory and in practice. I have listened with interest to testimony that new incentive designs are being tried out in practice with apparent success. The plans reflect some of the insights that analytical work has been able to identify, but others are missing. In this commentary I will briefly discuss aspects of practical design from the viewpoint of theory, in the hope of raising some questions for compensation and human resources practitioners to think about in their future pursuit of improved incentive plans.

Incentive Contracts—What For?

For analytical purposes, it is essential to begin by asking why incentive schemes are necessary in the first place. What are they meant to accomplish? Without a clearly identified purpose it is hard to contemplate any solutions, let alone judge their relative merits. Let me give a brief account of how economists rationalize the need for incentive schemes.

The main problem is the nature of labor as a productive input. It is unlike machines or raw materials in that its characteristics vary across individuals, often in an unobservable manner. The quality of labor differs from one person to another, partly because of innate differences

I am grateful to Haig Nalbantian for editorial assistance. The research was partially supported by grants from NSF and the Sloan Foundation.

in ability, partly because of the variation in effort people put into a job. Also, labor is team production either in the literal sense that it takes many people to get a job done, or in the sense that nature is an invisible partner causing the same labor input to result in different outcomes because of random disturbances. Consequently, the true value of labor input is hard to measure and therefore hard to pay for in the same way as we pay for most goods we regularly buy. Instead, labor exchange has to be mediated by more complex arrangements—employment contracts.

Employment contracts need to deal with the many problems that arise from an inability to measure and directly reward individual contributions. They must guard against opportunism as well as risk, and they need to respond in an effective way to information about ability and other unknown characteristics of the employee or the task he/she is assigned to. Needless to say, there is no single contract that can accomplish all objectives at once; that is why it is so important that practitioners clearly identify the specific problems they feel are of central concern. Is the primary aim to get an individual worker to exert more effort? Is it to induce cooperation among a team of workers? Is it to align employee risk preferences with those of the firm? Is it to screen for ability or some other relevant characteristic like willingness to work? The design of a contract will depend on which of these questions is the most relevant in any particular situation.

One more point on the need for contracts: people's incentives are not only guided by explicit short-term contracts, but also by longer-term considerations such as career objectives. Our competitive economy provides plenty of implicit incentives in the form of promotions and other discretionary rewards. Some would argue that these are sufficient inducements and that one should not tamper with them by adding explicit schemes. Theoretical work does not support such wishful thinking, but it is important to recognize that the design of explicit schemes is part of a much larger incentive framework, which must not be ignored in the design process.

Design Criteria

Whatever the source of the incentive problem, there are usually two conflicting objectives in designing a contract—at least as economists see it. One is that one would like to promote efficiency in the sense of maximizing the size of the pie that is available for sharing between the firm and its employees. The other is equity in the sense that one would not like external events to determine the distribution of proceeds. There is a conflict, because imperfect measures have to be used in the contract as proxies for the real variables one would like to contract on (such as true labor input or actual decisions made). The heavier one relies on the proxies the stronger are the incentive effects, but also, the more randomness there is. For instance, if profit sharing is used to motivate employees, more of it will induce a higher level of effort, but also make income less predictable. Since there is a lot of evidence that people dislike risk, the tradeoff is between incentives and risk-sharing (or fairness, as some would call it.)

In considering such trade-offs, the most important observation is that the design problem cannot be viewed narrowly from either the firm's or the worker's side. The conflict is between two incompatible economic objectives—efficiency and equity—and not between two parties—the firm and the worker. One should strive for arrangements that are mutually good rather than unilaterally good, because the surplus that is created can be redistributed to arrive at a fair division. Economists call this the principle of Pareto optimality, which simply means that a best scheme is one that cannot be improved for the benefit of both parties. An exclusive concern with the benefits of the worker side in bargaining, for instance, is at odds with this rational principle. If unions looked at the problem cooperatively, there would, I presume, be more to share, implying benefits for both the union and the firm.

Dimensions of Incentive Design

It is hard to go into further detail about incentive design without having a more specific subject in mind. Let me focus on executive compensation with the understanding that much of what I have to say has broader relevance. I have in mind a plan for the top executives in a corporation, including divisional managers.

The objective of executive incentive plans is to create shareholder value, i.e. to motivate executives to maximize total shareholder returns. There is no universal formula for creating shareholder value, however. Deciding on a good plan involves the kinds of trade-offs mentioned earlier. These trade-offs vary with the circumstances in which a firm finds itself at a particular point in time and also depend on the strategic objectives that are deemed appropriate for the situation at hand. Clearly, incentive plans should be designed in tandem with corporate strategic plans. The reason is that people react strongly to financial incentives and if there is a conflict between what is desired as expressed in words and what is actually rewarded in money, the latter tends to win out. Put differently, implicit in each incentive plan is a set of strategic objectives that are likely to be implemented independently of verbally expressed objectives. Properly used then, this correspondence makes incentive plans potent communicators of company objectives.

In designing the plan, I consider five important dimensions:

- *Risk posture*—the proportion of an executive's pay that is at risk, i.e. depends on performance.
- *Time focus*—the relative emphasis on short-term vs. long-term goals in the plan.
- *Flexibility*—the rigidity of the plan relative to new contingencies and changes in the environment over time.
- *Performance measures*—the measures used to assess the executive's contribution and to pay rewards.
- *Award instruments*—the rules for and forms of payment.

Risk Posture

Making the executive's compensation sensitive to corporate performance has motivational advantages: it induces a concern for the corporation's welfare and a willingness to expend effort to enhance it. But it also carries costs. An executive is not as efficient a risk-bearer as is the capital market. The cost of compensating the executive for carrying risk is higher than the risk premia charged in the capital market. (This is the reason we see broadly held companies in the first place.) Increasing executive risk must, therefore, be accompanied by a disproportionate increase in average (or expected) pay, creating a trade-off between incentive gains and compensation costs. The evaluation of this trade-off depends on such factors as the innate risk of the technology that the executive is controlling, the degree of influence that the executive has over the technology, and also how the executive feels about carrying personal risk. Other things being equal, a more risky technology or a technology that can be influenced less would call for a lower risk posture. The executive's own tastes for risk could be incorporated by having him determine, partly at least, the composition of his compensation package.

Of central concern in determining the appropriate risk posture is its influence on the executive's preferences for project selection. The particular form of the payment plan has much to do with this. Options that place a lower bound on earnings are likely to encourage risk taking, while stock rewards may well induce risk aversion. The proper mix will depend on what kind of risk-taking behavior should be encouraged, given general economic conditions and the corporation's or the business unit's market position at a particular point in time.

Time Focus

Executives should ideally have a long-term perspective on the firm's objectives, the more so the higher they are in the organization. Their time focus can be influenced by the choice of measures used to evaluate performance as well as the explicit horizon of the plan. Rewards that are based on market data (stock prices and their derivatives) will naturally induce a long-term concern, because they are not sensitive to extraneous, temporary changes in accounting data. Indeed, it would seem that basing performance on market data would be all that is necessary for inducing the right time focus at the highest levels of the corporation, but apparently that is not what executives and consultants think. Recently, so called performance plans, which link rewards to a set of explicit long-term accounting measures, have been introduced in many corporations.* I find it puzzling and would predict a short life for these plans except that markets also seem to have reacted favorably to them.

The situation is rather different at the divisional levels of a corporation. Here the need is to communicate operational strategic objectives and for this purpose one must rely on accounting measures such as sales, return on investment (ROI), earnings, etc. However, accounting measures are likely to induce short-sightedness unless explicit long-term objectives are embedded into the plan. How far into the future these goals should be set depends on the strength of top management's desire to be flexible in changing the goals as new information comes in. The appropriate horizon also depends on such technological factors as the natural cycle of the industry, how long it takes for investments to pay off, and the typical pattern of their returns. Of course, the division's strategic position is central, too. A division that is being "milked" may be controlled by very short-range incentives, while a growing division should have its sight set on long-term profitability.

In thinking about long-term incentives, a problematic issue arises with the transfer of jobs. How should one allocate responsibility between the incumbent and his successor if actions have long-term consequences? It seems that the practice is to cut off responsibility with the change of jobs, but that would seem to raise the possibility that the incumbent cares less about the future than he should. A theoretical analysis therefore suggests that rewards from a particular job should be stretched beyond its tenure. I can see some practical but not insurmountable difficulties with such arrangements, and perhaps practitioners should think about ways to implement lagged payment plans of this kind.

Apart from stressing the need to induce a concern for the future, long-term plans have another benefit. A typical problem is that it is hard to know what a division's true potential is. One has to rely on past performance, at least partly, for judging future potential. This may lead to a so-called ratchet problem if plans are revised too frequently. The division may not want to produce at its full potential for fear of raised objectives in the future. Allegedly, this is a severe problem in the Soviet Union, which suggests that it is a problem also in other bureaucracies.

---

*Editor's note: for a discussion of long-term incentive plans and some evidence on their effectiveness, see Rich and Larson, chap. 8, this volume.

One remedy for the ratchet problem is to let managers set their own goals with a direct reward for increasing desirable objectives. I presume this is what happens implicitly in firms, but it is not out of the question that some more explicit device for dealing with the ratchet issue (and more generally the issue of setting fair standards) would be helpful. I think theory could be useful in offering guidance on this matter if it is deemed important by practitioners.

Flexibility

In any business, unforeseen events occur and the question arises of how to deal with them in an incentive plan. Allowing a lot of flexibility, for instance by promising no definite rewards before an after-the-fact review by a compensation committee, has the benefit that gross errors in rewards can be avoided. However, it should not be overlooked that an extensive use of this option tends to dilute the strong incentive effects that an explicit and rigid compensation plan has. Flexibility is a two-edged sword and its use can easily backfire. It may take time to build up trust that fair judgements are going to be applied; what constitutes a fair judgement is not always easy to determine even after the fact, and people tend to disagree with the interpretations of facts, making flexibility a problem for morale. The apparent advice is to retain a right for *ex post* revisions, but to use it sparingly.

An alternative to using discretionary rules is to index contracts more heavily. Indexation preserves flexibility while maintaining the benefits of high-powered, explicit incentives. For instances, one could tie future objectives to overall economic conditions as well as the specific situation in comparable firms. It is hard for me to judge how costly it is to make such inclusions, particularly when there are many future contingencies to guard against. But it would seem that on the margin some form of indexing would be worthwhile. A less rigorous implementation of the same idea would be to spell out the general principles by which future objectives will be set. In either case, the benefit is to give divisions a clearer notion of the long-term consequences of their actions.

Indexation should also be considered in the direct payment of rewards. There is no reason to let executives, particularly on lower income levels, carry risk in their incentive contracts that could be easily filtered away. This can be done by including general economic indicators (such as Dow Jones averages, GNP, CPI) in the reward formula as well as by making comparisons to a relevant set of competitors. Note that the objective here is not fairness, but lower incentive costs. A corporation can carry risk more efficiently than individuals, and hence an indexed scheme can achieve the same incentive effects at a lower cost. Relative performance evaluations are becoming a bit more popular, but it is still surprising that their use is not more extensive in light of their compelling rationale. If it is because of a lack of experience in how to set relative standards, I would think that statistical models could be constructed to resolve that problem.

A warning is in order here. Indexation usually changes the economic evaluation of decisions and this must be taken into account in judging their use. For instance, indexing to prices of particular commodities such as oil would not necessarily be advisable because of the consequent distortions in the value of oil-related projects. Indexation must be done in a fashion that maintains approximate neutrality in relative values, which usually would seem to imply the inclusion of broad economic variables rather than narrow ones. Again, a theoretical analysis of this question should be able to resolve what type of indexation is safe and what type isn't.

Performance Measures

The general principle for choosing performance measures is simple: find measures that tell as accurately as possible how well the executive performed. Implicit in this statement is the acknowledgement that desired performance cannot always be measured accurately. This is less puzzling than it sounds. The point is that good decision making and hard work may not be easily identified in the corporate accounts because of uncontrollable events. Indeed, it is the confusion between luck and skill that makes the incentive problem difficult. Thus, the principle could also be re-expressed as finding measures that filter away as effectively as possible extraneous information that is beyond the executive's control. Interestingly enough, this does not mean that one should only use performance measures that the executive can influence, as standard responsibility accounting would lead us to believe. This was illustrated in the earlier discussion of indexation, where the executive's reward is explicitly made to depend on external uncontrollable events with the express purpose of making the indexed measure a more accurate account of his true contribution.

On the top level, measures should, of course, relate to overall corporate performance. There is hardly any substitute for market data in this regard. Stock prices reflect in an unparalleled way the true performance of the corporation. I have little regard for the use of accounting data, which has become more common in recent years. One might argue that accounting data is easier to control (which almost surely is true), but the bottom line is that top executives are hired to create shareholder value, not good accounting numbers. It is another matter, of course, that share prices are sensitive to external events. But this should again be dealt with by indexation rather than by going to entirely different measures.

On the divisional level, the argument for accounting measures has force for two reasons. First, the link between divisional performance and overall corporate performance is much weaker. If one used stock value, it would not reflect very accurately divisional contributions. The incentive effects would be weaker and the risk borne by the divisional manager too costly. Second, accounting measures are the right instruments for communicating strategic objectives as determined by the headquarters. Since strategic objectives can vary greatly from one firm to another, and even within a firm, there is nothing one can say in general about what particular accounting measures are good. It all depends on the circumstances, and one should not hesitate in using different measures as one sees fit. A warning is in order. Accounting measures, unlike market data, are easily manipulable and much thought should go into the choice so as to guard against the possibility of distortion. Presumably, accountants have had much experience with this problem in the past, and they should be able to give good advice.

One problem that is overlooked in the discussion above is the tension that may arise from the desire to hold individuals accountable for their own actions, and the recognition that the corporation as a whole is a team of performers. Stressing the team dimension dilutes individual incentives, while stressing unit performance may cause coordination problems. This could be used as an argument for holding divisions at least partly responsible for overall corporate performance. On the other hand, it could also be dealt with by making interrelated decisions on the corporate level. Such, of course, is the practice in allocating capital among divisions.

Award Instruments and Rules

Starting with rules, one good principle is to use simple ones. The value of a complicated rule is hard to assess, and it may also be more susceptible to manipulations. For instance, linear rules are simple, and they have the advantage of providing the same "incentive pressure" regardless of how well the performance has been to date. In contrast, non-linear rules may exacerbate the problems with manipulating accounting numbers. For instance, the typical practice is to have caps (both upper and lower limits) on the amount of bonuses awarded to executives during a year. This invites end-of-year maneuvering where accounts and decisions, such as investments in research and development and inventories, are transferred across periods to get maximal benefits from the bonus schemes. Incidentally, this is not something imagined. There is clear statistical evidence that such maneuvering happens in firms. To avoid it, I would take away the caps and replace them with some form of indexation (again) so that undue rewards or punishments are avoided.

What payment instruments (stocks, options, cash, deferred funds) should be used depends to a large degree on tax considerations and on individual preferences. I have little to say about these preferences except to note that in looking at tax gains one should consider joint benefits to the firm and the executive rather than just the benefits to the executive. This is the principle of Pareto optimality that I mentioned before; apparently it has not always been applied, causing misjudgments in the true gains from particular payment forms. Also, it should be recognized that tax planning is not a separate exercise. It clearly interacts with the incentive dimension. Paying in options rather than stock may have tax benefits, but it also changes risk preferences as I indicated before.

An "Ideal" Incentive Plan

As a way of summarizing my discussion, let me close with a sketch of an "ideal" incentive plan for executives (top level and divisional) based on what theory suggests.

The highest officers would be rewarded by indexed stock options, that is, options that have an exercise price that depends positively on the general stock market level (to filter out inflation and other general economic data) as well as on a composite index of the stock prices of competitive firms (to make a more accurate assessment of how well the executives have performed in the business they are in.) The weight on the composite index would be small if substantial shifts in the line of business (through divestments or acquisitions) would be a relevant option in the near future. Otherwise the weight could be substantial. I would use options rather than stock awards for tax advantage and also as an inducement for risk taking.

At lower echelons I would use accounting measures. The objectives would be pegged to similar measures in comparable firms and stretch over a horizon that is compatible with the corporation's strategic plan, say five years. This is to prevent myopic decision-making. The objectives would be expressed in a form that makes them automatically adjust to changes in economic circumstances (for instance, be a certain percentage point above the average of similar firms).

Managers who would shift tasks within the corporation would still receive partial bonuses from their former assignment for some years. Yearly bonuses would be linear in the underlying measures. They would have no explicit upper limit (except for measures for which more is not necessarily better; e.g. growth). The lower limit would be set with consideration for risk-taking. If risk-taking is to be induced, the limit would be relatively higher.

Discretion to adjust divisional objectives over time should, of course, be left with headquarters, but not be used indiscriminately. I would consider offering managers the option to "purchase" lower targets as well as raise targets in return for direct rewards. This could provide valuable information about true opportunities and aid in coordinating financial plans. Discretion to make changes in rewards should be retained by a compensation committee or corresponding body to avoid gross misassessments, but it should be exercised in genuinely exceptional circumstances.

Part IV

MACROECONOMIC IMPLICATIONS

11

The Role of Contracts in Macroeconomic Performance

John B. Taylor

Because prices are sticky, faster or slower monetary growth initially affects output. . . . But these effects wear off.
　　　　　　　　—Milton Friedman, *Newsweek*, July 12, 1982

Prices—including money wages—are sticky in the short run. . . . [This implies] that monetary and fiscal policies that add to demand will, in the short run at any rate, increase output and employment.
　　　　　　—James Tobin, *Asset Accumulation and Economic Activity:*
　　　　　　　　Reflections on Contemporary Macroeconomic Theory

Temporary wage and price rigidities play a central role in macroeconomic fluctuations. As the two epigraphs indicate, traditional Keynesians and monetarists are in agreement on this point. So are many economists who use rational expectations in their models, an exception being the "new classical" models. The traditional assumption in microeconomics, on the other hand, is that prices and wages are perfectly flexible: all markets—including labor markets—are like auctions. When monetary or fiscal disturbances affect supply or demand in such markets, prices and wages change quickly, possibly by large amounts, to keep resources fully employed. When prices or wages are temporarily rigid, or *sticky*, the economy responds slowly to disturbances. During the period when prices and wages adjust, the economy can be in a state of excess demand (a boom), or excess supply (a slump) for a year or more.

Labor contracts between firms and their employees are one of the

Some of the material in this essay is drawn from research and results reported in Taylor (1986), Taylor (1987), and Hall and Taylor (1986). A grant from the National Science Foundation at the National Bureau of Economic Research is gratefully acknowledged. I am grateful to Tamin Bayoumi for helpful research assistance.

main reasons for wage rigidities. As many of the papers in this volume illustrate, labor contracts are motivated by, and in turn influence, incentives and risk sharing. They can be shown to have a good microeconomic rationale. The part of the contract that is important for macroeconomics, however, is its stipulation of a fixed nominal wage payment for some period of time. This wage payment introduces economy-wide wage and price rigidities.

Some explicit contracts stipulate a wage rate for up to three years into the future. Most contracts are less formal and shorter, however, and stipulate a fixed wage for only a year or so. Whatever the length, during the period of the contract the wage does not adjust to changes in market conditions. If there is a recession, the same wage applies. If the recession causes a drop in sales and profits, the hourly wage will remain the same. With full cost pricing, the firm's price will be about as rigid as the wage since labor is by far the largest input to production.

For these reasons employment contracts—whether implicit or explicit—play an important role in macroeconomic fluctuations. Many proposals to improve macroeconomic performance, that is, to reduce the size and duration of economic fluctuations, have proposed that labor contracts be made more flexible. Tying the wage to prices, productivity, sales, or profits through indexing or sharing arrangements is one of the most frequent proposals for increased flexibility. According to those macroeconomic theories that are based on price and wage rigidities, such proposals, if implemented, would improve macroeconomic performance.

The purpose of this chapter is to review the empirical evidence that labor contracts are important for generating wage rigidities in the United States, to review the empirical evidence that these wage rigidities, in turn, are an important propagator of economic fluctuations, and finally to show that microeconomic research on contracts that emphasizes risk sharing and incentives, in its current form, does not fully explain these empirical observations.

1. Employment Contracts in the United States.

Union Contracts

Of the twenty percent of U.S. workers that are unionized, about half are involved in collective bargaining situations that include enough workers (1000 or more) to be regularly tracked by the Bureau of Labor Statistics (BLS). In total, this group consists of about 10 million workers. Although only 10 percent of the labor force, this group receives enormous attention in the media and in public policy discussions. The most common length of contract is about three years. Unless there is an early reopening or a delay in negotiating a new contract, the workers signing three year contracts will do so every three years; for example, the electrical workers negotiated contracts in 1976, 1979, and 1982 and so on. This pattern of bargaining activity gives rise to a three-year cycle. Every third year involves a relatively small group of workers.

All of the contract negotiations do not occur at the same time. Instead they are nonsynchronized—or staggered—over many different time periods. At any one time, only a small fraction of the workers are signing contracts; the remaining workers have either recently signed their contracts, or are about to sign their contracts in the near future. The period in which one contract is in force overlaps the period in which other contracts are in force. This staggered wage setting plays an important role in explaining both the persistence of economic fluctuations and the resistance of inflation to aggregate demand pressures.

For example, the United Mine Workers signed a contract with the bituminous coal operators in May of 1981. The contract affected about 160,000 workers and lasted 40 months, expiring in September 1984. The contract stipulated wage increases that averaged 11 percent per year. The wage increases were $1.20 in the first year, $1.10 in the second year, $1.00 in the third year, and $.30 in the last quarter. Part of the wage increase was deferred to the second and third year of the contract. These deferred increases indicate that management and labor had expectations of continued high inflation. There were no indexing provisions in the contract; these increases would occur regardless of economic conditions and indicate the extent of the nominal rigidity that such contracts impose on the economy. As with the coal contract, most other union contracts have a significant amount of the wage increase in the second and third years of the contract. There is some front-end loading, however, in that the largest increases occur in the first year of the contract period.

Part of this front-end loading occurs because some of the contracts have indexing clauses. These indexing clauses stipulate that the wage increase in the later years will be greater if the consumer price index increases. For example, the contract would increase the wage rate by .5 percent if the consumer price index increases by 1 percent. This would be 50 percent indexing. Because some inflation was generally expected when these contracts were negotiated, both management and labor would expect that the wage would increase because of indexing. For this reason, the more indexing the less of a deferred increase would be necessary. Other things being equal, the larger the expected wage increase because of indexing, the smaller will be the scheduled deferred increase. About 50 percent of the workers in this group had indexed contracts; most of these contracts had less than 100 percent indexing.

As is now well known, a long and serious recession occurred during the period of the 1981–84 coal contract. The unemployment rate increased dramatically from about 8 percent in mid-1981 to close to 11 percent by the end of 1982. Inflation began to come down. Yet the wage payments in this contract did not adjust throughout its entire term. The effect of the severe recession in the early 1980s is quite apparent in other contracts whose term expired during the recession and that were renegotiated. As a result, wage settlements overall dropped from nearly 10 percent to below 5 percent by 1984.

Most workers in large labor unions change their contracts about once every three years. Wage and salary decisions are made in collective bargaining meetings for which both management and labor leaders spend extensive time preparing. While the outcome of any one bargaining situation cannot be predicted with much certainty, a number of factors clearly influence the outcome in particular directions.

The first and perhaps the most important factor is the state of the labor market. If unemployment is high then labor will be in a relatively weak bargaining position. Conversely, if unemployment is low, then workers will be able to bargain for larger wage increases. The threat of a strike is more credible in good times than in bad. Moreover, firms are likely to settle for larger wage increases in tight market conditions, because they will be better able to pass on their costs in the form of higher prices.

A second factor influencing wage bargaining is the wage paid to comparable workers in other industries. Because not all contract negotiations are synchronized, there are two components of this comparison wage: the wage settlements of workers who have recently signed contracts, and the expected wage settlements of workers who will be signing their contracts in the near future. Looking back at the wage settlements in recently signed contracts makes sense in a current negotiation because those settlements will be in force during part of the contract period under consideration. This backward looking behavior tends to give some built-in inertia to the wage determination process. If one union group gets a big increase, then the next group of workers in the wage determination cycle will also tend to get a big increase. Lester Thurow describes the process as follows: "Suppose that this year the Machinists' union is negotiating a new three year contract. Last year the Auto Workers negotiated a three year contract for a 10% rise per year. No leader of the machinists can settle for less than 10% and still remain in office. And in two years time the auto leaders will be similarly imprisoned by what the machinists negotiate today" (*The Economist,* Jan. 1982). But looking forward at future settlements also makes sense, because the current contract will be in force when these changes take place. In other words, we would expect wage determination to combine elements of forward and backward looking behavior.

A third factor that influences wage decisions is the expected rate of inflation. If inflation is expected to be high, workers will ask for larger wage increases and management will be willing to pay them because their own prices are expected to rise. As with the effect of comparable wage increases, the effect of expected inflation will have both a backward looking element and a forward looking element.

In preparation for these negotiations management spends months surveying wages in other industries, estimating changes in labor productivity, forecasting changes in its own profits, and obtaining estimates of the general inflation during the upcoming contract period. To be adequately informed during the collective bargaining sessions, labor leaders must be equally and independently prepared; hence, they must also spend months preparing for negotiations. Moreover, there is the threat of a strike in almost every collective bargaining situation. An actual strike is obviously costly for both sides, but the mere preparation for a possible strike is also costly because the firm must accumulate and finance additional inventories. Hence, production will be abnormally high before negotiations, and abnormally low after negotiations as firms draw down inventories if a strike does not occur. These swings in production raise average costs to the firm. Given these high costs, it is understandable that many collective bargaining negotiations occur only once every three years.

Nonunion Workers

It is very common for workers who are not in unions to receive wage and salary adjustments once each year. Although there is no formal contract involved, it is unlikely that this wage decision will be changed before the next scheduled adjustment period. Hence, the nominal wage rigidity is very similar to that in the union contracts. One difference is that the entire wage adjustment usually occurs at one time rather than part being deferred as in the second and third years of the large union contracts. This is probably due to the shorter time between wage adjustments.

In preparation for a wage adjustment, the management of nonunion firms must obtain information very similar to that obtained by management of unionized firms preparing for a collective bargaining meeting. In a large private firm there are usually specialists called wage and salary administrators who must make a wage decision. They obtain information about the current labor market situation. They conduct wage surveys or subscribe to a wage survey performed by an outside group. They also attempt to forecast the rate of inflation.

Although the wage decision will usually be made under more competitive conditions than exist in a collective bargaining situation, these factors—the state of the labor market and wage and price inflation—will influence the final outcome in similar directions. If unemployment is very low and is expected to remain low for the next year, then management will know that it will have to pay a relatively high wage compared to other firms employing similarly skilled workers. An attractive wage will prevent workers from quitting and help lure workers from other firms if they are necessary for expansion. On the other hand if unemployment is high, there will be less worry that workers will quit to look for jobs elsewhere. Moreover, if sales projections for the coming year are poor, an expansion of production requiring more workers would be unlikely.

If wages are expected to be relatively high at other firms—either because of recent wage decisions at these firms or because of expected wage increases at other firms—then the wage will necessarily be higher. Information about both recent wage decisions and imminent wage decisions can be obtained from surveys.

Although there is little direct evidence on the scheduling of nonunion firms' wage increases, it is unlikely that they all occur at the same time. Hence, there is the same type of nonsynchronization that we observe for the union sector.

Many of the properties of formal negotiations pertain to the more informal wage setting procedures used by firms employing nonunion workers. A review of each worker's performance is costly, and obtaining survey information about wages paid elsewhere and forecasts of inflation requires time and expense. To make such an adjustment more than once a year is probably prohibitive for many firms. The same arguments against extensive contingency clauses also apply to this type of wage setting. Moreover, indexation would do little to improve the workings of annual wage setting arrangements; waiting less than a year to make an adjustment after the fact is usually adequate.

In a decentralized economy like the United States, firms and workers are left to their own to decide when their wages and salaries are adjusted. The fact that these decisions are not synchronized therefore seems natural; one would be surprised to see a coordinated wage (or price) adjustment without some centralized orchestration of such a move. Historical accident would be enough to explain why the auto workers always negotiate just before the machinists.

It is important to know, however, whether the lack of synchronization in the United States serves any microeconomic purpose. If it does not, then proposals for reforming the economic system to bring about more synchronization would be innocuous for microeconomic welfare, and could have some macroeconomic advantages.

Imagine what would happen if all wages and prices were set at the same time, and without a central planner to tell workers and firms what to do. A firm that thought that a relative wage increase was appropriate for its workers, would have a difficult time knowing what other wages would be in order to achieve that relative increase. A wage survey would be impossible because there would be no wages to survey. Similarly, a competitive firm suffering from a decline in productivity might want to cut the wage of its workers relative to the price of the firm's product. But in a fully synchronized setting, it would not know what the price of its products would be, and hence would not be able to set the right wage.

Staggered wage setting is a way to provide information to firms and workers about wages and prices elsewhere. Even though other wages will be adjusted before the current contract expires, there will be some period of time when the desired relative wage is in force. Nonsynchronized wage and price setting seems desirable in a real-world decentralized economy without an auctioneer to call out wages and prices and balance supplies and demands before the market actually opens.

Moreover, staggered wage setting adds some stability to wages. With full synchronization, all wages and prices would be up for grabs each period; there would be no base for setting each wage. Tremendous variability would be introduced to the price system. In sum, synchronized wage and price setting—without a central organization to provide a basis or target for prices from which wage and price decisions could be made—would not be desirable. It would make wage adjustments difficult and would increase the volatility of prices.

Other Countries

Differences between wage setting behavior in the United States and in other countries are frequently noted by researchers. For example, in Japan most contracts last about one year, like most implicit contracts in the United States. However, in Japan a large number of wage decisions are synchronized each spring when there is a "Shunto" or simultaneous wage adjustment for the large companies. According to recent data, about 40 percent of the labor force negotiates contracts in the second quarter. This fraction is larger than in the United States or other industrialized countries, but is significantly less than 100 percent, so that there is still much staggering of contracts. The government is actively involved in the Shunto. Prior to the Shunto, extensive deliberations take place to determine the appropriate wage adjustment for that year. Governmental participation is integral to this process.

In Italy about 30 percent of the labor force is unionized and most of these workers have three-year contracts. Until recently there was extensive indexing in these contracts, however, so that the effective duration was shorter. In Canada about 65 percent of unionized workers have one year contracts, and there is little synchronization. In France contracts typically do not have a set determination date, but are most frequently changed about once per year. There is little synchronization. In Germany and England there is also little synchronization, with one year contracts being the most typical.

Overall there are surprising similarities in the wage setting institutions in the major industrialized countries. Even the synchronization that has been noted in Japan leaves much staggering in wage setting, and the high degree of indexation in Italy seems to be less important than it was in the 1970s.

2. Evidence that Nominal Wage Rigidities are Important.

The above micro data on wage contracts indicate that they are indeed important factors in generating nominal wage rigidities in the economy. But what is the evidence that these nominal wage rigidities are important in economic fluctuations? As mentioned in the introduction, many structural macro models have been developed that show that such wage rigidities are capable of generating the observed fluctuations. An important result of these models is that staggered contracts of about the same duration as those observed in the micro data are capable of explaining business cycles. The consistency of these structural models with the data is clearly some evidence in favor of the importance of wage rigidities for macroeconomic fluctuations.

Direct empirical evidence on the relationship between output fluctuations and price and wage fluctuations provides additional support for the view that price and wage rigidities are an important aspect of economic fluctuations. Consider the experience of the major industrialized countries—Canada, France, Germany, Italy, Japan, the United Kingdom, and the United States—during the last 30 years. An effective way to summarize the output-inflation data is to look at the unconstrained infinite moving average relation between deviation of output from trend and inflation. The infinite moving average, which is reported for these 7 countries in Taylor (forthcoming), shows the dynamic interaction between inflation and output. The results are easily summarized: there is a striking similarity among the moving average representations in the countries. The effect of output shocks is to increase inflation, while the effect of inflation shocks is to decrease output. In other words the intertemporal cross correlation between inflation and output shocks reverses sign when we switch variables. The only exception is Japan, which we noted above has somewhat different wage-setting institutions than the other countries. With this one exception, the reverse cross correlation is apparently a central part of economic fluctuations.

An explanation for this finding is as follows: (1) positive deviations of output from the trend level represent periods of excess demand during which prices and wages tend to be bid up gradually, and then raise the inflation rate with a lag, and (2) increases in inflation are not completely tolerated by policy makers so that such increases result in less than fully accommodative policies that cause the economy to go into a recession after a lag. Less than fully accommodative policies could occur with monetary tightening in the face of inflation shocks, but fiscal policy could also be used. The story is similar in the case of shocks of the opposite sign: decreases in output eventually cause declines in inflation, and decreases in inflation eventually cause increases in output.

Particular realizations of these cross relationships are well known in these industrialized countries. For example, the increase in inflation in the late 1960s and during the two oil shocks in the 1970s all led to recessions. More recently, in early 1986, a surprise decline in inflation largely caused by reductions in the price of oil were expected to lead to high growth rates of real output. Most economic forecasters raised their forecast of world economic growth after observing the decline in oil prices in early 1986. These are all examples of the negative effect of inflation on output when inflation is dated prior to output.

On the other hand, inflation fell soon after the recessions in the 1970s and early 1980s. These are examples of the positive effect of output on inflation when output is dated prior to inflation.

Are these correlations consistent with other business cycle theories—such as the real business cycle theories described by King and Plosser (1984)? There are many structural explanations of any reduced form correlation, but in my view the above explanation is still more complete than alternative business cycle theories. It is clearly beyond the scope of this paper to discuss all alternative theories. Real business cycle theories do not attempt to deal with the timing relations between inflation and output that I documented and emphasized above. In principle, the negative relation between inflation and output could be due to shifts in the production function, rather than to the tightening of monetary policy. However, to focus on one example, it is difficult to think of a productivity shock that could have led to the large recessions in 1981–82. Moreover, shifts in productivity *per se* do not generate the timing relationship between inflation and output noted above.

3. The Optimal Contract Model.

The basic optimal contract model was originally put forth by Azariadis (1975) and Baily (1974) to give a microeconomic rationale for the nominal wage rigidities and the economic fluctuations discussed above. In this section I argue that the results available thus far do not provide such a rationale.

A basic property of a contract is that it specifies actions to be taken in the future, for example the wage to be paid the next year. Hence, in order to build a model of contracts it is necessary to consider a situation where some events explicitly take place in the future. At the time that the contract is written these events are unknown. The typical assumption is that future productivity growth is unknown. The labor contract must be written in advance of the time when the disturbance occurs.

Neither firms nor workers know in advance what type of a disturbance will, in fact, occur. They are likely to have some idea of the *probability* of a particular disturbance occurring. Suppose, for example, that everyone thinks that there is a 50 percent chance that a negative shock will occur, and a 50 percent chance that a positive shock will occur. It is as if a coin is tossed: heads, labor productivity shifts up; tails, labor productivity shifts down.

Suppose that the contract is one year in duration, and applies only to the next year when the uncertain disturbance will occur. Under these circumstances it is optimal for the contract to be written in the form of *contingency clauses* that stipulate what the level of employment and the wage rate will be in the case that the next period is a good year and in the case that it is a bad year. These contingencies will take the following form: if productivity is high, employ workers for X hours and pay real wage W. If productivity is low, employ workers for x hours and pay real wage w. This contingency provision is an important feature of optimal contracts and tends to make them more flexible than contracts that do not contain it. The fact that contracts can be made contingent tends to reduce their potential as a source of rigidity that can explain departures from potential GNP.

Both the workers and the firm will want the best contract that they can get. The workers will want to maximize their utility, and the firm will want to maximize profits. However, both utility and profits depend on the unknown productivity shock that will occur next year. Hence, both utility and profits are viewed as random from the perspective of the year when the contract is drawn up. Therefore, the firm must maximize the *expected value* of profits, and the worker must maximize the *expected value* of utility. Based on the contingencies written into the contract, the firm calculates its profits in the high productivity case and in the low productivity case. Because the probabilities of each case are the same, the firm's expected profits are just the average of the two cases.

The workers' assessment of their utility in the next period will also involve an averaging of the two future possibilities. However, the uncertainty about the future productivity shock has a special additional effect on the preferences of workers. Optimal contract theory assumes that workers are "risk-averse" when dealing with this uncertainty. In terms of their employment contract, this means that they would prefer a contract giving them lower average income if that contract also stipulated that the income would be the same amount in the high productivity case and in the low productivity case. Paying the same income whether the workers are more or less productive clearly reduces the risk to the worker.

While it is typically assumed that workers are risk-averse in the optimal contract model, firms are usually assumed to be "risk neutral." The reason for assuming that firms are not risk-averse (while workers are) is that firms are larger and probably find it easier to obtain insurance elsewhere.

From these conditions the specific form of the optimal contract can be deduced. First, the contingent levels of employment in the two productivity situations will be efficient in the same way that the auction market is efficient. The reason is that by using contingencies the firms and workers can fix their contract so that the employment level responds to the productivity shock just as in the auction model. Since it is in both the worker's and the firm's interests to have a contract that is efficient, and since the auction market is efficient, the contract will be set up this way. The important idea here is that contingent contracts allow for sufficient flexibility to obtain the efficient level of employment. This result shows that if contract theory is to provide a good explanation of economic inefficiencies, such as the departures of real GNP from potential, it must explain why these contingencies do not exist in the real world.

Second, the real wage that is paid to the workers in the two states is not the same as in the auction model. It will be such that the workers' income does not depend on the state of productivity. This property is entirely due to the risk-aversion assumption. It gives the workers some insurance against fluctuations in income as the economy moves from good to bad productivity situations.

Why Aren't Contingency Clauses More Common?

Few contracts seem to be negotiated contingent on events that may occur in the future. We have noted that some of the contracts in recent years have included cost-of-living adjustments whereby the wage is indexed to the consumer price level. However, these clauses rarely involve 100 percent protection from cost-of-living changes, and many contracts (about 50 percent) do not have any such clauses. Moreover, cost-of-living clauses represent only one of many possible contingency clauses. More pertinent to the central concerns of this volume, the contracts could be directly linked to the profits of the firm or to the workers' productivity.

The primary reason why more contracts are not indexed to the cost of living is that such indexing can be harmful if prices are rising because of supply side shocks. Suppose that the marginal productivity of labor is reduced because of a shift in the production function. Such a shift will eventually require a reduction of the real wage, so that it is equal to the marginal productivity of labor. But a 100 percent indexed contract will prevent such a decline. The escalator clause will call for an increase in the wage in the same proportion as the increase in prices. It is understandable that many firms and workers are reluctant to institute an arrangement that prevents necessary adjustments in the real wage. Of course if the reason for the increase in the price is a general monetary induced inflation, then there will be no need for a reduction in the real wage. Unfortunately there is usually no way to tell in advance whether the price rise is caused by monetary effects or shifts in the production process.

Why aren't more contracts linked to other variables such as productivity or profits? In many cases it is difficult to verify a fully objective measure of such variables. The firm may be tempted to modify its accounting and thereby affect profits in a way that would keep the wage down. Verification is usually costly for productivity measures as well.

A final reason that contracts do not have many contingency clauses is that they add complexity. There are good reasons to have a straightforward contract that the rank and file can easily understand and vote on. Similarly, contingency clauses appear to add uncertainty about the wage that the workers will actually earn. Many workers would object to this added uncertainty.

4. Historical Comparisons.

One way to test whether a more flexible wage system would improve economic performance is to look at United States economic history. Before the Second World War, macroeconomic performance was much worse than after. From 1952 to 1983 the standard deviation of output from trend was 3.6 percent. During the gold standard period from 1891 to 1914 the standard deviation was 4.8 percent. From 1910 to 1940 the standard deviation was 10.1 percent. Hence, the fluctuations in output and employment were larger in magnitude than in the postwar period.

However, wages and prices were also apparently more flexible in the earlier period. The institution of three-year labor contracts did not occur until after the war. Moreover, the data suggest that there was much less persistence of inflation. In the aggregate, wages and prices moved more quickly. Microeconomic studies by Cagan (1979) and others also suggest more flexibility in the earlier period.

The comparison therefore presents a puzzle. Less flexibility of wages and prices should lead to a deterioration in economic performance. The comparison suggests the opposite. Of course many other changes could have led to the improvement in performance. There were fewer bank panics in the postwar period because of deposit insurance. Automatic stabilizers made income fluctuations smaller. And monetary policy was conducted with the aim of promoting stability.

Nevertheless, the historical comparison should make one pause to think through the macroeconomic effects of more flexibility at the microeconomic level. DeLong and Summers (1986) have recently argued that more flexibility can be destabilizing because of its effects on expectations, and thus on real interest rates. The discussion of staggered wage setting in this paper indicates that volatility could be increased if wage setting were synchronized.

Economic performance would probably be improved if wages and prices became less rigid than they seem to be now because of a move to more flexible renumeration. More flexibility would mean that inflation could be controlled with fewer and shorter recessions. In the language of contemporary macroeconomic textbooks, price adjustment would occur more quickly so that contractionary monetary policy would have a smaller effect on output. But if wage setting became too flexible or too synchronized, macroeconomic performance might get worse because, with larger fluctuations in the real interest rate, investment demand would be subject to larger swings. Again to use textbook language, the aggregate demand curve might become more volatile.

References

Azariadis, Costas. "Implicit Contracts and Underemployment Equilibrium." *Journal of Political Economy* 83(1975): 1183–1202.

Baily, Martin N. "Wages and Employment under Uncertain Demand." *Review of Economic Studies* 49(1974): 761–82.

Delong, J. Bradford and Lawrence Summers. "The Changing Cyclical Variability of Economic Activity in the United States." In *The American Business Cycle: Continuity and Change*, edited by Robert J. Gordon. Chicago: The University of Chicago Press. Forthcoming.

Cagan, Phillip. "Changes in the Cyclical Behavior of Prices." In *Persistent Inflation: Historical and Policy Essays*. New York: Columbia University Press, 1979.

The Economist. January 23–29, 1982.

Friedman, Milton. Quotation appearing in *Newsweek*, July 12, 1982, p. 64.

Hall, Robert E. and John B. Taylor. *Macroeconomics: Theory, Performance, and Policy*. New York: W. W. Norton, 1986.

King, Robert and Charles Plosser. "Money, Credit and Prices in a Real Business Cycle." *American Economic Review* 74(1984): 363–80.

Taylor, John B. "Improvements in Macroeconomic Stability: The Role of Wages and Prices." In *The American Business Cycle: Continuity and Change* edited by Robert J. Gordon. Chicago: University of Chicago Press for National Bureau of Economic Research. Forthcoming.

Taylor, John B. "Externalities Associated with Nominal Wage and Price Rigidities." In *New Approaches to Monetary Economics*, W. Barnett and K. Singleton, eds. Cambridge: Cambridge University Press. Forthcoming.

Tobin, James. *Asset Accumulation and Economic Activity: Reflections on Contemporary Macroeconomic Theory*. Chicago: University of Chicago Press, 1980.

12

Macroeconomic Aspects of Profit Sharing

Martin L. Weitzman

When John Maynard Keynes came to sum up the central message of the *General Theory* for the economics profession, in a remarkable but long forgotten *Quarterly Journal of Economics* article of 1937, he began with a "general, philosophical disquisition on the behavior of mankind"—under uncertainty. Here as elsewhere, Keynes made it abundantly clear that he shared Frank Knight's distinction. "Uncertainty" did not mean "risk"—that which is, at least in principle, reducible to well-defined actuarial probabilities. By "uncertainty" Keynes intended, I believe, to convey the idea of "ignorance"—that which is essentially due to insufficient or precarious knowledge of the mechanism by which the future is generated out of the past.

The Keynesian scenario looks out over an economic world that is rife with uncertainty. In that world, expectations play an important dual role as both a manifestation of uncertainty and as a cause of it. Such expectations are arbitrary to some degree because they can be based on almost anything, including self-fulfilling expectations of the behavior and expectations of others. And, as Keynes pointed out, "being based on so flimsy a foundation," these expectations of expectations are "subject to sudden and violent changes."

It follows that while there may ultimately be some long-run forces drawing it toward full employment, capitalism may also have some deep-seated tendencies toward short-run instability. Unadulterated laissez-faire is likely to be out of equilibrium much of the time, and even when it is in equilibrium there is no guarantee of being in a "good" equilibrium. Whether in a state of "bad" equilibrium or merely in disequilibrium, such coordination failures generate undesirable macroeconomic consequences like unemployment, which can cause very significant losses in economic and social welfare. By the ultimate logic of this Keynesian world view, then, the stage is set for some form of government interven-

202

tion to recoordinate the economy into a better configuration. Any such government policy will inevitably introduce some economic distortions of its own, but as an empirical matter, it can be argued, these losses tend to be small relative to the enormous welfare gains from having an economy operate at its full employment level.

These general considerations do not indicate the best *form* of government intervention to stabilize the macroeconomy. Indeed, we do not currently have a general, realistic framework within which a meta-issue like that might properly be addressed. Nevertheless it is possible, I believe, to give some common-sense criteria for desirable forms of government intervention. It is my contention that economists have not been sufficiently imaginative in devising operational mechanisms or systems possessing advantageous macroeconomic properties. My thesis is that both the Keynesian policy revolution and the monetarist counter-revolution represent dazzling digressions around the main problem. In the long course of history I think it will increasingly come to be seen that, for all the wealth of practical policy options and theoretical insights they might offer, the common defect of Keynesianism and monetarism is that both are attempting to detour around the malfunctioning labor market by skillfully manipulating one or another financial aggregate. Discretionary macroeconomic policies can work, and sometimes they work very well, but I think their main attraction is as a temporary measure, not a long-term strategy to be relied upon with impunity for decades on end. The usual fiscal and monetary policies are, to my mind, sledgehammer-like tactics for controlling unemployment and inflation. They do the job, but clumsily, by brute force—and they can have harmful aftereffects. I think it is possible to find subtler alternatives that operate more cleanly and with a softer touch by taking a page from the book of Adam Smith.

A good mechanism for fighting unemployment and inflation should have several noteworthy characteristics. It should be decentralized, based on the natural microeconomic incentives of a market-like environment. It should work more or less automatically, keeping to a minimum the need for using discretionary government policy. And, in a highly uncertain world, it should be robust in retaining its desirable macroeconomic characteristics over a wide range of possible situations or circumstances—including some that are currently unforeseen.

I would argue that a superior form of government policy for combatting unemployment and inflation in our economies is to encourage, through exhortation and special tax privileges, the widespread use of profit sharing. A profit-sharing system has the potential to automatically counteract contractionary or inflationary shocks, while maintaining the advantages of decentralized decision making. And these desirable properties are robustly preserved throughout a variety of economic environments. At the very least, widespread profit sharing can be a valuable adjunct to traditional monetary and fiscal policies.

I believe we should seriously consider some new ideas about basic reform of the economic mechanism because our old ways of doing things are no longer adequate. The premier economic malady of our time is stagflation. Despite some abatement of its virulence in the immediate present, we still seem to be unable to reconcile, over a reasonably sustained period, high employment with low inflation. Even when economic conditions are on the upswing, significant pockets of unemployed workers remain throughout the Western capitalist countries. Western governments are afraid to aggressively push unemployment down to more humane levels for fear of reigniting inflation. The policy induced recession remains our only reliable method for lowering inflation rates. It is difficult to imagine a more costly, inefficient, or unjust waste of economic resources and human potential.

The coordination difficulty that can cause some systems to suffer involuntary unemployment is not inherent in laissez-faire private enterprise *per se*. It is closely tied to one particular property of a conventional wage payment system: namely, compensation of each firm's employees is stuck to an outside *numéraire* (whether money, a cost of living index, or other companies' products) whose value is immune from anything the firm does. Under the wage payment system, we try to award every employed worker a predetermined piece of the income pie before it is out of the oven, before the size of the pie is even known. Our "social contract" promises workers a fixed wage independent of the health of their company, while the company chooses the employment level. That stabilizes the money income of whomever is hired, but only at the considerable cost of loading unemployment on low-seniority workers and inflation on everybody—a socially inferior risk-sharing arrangement that both diminishes and makes more variable the real income of the working class as a whole. An alternative labor participation system where it is considered perfectly normal for a worker's income to be tied to an appropriate performance index of his or her firm, by contrast, puts in place exactly the right incentives to automatically resist stagflation. Profit sharing is one variant of such a system. It represents a way of building into the economy the kind of natural resistance to unemployment and inflation that could really disarm stagflation at its source.

At some risk of oversimplification, let me give a concrete if highly idealized (and extreme) example of what I have in mind. Suppose that wages plus fringe benefits of the average General Motors automobile worker come to $24 per hour. This means that the cost to GM of hiring one additional hour of labor, the marginal cost of labor, is $24. The extra hour of labor is used to produce more automobiles, which are then sold to yield increased revenue. If the increased (or marginal) revenue exceeds the increased cost, more workers will be hired; in the opposite case, workers will be laid off. Since GM is trying to maximize profits, it will take on (or lay off) workers to the point where the additional revenue created by the extra hour of labor is neither more nor less than the additional cost, in this case $24. The average revenue per hour of labor will naturally be higher, say $36, to cover overhead, capital, profits, and the like.

Now imagine that the auto workers agree to a different type of contract with GM. Instead of a fixed wage of $24 an hour, they go for a fixed two-thirds share of GM's average revenue of $36. At first glance there seems to be no difference between the two systems, since in both cases the workers get $24 an hour. However, GM's incentive to hire or fire is subtly but dramatically changed.

If GM now hires an extra worker, its revenue goes up by $24 as before, but its *total* labor cost in fact only increases by two thirds of $24, or $16. It clears a profit of $8 on the extra worker, and understandably wants to go on hiring and expanding output more or less indefinitely. There is a secondary effect: in order to sell the extra output, GM has to reduce the price of its cars.

The benefits for the whole economy are clear: the new labor contract means more output and jobs—and lower prices. Firms want to hire more workers for the same reason they would be keen to acquire more salesmen on commission—nothing to lose, and something to gain.

So what is the rub? Clearly the revenue per worker—and therefore pay—has declined because the marginal revenue brought in by the extra worker is less than the average revenue. Senior workers who are not unduly at risk of being laid off might resist the plan.

However, this conclusion does not necessarily follow if a large number of important firms introduce profit (or revenue) sharing, because as each firm expands and hires more workers, total workers' purchasing power rises, and so does the demand for GM's products. Not for the first time, the sum of the economic parts adds up to more than the parts themselves. The conclusions reached from this example readily generalize to formulas encompassing more realistic "mixed" compensation systems of base money wages plus shares of per capita profit (or revenue).

Somewhat more abstractly, consider a typical monopolistically competitive firm in a partial equilibrium setting. Suppose the wage is treated as a quasi-fixed parameter in the short run. If the firm can hire as much labor as it wants, it will employ workers to the point where the marginal revenue product of labor equals the wage rate. This is familiar enough. Consider, though, what happens with a profit-sharing contract that names a base wage and a certain fraction of profits per worker to be paid to each worker. A little reflection will reveal that if the profit-sharing firm can hire as much labor as it wants, it will employ workers to the point where the marginal revenue product of labor equals the base wage, independent of the value of the profit sharing parameter. (Note, though, that what the worker is actually paid depends very much on the value of the profit-sharing coefficient.) When a standard textbook (IS-LM type) macro-model is constructed around such a model of the firm, the following isomorphism emerges. A profit-sharing macroeconomy will find itself with the same output, employment, and price level as the corresponding wage economy whose wage is set at the profit-sharing economy's base wage level. In other words, the aggregate macroeconomic characteristics of a profit-sharing economy, excepting the distribution of income, are determined (on the cost side) by its base wage alone. The profit-sharing parameter does not influence output, employment, or prices, although it does influence the distribution of income. If the employed workers can be persuaded to take more of their income in the form of profit shares and less in the form of base wages, that can result in an unambiguous welfare improvement—with increased aggregate output and employment, lower prices, and higher real pay.

With identical-twin wage and wage profit-sharing economies are placed in the same stationary environment, with competitive labor markets, both economies will gravitate toward the same long-run full-employment equilibrium. But then perform the following thought experiment. In the typical style of disequilibrium analysis, disturb each economy and observe the short run reaction when pay parameters are quasi-fixed but everything else is allowed to vary. The profit-sharing economy will remain at full employment after a disturbance, while a contractionary shock will cause a wage economy to disemploy labor. It should not be hard to imagine why such characteristics make a profit-sharing system more resistant to stagflation.

This same point can be made yet another way. Consider the standard textbook macroeconomic (IS-LM type) model. Aggregate demand is determined, via the appropriate multipliers, as a function of autonomous spending injections and real money balances. The price level is determined as a degree-of-monopoly-power markup over wages. Wages are treated as exogenously fixed in the short run. Given the standard IS-LM type specification, the model grinds out (as a parametric function of the wage level) output, employment, and the price level. It is clear what happens within such a model if there is a *ceterus paribus* money wage cut. Output and employment are higher, while prices are lower. Yet this is exactly what occurs when an economy shifts toward profit sharing. The base wage determines the fundamental macroeconomic characteristics of the system: when there is an increase in profit shares at the expense of base wages, macroeconomic performance improves without loss of real labor income.

Here is one more way of seeing the differences between wage and profit-sharing systems in the short run when pay parameters are temporarily frozen. Consider the standard model of the monopoly firm. Suppose the government is initially imposing a tax on each unit of labor hired. Then the government switches some part of the labor tax to a tax on profits that raises the same tax revenue. We then expect the firm to expand employment, increase output, and lower price. But switching some part of the base wages over to profit sharing performs essentially the same experiment and should induce the same outcome.

Let me note in passing that a profit-sharing system does not eliminate unemployment by, "in effect," lowering wages to the point where equilibrium is automatically maintained. The driving force behind full employment in a profit-sharing system is not a disguised form of wage flexibility in the usual, classical sense of that term. A profit-sharing system will remain at full employment even when worker pay is above the marginal revenue product of labor. The point is not that one system operates closer to equilibrium that another, but rather that the *form* of disequilibrium response to unexpected disturbances is different. (In principle, a profit-sharing system is no less disequilibrated by shocks than is a wage system since both systems will likely exhibit some friction or inflexibility of contract parameters.) Roughly speaking, the short-term response of a share economy holds the quantity of hired labor (and output) at its full-employment level, with disequilibrium showing itself on the price (or value) side (workers are temporarily not paid their marginal value). Wage economies, on the other hand, tend to respond to contractionary shocks by holding equilibrium prices (or values) in line (workers are always compensated their marginal value) while the quantities of employment (and output) decline. In the long run, both systems tend to the same equilibrium, but their short-run behavior out of equilibrium is quite different. And, of course, it is far more important for overall economic welfare that the system as a whole maintains a full employment flow of goods and services throughout a contractionary shock than that some second marginal-value efficiency conditions on the level of the firm are being satisfied.

The theoretical identity between wage and profit-sharing systems in equilibrium is not just limited to static situations where the amount of capital is given. It also applies to establishing the stock of capital itself over longer time periods across which it can be treated as variable. It is true that if pay parameters were permanently frozen, then capitalists in a share system might underinvest relative to a wage system because any incremental profits would have to be shared with labor. But over the relevant time horizon for durable capital investment decisions, pay parameters are relatively plastic, essentially determined by long-run competitive forces. In both wage and profit-sharing systems, that will stimulate equal efforts toward output-increasing improvements. Actually, in a real world subject to disequilibrating shocks, a profit-sharing economy (whose aggregate output is perpetually stabilized at the full-employment, full-capacity level) is more likely than a fluctuation-prone wage economy to generate an enlarged steady volume of private investment.

I am aware that such short-run, fixed-pay-parameter disequilibrium models as I have been discussing will be unsatisfying to the economic theory purist who will want a full blown account of why one payment mechanism rather than another has been selected by society in the first place, and who will not rest content without understanding on a more fundamental level why pay parameters should be sticky in the short run. Such concerns have a legitimate place. But I do not think they should be taken to such an extreme that we are inhibited from examining what would happen in disequilibrium under alternative payment systems before first having firmly in hand a general, all-encompassing theory of economic systems and disequilibrium-like behavior.

What about the possible objections to profit sharing? Several are frequently voiced. I believe the objections can be successfully rebutted, even decisively rebutted, but I have space here to deal with only a couple of them, and at that rather skimpily.

The objection to profit sharing one hears most often from economists is that compared with a wage system, it represents a socially inefficient method of risk sharing. (Isn't it obvious that under a wage system the firm bears the risk, while under a profit-sharing system the worker bears the risk?) In my opinion the reasoning traditionally put forward to support this "insurance" argument is fallacious, being based on a partial equilibrium view that does not take into account the radically different macroeconomic consequences of the two systems for overall employment and aggregate output. The fixed wage does not stabilize labor income. What is true for an individual tenured worker is not true for labor as a whole. When a more complete analysis is performed, one that considers the situation not as seen by a tenured, high-seniority worker who already has job security but by a neutral observer with a reasonably specified social welfare function defined over the entire population, it becomes clear that the welfare advantages of a profit-sharing system (which delivers permanent full employment) are enormously greater than a wage system (which permits unemployment). The basic reason is not difficult to understand. A wage system allows huge first-order losses of output and welfare to open up when a significant slice of the national income pie evaporates with unemployment. A profit-sharing system stabilizes aggregate output at the full employment level, creating the biggest possible national income pie, while permitting only small second-order losses to arise because some crumbs have been randomly redistributed from a worker in one firm to a worker in another. Here is a friendly challenge to would-be critics. I challenge anyone to cook up an empirical real-world scenario, with reasonable numbers and specifications, where a profit-sharing system does not deliver significantly greater social welfare than a wage system.

As if this argument alone were not enough, you must bear in mind what a mistake it would be to extrapolate the demand variability now observed in the firms of wage economy to a share economy. Such cyclical industries as machine tools, metals, building materials, construction, and the like would not fluctuate nearly so much, since the share economy is permanently operating at or near full capacity. Every firm of a profit-sharing system would exhibit significantly greater demand stability than we are now accustomed to because a budding recession cannot feed upon itself in a fully employed economy. In addition, enterprising insurance companies are sure to offer to reduce risk further for the employees of big profit-sharing corporations by offering neatly packaged policies that will insure income fluctuations for a premium.

A second frequently voiced objection to profit sharing goes something like this. The good macroeconomic properties of a profit-sharing system come from the fact that share firms have a financial incentive at all times to maintain, or even to increase employment because, in effect, the average cost of labor, or pay, is lowered when additional employees are hired. But why would workers accept a profit-sharing scheme with no restriction on hiring? Wouldn't the senior workers of a share firm resent and try to resist the new workers coming on board who, in effect, lower the pay of all the employees? In addressing this issue we must first of all distinguish between abstract economic properties that might be apparent in an environment of just one profit-sharing firm, and readily observable behavior in a profit-sharing milieu. When an entire economy of share firms is geared up and functioning smoothly, there is a significant excess demand for labor as a whole and there are no long-term jobless people to be picked up easily. New labor must come primarily from other share firms, presumably yielded up in grudging amounts. In that environment, the tenuous aftermath of hiring a few more workers in one firm will scarcely be noticed, disguised as it must be behind a myriad of seemingly more important economic changes that directly influence the income of an individual firm. Besides, even should the subtle connection be made, it becomes an issue only when the senior workers are trying to protect a noncompetitive pay level held artificially above the going market rate of that job category; new workers will have no incentive to join the firm in the first place unless they can receive a higher pay there than elsewhere. A profit-sharing system can be the centerpiece of a program of prosperity for working people. The rules of the new game, of the new social contract, say that everyone will be able to find a job at the going rate. But, to put it bluntly, workers in a share firm simply cannot expect over the long run, for decades on end, to be continually paid above the competitive rate for their skill and experience level—the firm will naturally try to offset that possibility by drawing in more labor.

I am under no illusion about the political realities involved in making an economy-wide transition to a system based on profit-sharing principles. Some people are hurt by change, any change, and they will shout loudest to preserve the status quo even though, as with free trade, a share system is highly beneficial to the population as a whole. I believe that pure self interest based on strong tax incentives in favor of profit-sharing income will go a long way toward convincing unions and others to look favorably upon a system that guarantees that aggregate output will be produced, and consumed, at the full-employment level even if it erodes the monopoly rent above competitive pay, which they currently enjoy. If the tax incentives are strong enough, a unionized firm will not only be enticed to join the share economy, but, in a sense, will be driven to enroll. It will be compelled because, if many other firms adopt share plans and if the pecuniary advantages in the form of tax savings are significant enough (larger than the union premium), a union will be unable to compete for members without following course. And the potential tax benefits could be made extremely attractive without doing fiscal harm to the federal budget since the increases in government revenues and decreases in outlays obtained from maintaining permanent full employment are so enormous. No union would be compelled to petition for the special tax status of a share plan. But when it chooses to participate, a union cannot enjoy the tax benefits without forswearing any restrictive hiring practices. This is a logical requirement for the government to insist on, since the entire rationale of the differential tax treatment is to encourage increased employment. When all is said and done, no matter how well designed are the incentives, such change will require genuine consensus, a general agreement cutting across left/right political lines, that the broad social gains of permanent full employment without inflation are worth more than the narrow private losses that will inevitably be incurred here and there.

The superior profit-sharing variant of capitalism is practiced, to some extent, in the immensely successful economies of Japan, Korea, and Taiwan. While these countries are not identical clones, their economies do share certain important characteristics. In each case, workers receive a significant fraction of their pay in the form of a bonus. The bonuses are large, averaging over good years and bad about 25% of a worker's total pay in Japan and about 15% in Korea and Taiwan. The degree to which the bonus is actually determined as a function of current profits per worker varies from firm to firm, and depends upon the country.

(For example, in some Japanese companies the bonus is almost a disguised wage, but this is not true for most Japanese companies, and it appears to be hardly true for any Korean companies.) Bonuses, like dividends, respond to corporate earnings, but with a complicated lag structure not easy to quantify by any rigidly prescribed rule. Overall, there is very little question that profit sharing is a significant feature of the industrial landscapes of these "Japanese-style" economies.

While it is difficult to quantify the exact magnitude of its contribution out of a host of reinforcing tendencies, the bonus system is almost surely one major reason (although, most likely, far from the only reason) for the outstanding economic performances of Japan, Korea, and Taiwan. Their flexible payment system helps these economies to ride out the business cycle with relatively high, stable levels of employment and output. Their governments enjoy greater leeway for fighting inflation without causing unemployment. Levels of saving (and investment) are very high without causing dreaded Keynesian unemployment. The variability of real pay per member of the potential labor force has actually been reduced. Over time, a more equitable distribution of income has emerged than is found in other capitalist countries.

I believe that we in the West, instead of giving lessons as we are accustomed to doing, now must be prepared to take a lesson from the East. We should consciously tilt our economies toward this superior variant of capitalism. We ought to adopt a new social contract that promises our working people full employment without inflation but asks, in return, that workers received a significant fraction of their pay in the form of a profit-sharing bonus.

But, the typical economist will ask, why, if a profit-sharing system represents a far better way of operating a market economy than a wage system, don't we see more examples of share economies? After all, even in Japan, Korea, and Taiwan only modest (although significant) steps have been taken in this direction. The rest of the advanced capitalist countries are predominantly wage economies. Why, if profit sharing is so beneficial, does not self-interest automatically lead firms and workers in this direction?

The answer involves an externality or market failure of enormous magnitude. In choosing a particular contract form, the firm and its workers only calculate the effects on themselves. They take no account whatsoever of the possible effects on the rest of the economy. When a firm and its workers select a labor contract with a strong profit-sharing component, they are contributing to an atmosphere of full employment and brisk aggregate demand without inflation because the firm is then more willing to hire new "outsider" workers and to expand output by riding down its demand curve, lowering its price. But these macroeconomic advantages to the outsiders do not properly accrue to those insiders who make the decision. Like clean air, the benefits are spread throughout the community. The wage firm and its workers do not have the proper incentives to cease "polluting" the macroeconomic environment by converting to a share contract. The essence of the public-good aspect of the problem is that, in choosing between contract forms, the firm and its workers do not take into account the employment effects on the labor market as a whole and the consequent spending implications for aggregate demand. The macroeconomic externality of a tight labor market is helped by a share contract and hurt by a wage contract, but the difference is uncompensated. In such a situation there can be no presumption that the economy is optimally organized and society-wide reform may be needed to nudge firms and workers towards increased profit sharing.

This much-needed reform will not come about easily. Persuading workers and companies to fundamentally change the way labor is paid in the name of the public interest will demand political leadership of a very high order. Material incentives, such as favorable tax treatment of the profit-sharing component of a worker's pay, will probably be required. Yet the benefits of full employment without inflation are so enormous, the increased income is so great, that we cannot afford not to move in this direction.

References

Keynes, John Maynard. *The General Theory of Employment, Interest and Money.* London: Macmillan & Co., 1936.
———. "The General Theory of Employment." *Quarterly Journal of Economics* 51 (February, 1937): 209–223.
Knight, Frank. *Risk, Uncertainty and Profit.* Boston and New York: Houghton Mifflin Company, 1921.
Weitzman, Martin L. "Some Macroeconomic Implications of Alternative Compensation Systems." *Economic Journal* 93 (December, 1983). This is a technical discussion of the microeconomic foundations of profit-sharing's macroeconomic properties.
———. *The Share Economy.* Cambridge, Mass.: Harvard University Press, 1984. This book is intended to be understandable by the lay person.
———. "The Simple Macroeconomics Profit Sharing." *American Economic Review* 75 (December, 1985): 937–53. Technical treatment of comparison between the macro behavior of wage and profit-sharing economies.

13

Business Cycles and Wage Determination in the United States

Clive Bull

1. Introduction

The modern view of macroeconomic fluctuations and the unemployment they create focuses almost exclusively on the labor market. How wages and layoffs are determined at the level of the firm is regarded as crucial in determining how the economy as a whole will respond to macroeconomic shocks such as large changes in the money supply or sudden changes in the price of oil. Given this view it is only natural to ask how the widespread introduction of profit- and gain-sharing incentive schemes might effect, not just the efficiency of the individual firms, but also the macroeconomic efficiency of the economy as a whole. Categorical answers to this question cannot be given because economists have only a poor understanding of what causes the business cycle and how macroeconomic shocks are propagated over time. Nevertheless, the question is an important one and, as Martin Weitzman has eloquently argued, we cannot wait around until macroeconomists have advanced far enough to give us a definitive answer. For policy purposes, we need to make informed judgements about the macroeconomic effects of profit and gain sharing now. In order to make such judgements we need to understand how the labor market operates and how wages and unemployment behave over business cycles. The purpose of this chapter is to provide a short summary of what we do and don't know about wage behavior and to show how this information should affect our evaluation of the macroeconomic impacts of the spread of profit- and gain-sharing plans.

The standard explanation for the existence of business cycles is that nominal aggregate demand fluctuates over time. These fluctuations can come from many sources such as changes in the growth rate of the money supply or changes in the fiscal stance of the government. Whatever their causes, these fluctuations in nominal aggregate demand are

This research was supported by grant SES 8409276 from the National Science Foundation.

thought to then cause fluctuations in real GNP and employment because nominal or dollar wages are not sufficiently flexible. That is, nominal wages are thought not to respond fast enough to changes in business conditions. For example, a reduction in the growth rate of the money supply will slow the growth rate of nominal aggregate demand. This will slow the growth rate of prices. However, the growth rate of nominal wages will slow only with a lag with the result that the relative price of labor will rise. This will, in turn, cause firms to cut back output and employment and the economy will go into a recession.

This story has been the common stock-in-trade of postwar macroeconomists.[1] The chapters of John Taylor and Martin Weitzman in this volume and in their previous work (Taylor 1980 and 1983, Weitzman 1984 and 1985) are good examples of this modern approach to macroeconomics. Clearly, wage determination and, in particular, nominal wage rigidity plays a crucial role in this type of analysis. If this analysis is correct, then the introduction of profit- and gain-sharing incentive schemes, which tie nominal wages indirectly to product demand, would, by making nominal wages more flexible, reduce the severity of the business cycle.

I will argue in section 2 of this chapter that, in contrast to the usual presumption, there is very little empirical evidence to suggest that the relevant wages, namely those for the marginal labor inputs, are inflexible and that, moreover, increased rigidity of the average wage paid to workers seems to have little effect on macroeconomic performance. Thus, this tradition of appealing to sticky or rigid nominal wages as the source of macroeconomic instability seems to be empirically irrelevant. If the relevant wages are already flexible, then the macroeconomic impact of the introduction of profit- and gain-sharing schemes cannot lie directly in increasing the flexibility of nominal wages.

Even if nominal wages are flexible, wage and employment practices can still have significant macroeconomic implications. An increase in the costs of laying off workers, for instance, will make firms less willing to release workers when business turns bad and less willing to hire new workers when business turns up. Thus two economies that differ in their hiring costs, for instance because of government regulations on severance pay, will differ in the responsiveness of employment to a business cycle downturn. On the wage front, compensation systems, such as profit and gain sharing that tie infra-marginal workers' pay to business conditions will make their income streams more variable. This increased variability of income will induce changes in savings and consumption behavior that may have direct effects on the macroeconomic behavior of the economy.

In order to predict the true macroeconomic impacts of profit- and gain-sharing schemes, one must first understand the forces that have given rise to the current compensation systems. While our understanding of these forces is still incomplete, the third and fourth sections of this chapter will describe some of these forces and the wage and employment practices they have generated both in the union and nonunion sectors. The forces at work in these two sectors are quite distinct. In the United States, labor in the unionized sector is traded under contracts while in the nonunion sector it is generally not. This means that the set of trades that can be carried out in the union sector differs from that of the nonunion sector. More obviously, the union sector is, by definition, monopolized while the nonunion sector is not.

In section 5 I look at a new class of explanations of labor market behavior called efficiency wage models. These models begin by noting that the wage paid to a worker often has to fulfill two roles. Most obviously the wage must attract labor to the firm; that is, the wage serves to allocate workers across firms. However, the wage often has to fulfill a second role, namely that of providing the right incentives for hard work on the part of workers. Efficiency wage models draw out the implications of this observation. It is quite conceivable that the wage cannot simultaneously and perfectly fulfill these two functions. For instance, if lowering the wage at a firm causes workers to leave, the wage successfully performs its allocative role; but if lowering the wage results in shirking by the workers that remain, the wage fails in its incentive role. Thus, in the face of a fall in demand, firms may lay off workers rather than lower wages so as to avoid the costs of shirking. In short, the conflict between the incentive and allocation roles of the wage may result in equilibria in which there is unemployment. Clearly, if this is the case then the introduction of sophisticated incentive systems may relieve the base wage of its incentive role and result in a lower level of unemployment.

Finally, section 6 tries to identify those areas of labor market behavior where our ignorance is greatest and that promise to be most important for analyzing business cycles and the impacts of profit-sharing schemes.

2. Are Nominal Wages Rigid and Does it Matter?

There seems to be no doubt that in the United States nominal wages are rigid in the sense that their time path responds only slowly to changes in macroeconomic business conditions. Certainly this is a commonly held belief among macroeconomists. Weitzman has made an unusually clear statement of this belief.

> Our macroeconomic problems trace back, ultimately, to the wage system of paying labor. We try to award every employed worker a predetermined piece of the income pie before it is out of the oven, before the size of the pie is even known. Our "social contract" promises workers a fixed wage

independent of the health of their company, while the company chooses employment. (1985, p. 42)

This belief really consists of two independent beliefs: first, that nominal wages respond very slowly to movements in business conditions, i.e. the piece of the nominal pie going to workers is predetermined; second that this wage rigidity causes, or at least worsens, our macroeconomic problems. Yet surprisingly, given the strength with which these convictions are held, there is little or no evidence to support either of these beliefs.

Consider the first of these beliefs, namely that nominal wages are sluggish or rigid. There is considerable empirical work to support the contention that the *average* wage of those employed responds very little to macroeconomic conditions. See, for example, Branson and Rotemberg (1980), Gordon (1982), and Sachs (1979).[2] However, for most macroeconomic models, for example Weitzman's, the behavior of the average wage is not of much interest. What matters for the determination of output and employment is not the average wage but the *marginal* wage that must be paid for additional labor services.[3] To see this, consider a firm that is contemplating an expansion of output. In order to raise output, the firm must use more hours of labor services. These extra hours can come either from existing employees working longer hours (the "intensive" margin) or from hiring additional workers (the "extensive" margin). The firm will, if it expands output, use labor first from whichever margin is cheapest. Whether it will expand output or not depends on the cost of this marginal labor, that is to say the marginal wage. This marginal wage can be very different from the average wage paid by the firm. Using more hours from the existing labor force may involve paying overtime, for instance. Thus the lack of flexibility in the average wage need not imply that the marginal wage is rigid.

As far as I know there has been no major econometric research on the rigidity or otherwise or marginal wages. Despite this hole in our econometric research there is some less rigorous information that strongly suggests that marginal wages are considerably more flexible than average wages. At the intensive margin, i.e. variations in hours worked of existing workers, the marginal wage can be as low as zero in a recession if there is underutilized labor in the plant. At the very least, during such periods of labor hoarding, the marginal wage will be considerably below the average wage.[4] In contrast, during the peak of a business cycle, utilizing the internal margin will involve workers doing overtime and being paid wage premia. These premia drive the marginal wage above the average wage. Thus, at the internal margin, the marginal wage is highly variable over a business cycle.

While the wage at the internal margin may be highly flexible it will not be the relevant margin of adjustment for the firm at all stages in the business cycle. At some point in a recession, increased labor hoarding becomes unprofitable and layoffs will occur. Similarly in a growth period there comes a point where further extension of overtime working becomes too expensive to be feasible and new workers will be hired. At these points it is the extensive margin, i.e., changes in the size of the labor force that become the relevant margin of adjustment for the firm. Is the marginal wage, when the firm is adjusting at the extensive margin, flexible? If the firm adjusted its labor force by hiring or laying off $x\%$ of workers in all job classifications, then the observed rigidity of the average wage would imply that the marginal wage was also rigid. In fact, changes in the labor force do not occur in this "scaling up and down" fashion. Rather, the changes in the labor force are usually concentrated in certain jobs known in the internal labor market literature as "ports of entry." These jobs are typically low skilled and occupied by young workers with little experience. Except in the union sectors,[5] it is commonly thought that it is precisely at such "port of entry" jobs that wages are most strongly market determined. (See Doeringer and Piore, 1971, p. 46.) Bils (1985) found that the real wages of those who change jobs are almost twice as sensitive to changes in aggregate business cycle conditions as the wages of those workers who do not change jobs. Certainly, the wages of temporary workers are most unlikely to be anything other than market determined. Such wage flexibility at the "ports of entry" is quite consistent with observed average wage inflexibility because the percentage increases and reductions in the labor force of a firm over a business cycle are typically small and so the wages of these marginal workers will have only a small impact on the average wage of the firm's workers.

Given the dearth of empirical evidence on the flexibility of marginal wages, one cannot say categorically that they are or are not rigid. However, as we have seen, there is every reason to believe that marginal wages are very much more flexible than average wages. But even if they are rigid, is the second belief (typical of macroeconomists) that paying workers rigid wages causes or amplifies our macroeconomic problems empirically plausible? There are two ways of evaluating this. One can either look at the behavior of the U.S. economy over time or compare its behavior across countries. Let's take each set of evidence in turn.

Since World War II, average nominal wages appear to have become far more sticky. This is best illustrated by the development and widespread adoption of the three-year contract in the unionized sector. Many explanations have been put forward for this phenomenon. (See Mitchell, 1985 a, b.) If, to paraphrase Weitzman, our macroeconomic problems are ultimately caused by marginal wage rigidity, then the macroeconomic performance of the U.S. economy should have worsened markedly after 1945. At least to those readers who can recall the Great

Depression, it will come as no surprise to hear that, in fact, the macroeconomic performance of the U.S. economy, when measured by the severity of recessions, improved dramatically after 1945. Measuring macroeconomic performance by the variation of real GNP around its trend, DeLong and Summers (1984) found that post-1945 performance was better than that during the interwar period and that prior to WW I. Moreover, they could not account for this improvement by such obvious structural changes as the decline in the share of agriculture in GNP. Of course, many other things have changed in the economy since the war, notably the conduct of countercyclical monetary and fiscal policies, which may have offset the detrimental effect of increasing wage rigidity. However, if the latter and notably three-year overlapping union contracts are so important, then it is quite remarkable that it has not shown up as a deterioration in macroeconomic performance.

If we look across countries, similar puzzles emerge. Several studies, notably those by Branson and Rotemberg (1980) and Gordon (1983), have identified the U.S. as having unusually inflexible nominal wages compared with other major OECD countries. This could be for one of several reasons. For instance, no other OECD country has three-year, legally enforceable union contracts. Also in several countries, such as Austria, Sweden, and Germany, union wage setting is carried out with a clear concern for macroeconomic conditions. This higher flexibility of nominal wages in other OECD countries would suggest that they should have far better macroeconomic performance than the United States. Yet, at least since the first oil shock of 1973–74, the reverse has been the case.[6] For instance, in the recessions immediately following the two oil shocks, 1973–75 and 1979–83, the German unemployment rate rose by 260% and 139% respectively, while the U.S. unemployment rate rose by only 73% and 65% (OECD, 1984). Admittedly, the example of Japan where wages are notably flexible does, in contrast, support the role of wage flexibility.[7] Again many other factors (which certainly cloud the interpretation of the data) differ across these countires. Nevertheless, if the effect of wage stickiness were so strong, then one would expect it to show through.

While none of the evidence above proves that marginal wages are flexible or that wage flexibility has no role to play in macroeconomic performance, it does show that there is remarkably little evidence either in favor of the phenomenon of marginal wage rigidity or for the allegedly adverse impact of average wage rigidity. To cast wage rigidity as *the* villain of the macroeconomic piece at this stage of our knowledge is an act of faith rather than a deduction from the data.

Part of the problem with appeals to wage rigidity as a cause of business cycles is that they occur in very abstract models that deal with "the" labor market. Even if there were realistically one such market, it is represented so simplistically in most macromodels as to be of little empirical relevance. Thus, if we are to understand the impact of changes in the way wages are set, for instance the introduction of gain-sharing schemes, we must first understand the forces that gave rise to current wage-setting practices. Some of these practices in the union and nonunion sectors are described in the next two sections.

3. Union Wage Setting

For many reasons, most of the research on wage setting and its macroeconomic effects has concentrated on the union sector. John Taylor, for instance, has very thoroughly investigated the impact of the overlapping, three-year union contracts on macroeconomic behavior (1980, 1983).* However, perhaps the single most important feature of the union sector as far as macroeconomic performance is concerned is its size. Union contracts now cover less than 20% of the U.S. labor force and that share shows a strong downward trend. While 20% of the labor force is certainly not a macroeconomically insignificant share, it is far from overwhelming. Indeed, it would be quite remarkable if wage setting in the union sector dominated the macroeconomic behavior of the U.S. economy.

Although unlikely to be of much macroeconomic significance, wage setting practices in the union sector are of interest. In particular, the union sector represents the only significant part of the U.S. labor market in which workers' compensation contains a major element of what we may call *de facto* profit sharing. Although there are relatively few formal profit-sharing schemes in the union sector, the premium of union wages over nonunion wages represents a share of corporate profits going to workers. A union can only extract wages above the nonunion rate if it unionizes a firm whose discounted stream of economic profits prior to unionization is positive. By unionizing the firm's labor force, the workers capture a share of those profits, the size of the share depending on the outcome of wage bargaining. Thus, the union members, in effect, become "shareholders" and own a fraction of the discounted profit stream of the firm.

There are, of course, significant differences between the shares of the union members and those traded on the stock exchanges. For instance, union members cannot sell their shares or use them as collateral against loans. Perhaps the most obvious difference lies in the stream of dividends paid to the union shareholders. What we do *not* see is this

---

*Editor's note: a summary of this research is found in Taylor's contribution to this volume, chap. 11.

dividend, the premium over the nonunion wage, varying substantially with the year-to-year profits of the firm in the way that dividends to ordinary shareholders do. It seems that union members own something closer to preferred rather than ordinary shares. Why union choose to receive their share of discounted profits in this way is not well understood. One reason could be that the union members have less access to capital markets than do regular shareholders so that the latter are better placed to smooth out the stream of income generated by the firm.[8] Although attractive, this explanation has some weaknesses. By saving, workers themselves may be able to smooth out their consumption stream in the face of a fluctuating stream of income (Topel and Welch, 1983). Moreover, while this explanation would account for the unions' desire to receive a smooth stream of *real* income, it does not explain why unions appear to concentrate on smoothing out the stream of *nominal* income.

Whatever the reason for the union deciding to take its share of profits as a smooth stream of nominal income, the fact remains that nominal union wages are sticky in the sense that they respond little to business conditions except, as in the last recession, when the latter become catastrophic. Surely this has a detrimental impact on the macroeconomic performance of the economy. The reason why this type of wage setting is believed to be bad for the economy is that a reduction in nominal demand will result in layoffs rather than a decline in wages and that these layoffs will then result in a decline in output and a rise in unemployment. This is precisely Weitzman's complaint. Two points must be noted, however, that contradict this presumption that such wage setting is bad.

If one claims that the existing wage-setting behavior is inefficient, then the first problem that must be faced is that these wages are the outcome of a bargaining process. As such, there must be a strong presumption that the parties to the bargain have found, over a period of years, rigidity of the nominal wage to be desirable. If they thought that flexible wages would lead to a more desirable situation, then presumably they would have adopted flexible wages. A corollary of this observation is that imposing a flexible wage system on firms and unions would make both parties worse off.

Why do unions and employers choose a system of rigid nominal wages despite the fact that this system results in larger fluctuations in employment than would occur under a flexible wage system? One plausible explanation is risk sharing between senior and junior workers. Senior workers typically have large financial commitments,[9] e.g. mortgages, education fees, and few alternative employment opportunities because, for instance, of low geographic and occupational mobility. Young, single workers without children, in contrast, have low expenditure commitments and are highly mobile both geographically and occupationally. Other things being equal, these facts imply that young workers are better able to adapt to fluctuating incomes than senior workers. Economically, this means that in a firm that contains both types of worker it is efficient to choose a wage and layoff policy that transfers most of the business conditions-induced income risk to the young workers. This is precisely what a fixed wage contract together with a first-in/last-out layoff policy does. Thus one consequence of adopting a Weitzman-type compensation system would be that income risk would be shifted from those most willing and able to bear it, young workers, onto those least able to bear it, senior workers.

Although increased wage flexibility may result in a poorer allocation of risk at the level of the individual worker or union, this need not mean that increase wage flexibility is a bad thing. There are many examples in economics of individually suboptimal constraints resulting in large aggregate benefits. Individually, we might each be slightly worse off if there were an enforced ban on dropping litter at the beach. However, the aggregate result, namely a clean beach, could more than outweigh the inconvenience of not being able to drop litter. Similarly, if the inability to shift income risk to those best able to bear it resulted in a great enough reduction in the variability of aggregate income, then the net result could well be an increase in welfare. This brings us to the second point that must be made about proposals for increased wage flexibility: will increased nominal wage flexibility reduce the severity of macroeconomic fluctuations?

Unfortunately, our understanding of the macroeconomy is so incomplete that a clear answer to this question is impossible. What does deserve to be emphasized, however, is that the answer to this question is *not* obvious. Even on strictly Keynesian grounds, inflexible nominal wages may be a good thing. If the layoffs that result from the existing wage system are small relative to the size of the wage cuts that would be required to avoid them, the wage bill of the firm may be higher with layoffs than with flexible wages. If workers consume a constant fraction of their income, this means that aggregate consumption expenditure under rigid wages and layoffs will be less variable than under flexible wages. This in turn should lower the variability of aggregate demand and output. This is, of course, part of Keynes' argument against cutting wages in the face of a recession and is related to the arguments used by supporters of underconsumption theories of the business cycle. These latter arguments played a large role in the formulation of U.S. labor law, e.g. the Wagner Act (Mitchell, 1985, p. 37). Thus the case for the adverse macroeconomic impact of wage setting as carried out in the union sector is far from proven.

4. Nonunion Wage Setting

Given that it accounts for 80% of the U.S. labor force, it is wage setting in the nonunion sector that will, if wage setting has any impact, most significantly affect the macroeconomic performance of the economy. Unfortunately, this is precisely the sector about which little is known in terms of wage setting. What we do know is that labor contracts are rare in this sector and so employers are legally free to change the wages that they pay more or less at will. Despite this freedom, it appears that an annual wage-setting cycle is followed and that nominal wages are not indexed. The paucity of data on this sector makes theorizing about the wage-setting mechanism of dubious value. We do not know whether the wages of new hires are or are not flexible. We do not know why a one-year wage-setting cycle is used. We do not know to what extent labor market conditions play a role in setting the wages of inframarginal, typically senior, workers.

There is, however, indirect evidence that for the bulk of senior workers wages are only loosely related to current labor market conditions. Hall (1982) has documented the fact that in the U.S., at least for prime age males, tenure in a job is long, e.g. over 50% of men aged 40 or older are in a job whose tenure is expected to be 20 years or longer. If wages were determined as on an auction market, we would not expect to see such a degree of employment stability. As business improved temporarily in one firm and declined in another, we would expect to see a flow of workers from the latter to the former. We do not see this behavior except for young workers who have just entered the labor force (Topel and Ward, 1985). Clearly, most middle-aged workers are like the machines bolted to the factory floor, quite firm-specific and therefore costly to move between employers. As Oi (1963) and Hall (1980) pointed out several years ago, this means that there are no productive efficiency gains from making the wages of these workers highly flexible. Like the machines, they will not be thrown out of the factory in response to temporary downturns in business. Thus there is little reason to believe that fixing these workers' wages with little regard for the seasonal or business cycle elements of current business conditions should have any adverse impact on the macroeconomic performance of the economy.

The same is not true for new entrants to the labor force. Economic efficiency requires that those workers with the least firm-specific skills and the lowest costs of moving between jobs be the ones who reallocate themselves across firms as relative product demands change. These workers are typically young and single, or married but without school age children, and new to the labor force. Similarly, if a macroeconomic shock hits the economy and reduces the equilibrium level of employment then it is those workers whose market productivity is lowest relative to their nonmarket productivities that should drop out of the labor force. For instance, women with young children have relatively high productivity outside the labor market and, because of their generally lower education and shorter work experience, relatively low productivity in the labor market. The same is true for teenage workers who are in high school or college. These then are the workers for whom it is most efficient to move in and out of the labor force as conditions change. Unsurprisingly, this is exactly what we observe these groups doing. Because it is important for economic efficiency that these young and marginal workers do move across firms and in and out of the labor market, it is correspondingly important that the wage system do nothing to blunt the incentives for such moves.

There is no evidence that wage setting in the nonunion sector prevents such reallocations of labor. On the contrary, the data show considerable movement between jobs in this segment of the labor market. For instance, Topel and Ward (1985, p. 4) have found that young males hold an average of five jobs in the first ten years of labor market activity and that for this group of workers more than one third of new jobs end within three months. This mobility probably reflects the fact that these junior workers' wages are, in fact, flexible. Precisely because firms find workers at the entry level easy to substitute for each other, they will not pay workers with low tenure wages above the market wage. Similarly, the mobility of such workers means that they will not stay with a firm whose wages fall out of line with the market. There are, then, reasons for presuming that the wages of these workers will be sensitive to business conditions. However, the flexibility or otherwise of the wages of these marginal workers is ultimately an empirical issue that is as yet unresolved.

5. Incentives and Unemployment

A remarkable feature of the usual macroeconomic discussions of wage setting is that emphasis is placed exclusively on the allocational role of wages. Does the wage-setting mechanism encourage workers to move to where they are most valuable and, in particular, does it enable them to work when the wage at which they are willing to work is less than their productivity on the job? However, a crucial factor in the choice of compensation systems is often the incentive effects of the compensation package, not its effect on allocative efficiency. The questions usually asked of compensation schemes are whether they provide the workers with the right incentives in terms of the effort they put into their jobs, taking initiative and doing high quality work. Recently, economists have come to examine whether there might be a conflict between the role of a compensation package as a provider of incentives for worker performance and as a provider of incentives for workers to allocate themselves efficiently across firms. The literature that has developed goes by the name of "efficiency wage" models. See Yellen (1984) for a short survey of this work. See also Guillermo Calvo's chapter (4) in this volume.

Take a situation in which workers are imperfectly monitored and so are tempted to provide less than the level of effort laid down for the job. Whether they will give in to this temptation depends, in part, on the penalty they will receive should they be caught. One penalty that will not discourage cheating is lowering the worker's wage. If the worker was willing to risk being caught and losing his or her higher original wage, there is no doubt that the worker will be willing to take that gamble at the new, lower wage. How about threatening to fire the worker? This is a threat only if the worker is either currently earning more than the wage he or she could get elsewhere, or if upon being fired the worker could not get a new job quickly and so would have to spend a period of time unemployed. Notice that by definition all employers cannot pay wages above the market rate and so, if firing is to work as a threat, it must be because fired workers cannot immediately find jobs at the wage at which they had previously been employed. One equilibrium outcome, there-fore, in this labor market would be for the market wage to be set above the amount an unemployed worker receives and for there to be a positive level of unemployment at that wage. Although each unem-ployed worker would be willing to work at a wage below that paid to currently employed workers, no firm would be willing to hire such a worker because they know that at that lower wage he or she would find it attractive to gamble and provide low effort.[10] Thus involuntary unem-ployment arises as an equilibrium phenomenon.

There are many other types of efficiency wage stories but they all share the feature that the wage is asked to do too much. It is asked both to provide the worker with correct incentives to supply effort, and simultaneously to clear the labor market so as to prevent involuntary unemployment (achieve allocative efficiency). Because it cannot simulta-neously do both things perfectly, the result is unemployment.[11] These models are a significant advance in our understanding of wage-setting and personnel policies and their impacts. They identify a potentially serious trade-off in the economy between micro efficiency at the level of the firm and a kind of macro inefficiency in the form of underutilization of labor. The question that remains to be answered though is what the issues raised in the literature imply for macroeconomic performance.

One problem with answering this question is that in all cases the wage that is the focus of attention is a real wage and not a nominal wage. This means that there is no obvious reason within these models why a fall in nominal aggregate demand should result in an increase in unemploy-ment. A second problem is that these models, as they stand, provide an explanation for the average level of unemployment but not for how and why it fluctuates over the business cycle. We are told that the equilibrium real wage will be set so high that it will generate unemployment, but we are not told how it will respond to changes in business conditions. The existing models give us no reason to believe that real wages will be sticky in the face of such changes. So although these models have provided considerable insight into wage setting and incentives they have not yet given similar insights into business cycle behavior.

6. Conclusions

If only to encourage the supply of research funds, economics papers usually end with a call for further research. I think the review of the state of our knowledge of wage setting and its role in macroeconomic fluctuations in this chapter should have made it abundantly clear that more research is desperately needed. At the empirical level we do not know whether the relevant marginal wages in the economy are rigid in either nominal or real terms. Those economists (such as Weitzman) who think that rigid wages are important in propagating business cycles may be right in saying that if these marginal wages were rigid they would generate serious business cycle problems. Perhaps the large scale introduction of profit or gain-sharing plans would make these marginal wages more flexible and business cycles less severe. However, no one has yet shown empirically that marginal wages are rigid.

The second area where our empirical knowledge is extremely weak is in the wage-setting policies used in the nonunion sector. Without this information, macroeconomists of the rigid wage persuasion are forced to model the union sector as John Taylor has done. But this sector is very modestly sized and declining. Clearly, we need to have more empirical information about the nonunion sector, the sector that matters for the macroeconomic behavior of the economy.

While these empirical areas of research are perhaps the highest priority tasks, there are several more theoretical areas that are also badly in need of further work. Those macroeconomists who feel that rigid wages are important need to show in the context of a macroeconomic model that it is indeed a robust result that slowly moving nominal or real wages exacerbate business cycles. At a more microeconomic level we need to understand much more about how the nonunion sector works. Remember that in this sector labor contracts are rare, and yet long-term relationships requiring large investments on either side are built up between employers and workers. How are these long-term trades, which require considerable trust on both sides, carried out without the use of contracts? We simply do not know yet (see Bull 1987). It is very likely that these trades involve some kinds of commitments about how wages will vary over time and what will be done, e.g. layoffs, as business conditions vary. Thus finding out how these trades can be conducted is directly relevant to the question of how wages are set and how layoff policies are determined.

The importance of gaining such an understanding of behavior in the nonunion, and so noncontractual sector of the labor market can be exemplified by considering Martin Weitzman's proposal for a share economy. Let us assume that employers did switch over to offering such shares or revenues as payment for labor services. How would the individual worker be able to check that the firm fulfilled its promise? Note that in the union sector unions employ highly trained professionals to monitor compliance by the firm with the labor contract. In the nonunion sector it would be left up to the individual worker to monitor compliance and, if necessary, litigate to get accurate performance data from the firm. It is highly unlikely that most workers would have the skills to monitor the firm and, moreover, each worker might well rely on some other worker taking the trouble to monitor. Of course, if all workers take this route, the firm will not be monitored and so will be tempted to cheat.

This argument suggests that revenue sharing in the nonunion sector is highly unlikely to be a practical proposition. On the other hand, there are some very long-term implicit contracts made between workers and firms in this sector. Workers invest in firm-specific rather than widely marketable skills thereby opening themselves to exploitation by the firm after the investment has been made. Such investments must be based on promises or implicit contracts about what the firm will do in the future and for some reason workers trust these promises. If we understood the mechanism by which this kind of trade was successfully carried out then we might well conclude that, despite its obvious problems, Weitzman-style revenue sharing promises by firms in the nonunion sector might be valued by workers. Conversely, without such an understanding we have no reason to believe that workers will believe unverifiable promises by firms to share revenues or profits.

Notes

1. This in itself is a historical departure from traditional business cycle theory. The great names in this tradition such as Wicksell, Hayek, Pigou, and Keynes gave little attention to the labor market and concentrated instead on the capital market as the market most closely linked to the propagation of business cycles.

2. The aggregation involved in the construction of the average wage series seriously biases results concerning wage rigidity. See Stockman (1983) and Bils (1985).

3. See Heckman, 1984, p. 217 and Oi, 1984, p. 166, for a similar point.

4. The presence of labor hoarding does not imply any lack of efficiency on the part of

the firm if there are hiring costs and a positive probability that a laid off worker will not respond to a recall notice. See Bull and McCarthy, 1985.

5. The rapid rise in the use of "two-tier" clauses shows that even in the union sector there can be variation in the wages paid to new hires.

6. Note that it is important to distinguish clearly between the *level* of unemployment and the cyclical *changes* in unemployment. Austria, Germany, and Sweden have had average unemployment rates below those in the U.S. until quite recently.

7. Note that this flexibility is not due to the bonus system, which covers only a small part of the Japanese labor force.

8. This is the explanation used in the implicit contract literature pioneered by Azariadis (1975), Baily (1974) and Gordon (1974).

9. Precommitments to expenditures can induce considerable risk aversion in otherwise risk-neutral people. See Eden, 1977.

10. This is a loose description of the model presented in Shapiro and Stiglitz (1984).

11. Of course, one might expect other devices to be found in order to relieve the wage of this double burden. In the simple example given above requiring all new hires to provide truthful letters of recommendation from their previous employer would solve the problem.

References

Azariadis, Costas. "Implicit Contracts and Underemployment Equilibria." *Journal of Political Economy* 83 (December 1975): 1183–1202.

Baily, Martin N. "Wages and Employment under Uncertain Demand." *Review of Economic Studies* 41 (January 1974): 37–50.

Branson, William H., and Julio J. Rotemberg. "International Adjustment with Wage Rigidity." *European Economic Review* 13 (May 1980): 309–32.

Bils, Mark J. "Real Wages over the Business Cycle: Evidence from Panel Data." *Journal of Political Economy* 93(4) (August 1985): 666–89.

Bull, Clive. "The Existence of Self-Enforcing Implicit Contracts." *Quarterly Journal of Economics*, 102(1) (February 1987): 1–11.

Bull, Clive, and Mary McCarthy. "Layoffs and Labor Hoarding: The Effects of Job Changes by Workers on Layoff." New York University, April 1985, Mimeo.

DeLong, Bradford J., and Laurence H. Summers. "The Changing Cyclical Variability of Economic Activity in the United States." NBER Working Paper, #1450, September 1984.

Doeringer, Peter B., and Michael J. Piore. *Internal Labor Markets and Manpower Analysis.* Lexington: Heath Lexington Books, 1971.

Eden, Benjamin. "The Role of Insurance and Gambling in Allocating Risk over Time." *Journal of Economic Theory* 16 (December 1977).

Gordon, Donald F. "A Neo-Classical Theory of Keynesian Unemployment." *Economic Inquiry* 17 (December 1974): 431–59.

Gordon, Robert J. "Why U.S. Wage and Employment Behavior Differs from that in Britain and Japan." *Economic Journal* 92 (March 1982): 13–44.

———. "Wage and Price Dynamics and the Natural Rate of Unemployment in Eight Large Industrialized Nations." NBER Working Paper, October 1983.

Hall, Robert E. "Employment Fluctuations and Wage Rigidity." *Brookings Papers on Economic Activity* 1, 1980.

———. "The Importance of Lifetime Jobs in the U.S. Economy." *American Economic Review* 72 (September 1982): 716–24.

Mitchell, Daniel J.B. "Wage Flexibility in the United States: Lessons from the Past." *American Economic Review* 75(2) (May 1985a): 36–40.

———. "Wage Flexibility: Then and Now." *Industrial Relations* 24(2) (Spring 1985b): 266–79.

O.E.C.D. *Main Economic Indicators: Historical Statistics.* Paris, 1984.

Oi, Walter. "Labor as a Quasi-Fixed Factor." *Journal of Political Economy* 70 (1963): 538–55.

Sachs, Jeffrey D. "Wages, Profits, and Macroeconomic Adjustment: A Comparative Study." *Brookings Papers on Economic Activity*, 1979.

Shapiro, Carl, and Joseph E. Stiglitz. "Equilibrium Unemployment as a Worker Discipline Device." *American Economic Review* 74(3) (1984): 433–44.

Stockman, Alan C. "Aggregation Bias and the Cyclical Behavior of Real Wages." Conference Paper, Cambridge, Mass., National Bureau of Economic Research, July 1983.

Taylor, John B. "Aggregate Dynamics and Staggered Contracts." *Journal of Political Economy* 80 (February 1980): 1–23.

———. "Union Wage Settlements During a Disinflation." *American Economic Review* 73(5) (December 1983): 981–93.

———. This volume, chapter 11.

Topel, Robert, and Finis Welch. "Self-Insurance and Efficient Employment Contrasts." University of Chicago, mimeo, 1983.

Topel, Robert H., and Michael P. Ward. "Job Mobility and the Careers of Young Men." Graduate School of Business, Chicago University, mimeo, February 1985.

Weitzman, M. L. "Some Macroeconomic Implications of Alternative Compensation Systems." *Economic Journal* 93 (December 1983): 763–83.

———. *The Share Economy.* Cambridge: Harvard University Press, 1984.

———. "Profit Sharing as Macroeconomic Policy." *American Economic Review* 75(2) (May 1985): 41–45.

———. This volume, chapter 12.

Yellen, Janet L. "Efficiency Wage Models of Unemployment." *American Economic Review* 74(2) (May 1984): 200–05.

Contributors

Haig R. Nalbantian conceived and organized the conference program on which this volume is based. An economist with a specialization in industrial organization and monetary economics, he has been on the faculty of economics at New York University and an assistant research scientist at the C. V. Starr Center for Applied Economics, New York University. He currently retains his affiliation with the Starr Center as an adjunct member. A member of the American Management Association, his particular interest is in the design and implementation of incentive compensation systems.

Mr. Nalbantian is a graduate (Phi Beta Kappa, honors in English) of New York University and has pursued his graduate studies at Columbia University where he earned his M.A. and M.Phil. degrees. His current work is on incentives and employment contracts.

Sarah J. Armstrong has managed employee relations programs in industry since 1969. She has served as Corporate Personnel Manager for IU International Corporation, Director of Employee Relations and Employee Compensation for ITT Corporation, and was appointed Director-Compensation for Campbell Soup Company in 1986. Mrs. Armstrong designs compensation and reward systems that are customized to specific business objectives and strategies and are administered on a decentralized basis with control in the hands of the users; these systems emphasize recognition that jobs are known best by the individuals performing them and that performance should be measured and rewarded as close to the event as possible. Mrs. Armstrong received a bachelor's degree in government and philosophy from Cornell University in 1966 and pursued graduate study in human development at the University of Rhode Island. She is a member of the American Compensation Association, and the National Food Processors Association. In 1983, she received the YWCA Tribute to Women in Industry award.

Clive Bull is associate professor of economics at New York University. He is currently on leave from New York University in order to serve as Senior Analyst in the Fixed Income Financial Strategy Group at PaineWebber Inc. where he is in charge of options research. Professor Bull specializes in economic theory; his chief areas of research are noncontractual agreements, especially in the labor market, and the internal organization of the firm. His major publications have appeared in the *American Economic Review*, the *Quarterly Journal of Economics*, and the *Journal of Political Economy*. Professor Bull earned his Ph.D. from UCLA in 1980.

Guillermo A.R. Calvo earned his Ph.D. from Yale University in 1974. He is now professor of economics at the University of Pennsylvania. From 1973 to 1986, he taught in the department of economics at Columbia University in New York City. He has been a visiting professor at the University of Chicago and a visiting researcher at the Institute for International Economic Studies, University of Stockholm. Professor Calvo's research has spanned the economics' discipline. A specialist in macro and monetary economics and in international trade, he has conducted seminal research in optimal growth theory and the economics of internal organization. Professor Calvo has published extensively in many of the leading academic journals.

Richard A. Guzzo, associate professor of psychology, New York University, special-izes in industrial/organizational psychology. He joined New York University in 1980 after spending two years at McGill University as a member of the Faculty of Management. Productivity in organizations is a common theme in Dr. Guzzo's research. Of special interest is effective performance by individuals at work and by groups or teams of employees. He is the author of several books and numerous articles on motivation, productivity, and group performance. He received his Ph.D. from Yale University in 1979.

Bengt Holmstrom is the Edwin J. Beinecke Professor of Management Studies at the School of Organization and Management, Yale University. He is internationally known for his research on the design of incentive plans, labor contracts, and the theory of the firm, and has consulted for government and private firms on the same subjects. He is associate editor of *Econometrica,* the *Journal of Economic Theory,* and *The Rand Journal of Economics,* and is a fellow of the Economics Society.

Raymond A. Katzell was recently named Professor Emeritus of Psychology at New York University after having been on its faculty for more than twenty-five years, nine as head of that department. His career has spanned industry, government, and education, and has included the U.S. War Department; Illinois Central Railroad; Richardson, Bellows, Henry & Co.; Syracuse University; and the University of Tennessee. He has published more than fifty books and articles on the topics of personnel selection, training, performance evaluation, productivity and work atti-tudes and motivation. He is, at present, editor of an annual series sponsored by the Society for Industrial Organizational Psychology, the most recent volume being on career development in organizations.

John W. Kendrick received his Ph.D. from The George Washington University and has been a professor of economics there since 1956. He is also an adjunct scholar at the American Enterprise Institute and has also served as Chief Economist for the U.S. Department of Commerce, as Vice-President for Economic Research at The Conference Board, and as an economist with the National Resources Planning board. Dr. Kendrick is a fellow of the American Statistical Association and the National Association of Business Economists, and is a member of Phi Beta Kappa, the American Economic Association, and the Southern Economic Association. He is the author of several books, and has published over 100 articles in professional journals, and has lectured on economics, particularly productivity, in many countries of the world.

John A. Larson received his bachelor's degree in economics from Holy Cross College in 1969 and an M.A. in economics from the University of Wisconsin in 1971. After completing six years in the U.S. Navy, he received an M.B.A. from the Wharton School in 1979. Mr. Larson has published in the areas of labor relations, new business ventures, and executive compensation. He is currently the vice-president for market-ing of the Ivy Medical Group. Prior to this, he was an associate at McKinsey & Co., the management consulting firm.

Edward E. Lawler III received his Ph.D. from the University of California at Berkeley in 1964 and joined the faculty of Yale University. In 1972, he became professor of psychology and Program Director in the Survey Research Center at the Institute for Social Research at the University of Michigan. He is now professor of management and organization in the Business School at the University of Southern

California where he founded and became the director of the University's Center for Effective Organizations. In 1982, Dr. Lawler was named Research Professor at USC. Dr. Lawler is on the editorial board of five major journals and has consulted extensively on employee involvement; he is the author and co-author of 15 books and over 150 articles.

Jude T. Rich is president of Sibson & Company. Before joining Sibson, Mr. Rich spent ten years in the New York office of McKinsey & Company where he was a partner and leader of the firm's practice in human resource management. Mr. Rich has broad corporate experience including responsibility for all aspects of human resource management—compensation, manpower management and development, employment, sales and management training, and labor relations. In the compensation area, he developed and implemented company-wide salary and incentive programs for all levels of employees, particularly management and sales personnel. Mr. Rich's consulting experience spans a wide variety of industries, including consumer products, publishing, petroleum, pharmaceuticals, financial institutions, transportation, forest products, and utilities. Mr. Rich is a graduate of Rutgers University where he received a B.A. in business and an M.B.A. in general management.

Joseph E. Stiglitz is professor of economics at Princeton University and research associate at the National Bureau of Economic Research. He is a leading economic theoretician whose work has covered numerous fields within his discipline, most notably, the economics of information and uncertainty, public economics, the distribution of income and wealth, growth and capital theory, economic development and trade, and macroeconomics. His previous academic appointments include Drummond Professor of Political Economy, Oxford University; professor of economics, Stanford University; visiting scholar, The Hoover Institution, Stanford University; professor of economics, the Cowles Foundation, and the Department of Economics, Yale University. Professor Stiglitz is a former Guggenheim Fellow and a fellow of the Econometric Society. He has been a consultant to various governmental bodies and international organizations and is the author or co-author of over 225 articles, many of which have been published in the major academic journals. Professor Stiglitz earned his Ph.D. from MIT in 1967.

John B. Taylor, professor of economics at Stanford University and research associate at the National Bureau of Economic Research, specializes in macroeconomics, monetary economics, and econometrics. Prior to joining the Stanford faculty in 1984, he was professor of economics at Columbia University, professor of economics and Public Policy at Princeton University, and visiting professor of economics at Yale University. A former Guggenheim Fellow, he is now a fellow of the Econometric Society and has published over fifty articles in leading professional journals. He was senior staff economist at the Council of Economic Advisors under Presidents Ford and Carter and has served as a member of the Brookings Panel of Economic Activity, and of the Advisory Panel on Economics of the National Science Foundation. He received his Ph.D. from Stanford in 1973.

Andrew Weiss received his Ph.D. from Stanford University in 1976 and then combined a career in the private sector at Bell Laboratories and Bell Communications Research with academic appointments at Columbia University. His research has focused on the effects of informational imperfections on labor and credit markets. In publications appearing in leading journals, he has developed information-theoretic models of the relationship between wages and unemployment, job tenure, and education. He has also estimated the empirical significance of these informational assymetries.

Martin L. Weitzman is Mitsui Professor of Economics at M.I.T. and visiting professor at Harvard University for the academic year 1986–87. Professor Weitzman's primary specialty is Comparative Economics Systems, but he has done work in many areas of economics, especially economic theory and its applications. In the past few years his research has centered on the microeconomic and macroeconomic implications of alternative compensation arrangements, with particular emphasis on profit sharing. Professor Weitzman has published a number of articles and books in this area. He has been at M.I.T. since 1972 and was at Yale University from 1967–72, having earned his Ph.D. from M.I.T. in 1967. He is a Fellow of the Econometric Society and a former Guggenheim Fellow.

Index